FORGIVENESS IN PRACTICE

of related interest

The Forgiveness Project
Stories for a Vengeful Age
Marina Cantacuzino
Forewords by Archbishop Emeritus Desmond Tutu and Alexander McCall Smith
ISBN 978 1 84905 566 6 (hardback)
ISBN 978 1 78592 000 4 (paperback)
eISBN 978 1 78450 006 1

Forgiveness is Really Strange
Masi Noor and Marina Cantacuzino
Art by Sophie Standing
ISBN 978 1 78592 124 7
eISBN 978 0 85701 279 1

Violence, Restorative Justice, and Forgiveness
Dyadic Forgiveness and Energy Shifts in Restorative Justice Dialogue
Marilyn Armour and Mark Umbreit
ISBN 978 1 78592 795 9
eISBN 978 1 78450 795 4

Restorative Justice
How It Works
Marian Liebmann
ISBN 978 1 84310 074 4
eISBN 978 1 84642 631 5

God-Curious
Exploring Eternal Questions
Stephen Cherry
ISBN 978 1 78592 199 5
eISBN 978 1 78450 473 1

Introduction to Counselling Survivors of Interpersonal Trauma
Christiane Sanderson
ISBN 978 1 84310 962 4
eISBN 978 0 85700 213 6

Spiritual Care at the End of Life
The Chaplain as a 'Hopeful Presence'
Steve Nolan
ISBN 978 1 84905 199 6
eISBN 978 0 85700 513 7

FORGIVENESS
IN PRACTICE

Edited by Stephen Hance

Jessica Kingsley *Publishers*
London and Philadelphia

First published in 2019
by Jessica Kingsley Publishers
73 Collier Street
London N1 9BE, UK
and
400 Market Street, Suite 400
Philadelphia, PA 19106, USA

www.jkp.com

Library of Congress Cataloging in Publication Data
A CIP catalog record for this book is available from the Library of Congress

British Library Cataloguing in Publication Data
A CIP catalogue record for this book is available from the British Library

ISBN 978 1 84905 552 9
eISBN 978 0 85700 983 8

Printed and bound in Great Britain

Contents

INTRODUCTION

Stephen Hance

We might be tempted to think of forgiveness as a story. There is a beginning (the scene is set, everything is order), a middle (this peace is disrupted by the hurtful actions of a perpetrator) and an end (forgiveness is offered and received, and order is restored). Often we feel as if this story should be like a fairy tale with a happy ending, with forgiveness playing a magic role to restore an order that had been threatened by events and villains outside our control. But when we look at forgiveness more closely, just as when we look at fairy tales more closely, we find that the story is darker and more slippery than it first appears.

Fairy tales are set in fantastical yet self-contained worlds – boundaries are fixed, resolutions are tidy, characters are limited – and where normal rules don't apply – cats speak, pumpkins turn into coaches and wishes are granted. Forgiveness is played out in our world and cannot be isolated from the real challenges of a messy life. Characters have inner lives and motivations. They come with their own emotions and experiences that are invisible to us but affect each of their actions. Wishes are not always granted and resolutions must be worked out between individuals and groups. The desire for a simple model of forgiveness is understandable. We do not tend to worry about forgiving the person in the crowd who steps on our foot; we worry about forgiveness when life is at its most difficult and we are deeply hurt. At these points, a quick and tidy resolution with a happy ending seems very attractive.

Many books have been written promoting the healing powers of forgiveness or recommending forgiveness as a means to increase our well-being. This view is, of course, attractive and there may be some truth in these but it would be dangerous to presume that forgiveness can be a quick-fix solution. Marina Cantacuzino, in her introduction to *The Forgiveness Project*, is wary particularly of the flipside of this where not forgiving is linked to physical and spiritual disease. The implication is that you have an obligation to yourself for the sake of your own well-being to forgive. Quoting Rowan Williams, Cantacuzino warns us against forgiving too easily, 'if forgiveness is easy it is as if the suffering doesn't really matter' (Cantacuzino 2015, pp.14–16).

As the final chapters of this book were being completed, the area in which I lived and worked came under attack from terrorists. Three men in a van deliberately mowed down pedestrians on London Bridge, before crashing the van into railings near Southwark Cathedral. They then jumped out of the van, embarking on a rampage through Borough Market, stabbing and slashing at people randomly. Within eight minutes of the first call to the emergency services, the three terrorists were dead, shot by courageous police. Six people, ordinary people caught in an extraordinary event, were dead at the terrorists' hands, a death toll that rose to eight over the next few days.

On the Monday after the attack I travelled to Derby Cathedral to be introduced to the cathedral and city as the new dean. Local media took an interest, and even more so when they found out that I was moving from Southwark Cathedral, the attack still leading every news bulletin. So I found myself at 8 o'clock in the morning, live on BBC Radio Derbyshire, being asked a challenging ethical and spiritual question. When you find yourself caught up in a situation such as the London Bridge attack of 3 June 2017, isn't it incredibly hard to forgive? The interviewer might have continued, is it even morally right to think about forgiveness in the face of such evil?

Less than two weeks later London was to wake to the news of a fire at Grenfell Tower, a 24-floor housing block in West London. While television crews arrived to film live scenes of the burning tower, it was not known the fate of the families living inside the 129 flats. As the story developed, and with the building still burning, we learned about the concerns that the local residents' association had raised about the fire safety regulations. We learned that the families were instructed to stay in their flats as this would be the safest course of action. Staying put was fatal for 72 residents of this tower. Soon discussions in the media began to turn to how the fire had spread so quickly, and attention was focused on the cladding added to the tower in recent renovations. Tests conducted after the fire found that cladding and the insulation failed fire tests, but had previously been approved by the Royal Borough of Kensington and Chelsea as conforming to the relevant standards. The Borough Council was subject to great scrutiny both for its role alongside the tenancy housing organisation in ensuring the safety of the building but also for the initial response to these horrific events, which many saw as inadequate. Thinking about forgiveness in the immediate aftermath of these tragic events is incredibly hard.

But it is not whether it is hard to forgive or not which is the interesting question. To know that it is hard to forgive doesn't tell us *in what ways* it is hard to forgive or *what makes it* hard to forgive. There is, of course, the emotional difficulty of coming to forgiveness, and this is not something that should be underestimated. Many of the chapters in this book, including those by Richard Carter, Steve Nolan, Robin Shohet and Amanda Boorman, trace the emotional journey that accompanies the process of forgiving. But this book explores some of the other ways in which forgiveness in practice is hard, and shows how the morality of forgiveness is more complex than it may seem at first glance. I wasn't a victim of the direct actions of the attackers on London Bridge in June 2017 but my place of work was. Southwark Cathedral, the scene of daily worship for 1500 years, had to close its doors to its parishioners, who themselves had to close their businesses for 11 days. We were not able to offer the comfort and sanctuary of the cathedral to those people in the greatest need. Even if I had been in a position to forgive, is it possible to forgive the terrorists who were already dead? Forgiveness here would not affect the relationship between the victim and wrongdoer, as this was no longer a relationship that could exist. Nor would there be any possibility of the perpetrators repenting. But an attitude of forgiveness, despite this difficulty, may work in a different way and offer a release from the turmoil and distress. This is something I explore in my chapter.

If we were to think about forgiveness after Grenfell, it is not clear who should be forgiven, or even if there are individuals who are considered responsible. The inquiry into the fire may shed some light on these issues, but the involvement of different institutions, organisations and systems complicate this further. If we are to seek to forgive, from whom do we expect to hear repentance or apology? Is it even possible to forgive a group or an institution? Who, if anyone, can speak for the dead? And who is able to speak on behalf of the group in offering forgiveness? As Stephen Cherry in his chapter asks, if victims are not of one mind when it comes to forgiving the perpetrator, what does this mean for the perpetrator – are they forgiven or not?

In the south-west corner of the nave in Southwark Cathedral a memorial to the victims of *The Marchioness* disaster can be found. Here can be found the names of the 51 victims who drowned after a dredger collided with the pleasure boat *The Marchioness* in the early hours of 20 August 1989. Jonathan Phang had organised a birthday party for his best friend Antonio de Vasconcellos and invited many friends and colleagues from the fashion industry. This tragic disaster left so many dead and many survivors traumatised. Jonathan lived with the knowledge that it was his party; he had organised it. Twenty years later, finally Jonathan felt that he had forgiven himself (Jones 2009).

The difficulty posed by self-forgiveness is unlike the challenge of forgiving those who are already dead, or working out how to forgive a group or on behalf of a group. One and the same person are forgiving and being forgiven. On the surface this may seem easy, in fact so easy that it really doesn't count as forgiveness. We do not need to wait for apology from another, or acceptance of our forgiveness. We do not make ourselves vulnerable by giving up our feelings of revenge or clinging on to a desire for retributive justice. In practice, as several chapters in this book testify (most directly Stephen Cherry's but also Marian Liebmann's, Deborah Bowman's and Christiane Sanderson's) forgiving oneself is central to our experience of forgiveness. If we are to understand how we think about forgiveness then we need to carefully consider this category alongside traditional models of interpersonal forgiveness. Whether self-forgiveness should be considered a form of forgiveness, or perhaps would be better redefined as self-acceptance, is a question which this volume will explore.

The idea for this book came out of a Justice and Development Forum I chaired in 2013 at Southwark Cathedral. The three speakers, Marina Cantacuzino, Rabbi Jonathan Wittenberg from the New North London Synagogue and The Very Reverend Professor Iain Torrance, Pro-Chancellor of Aberdeen University and previously Convenor of the Church of Scotland, offered radically different perspectives on a word which many of us present may have assumed we understood. These differences generated energy and great discussion. What forgiveness looked like, and what rules applied differed greatly given the Christian, Jewish or non-religious backgrounds and the experiences of the speakers. Yet what struck us from this forum was the amazing mysteriousness of something that affects so many of us each day, and in all parts of our lives. To understand what forgiveness looked like from the different points of view and coming from different experiences in life seemed important, and perhaps urgent. We do often assume that when someone uses the word 'forgiveness', they mean it in the same way as we do. These three short presentations proved that this is a mistaken position to hold, and that a lot can be lost by such thinking.

It is often assumed even by mentioning the word that one is automatically advocating forgiveness. That is not the purpose of this book. Nor is the book's aim to provide guidance which can be translated into your situation so you can easily work out what forgiveness will look like and follow the steps to achieve it. Rather, this is a book that intends to encourage the reader to reflect on forgiveness and to challenge their assumptions. Many of the chapters identify assumptions based on the religious context of forgiveness. Honor Rhodes explicitly identifies this in her opening words and links an understanding of a religious injunction to forgive to instances of 'pseudo-forgiveness' (or 'premature forgiveness' as Christiane Sanderson calls it). These are those cases where an offer of forgiveness is given out of obligation but does not truly reflect the feelings of the forgiver.

The opening chapters of the book explore what forgiveness looks like in Islam, Judaism, Christianity and Buddhism and therefore what many members of our society may carry with them in terms of assumptions about what forgiveness means. They also introduce us to some of the issues taken up in the later chapters.

These chapters attempt to explore what forgiveness really looks like in practice. When relationships have broken down, when groups are divided by conflict, when we come to recognise our own wrongdoings or when we are consumed by feelings of revenge, how is forgiveness thought about and spoken about? The chapters in this book are written by people who have come across the challenge of forgiveness in their professional lives, including psychiatrists, therapists, social workers, politicians, chaplains, psychologists and religious ministers. In these chapters, they reflect on what forgiveness looks like across the different spheres of public and private life. These reflections pose challenging questions. How do we talk about forgiveness? Should we talk and discuss forgiveness openly in our professional work? Is forgiveness a duty or a gift? Can forgiveness help you heal? Is self-forgiveness possible or wise? Must forgiveness be preceded by apology? Should forgiveness always be encouraged? What are the dangers that come with forgiving? Inevitably the chapters don't agree on answers to these questions. The reality is that forgiveness is a slippery subject and in showing the range of divergent interpretations, this book has achieved one of its aims, namely to demonstrate the complexity and variety of ways in which people actually think about forgiveness.

Through reading these chapters it is hoped the landscape of forgiveness may become clearer to the reader, each chapter revealing a different aspect of and perspective on forgiveness so that by the end our own assumptions about what forgiveness looks like might be challenged and accompanied by new perspectives and examples. The map of the landscape this book provides is not complete; some territories are yet to be explored, some areas are loosely sketched and others may in fact be distorted. I hope that understanding forgiveness like this will leave the reader with a richer appreciation of this complex phenomenon that lies at the heart of human experience and relationships.

References

Cantacuzino, M. (2015) *The Forgiveness Project*. London: Jessica Kingsley Publishers.

Jones, L.-A. (2009) 'I've finally forgiven myself for my friends' cruel deaths on Marchioness'. *Daily Express*, www.express.co.uk/expressyourself/133363/I-ve-finally-forgiven-myself-formy-friends-cruel-deaths-on-Marchioness, accessed on 29/12/2017.

Chapter 1

REFLECTIONS ON FORGIVENESS
Some Jewish Perspectives

Howard Cooper

I was a young assistant rabbi in my first rabbinic post – in a large, formal, suburban congregation in London – leading the most awesome service in the Jewish liturgical year: the *Kol Nidrei* service for the eve of *Yom Kippur*, the Day of Atonement. After five years at the Leo Baeck College, which provided trainee rabbis with a good grounding in a range of traditional texts and traditions, I was keen to try out some of my own ideas; and enthusiastic about transforming the staid, institutionalised Jewish life that Reform Judaism in the UK represented for me at the time.

This was supposed to be the holiest evening of the year. Its themes – so the tradition said – were personal and collective repentance for wrongdoing, seeking forgiveness from God, repairing our relationships with each other and our maker. This was serious business. But how could I make these abstract ideas personal, religiously alive, for myself and members of the community? I thought I would ask the assembled congregation, gathered in their festive finery, to do something more than merely mouth the words of the prayers or listen contentedly to the choir's well-rehearsed performance.

The drama of the opening *Kol Nidrei* prayer was over, the Torah scrolls were returned to the Ark where they normally reside, the strains of the traditional melodies faded into stillness.

All was hush and expectation. I decided to draw the community's attention to a Talmudic passage quoted in our liturgy. It states that 'For transgressions between an individual and God, the Day of Atonement effects atonement; but for transgressions that are between one individual and another, the Day of Atonement effects atonement only if one person has regained the goodwill of the other'[1] – forgiveness must not only be prayed for, it must be enacted.

So before we proceeded with the rest of the service, I said, we needed to take to heart this rabbinic text and turn to those around us – family, friends, other members of the community – and acknowledge anything that was lingering in our relationships that we wanted to apologise for, or put right, or for which we wanted to seek forgiveness. I suggested that we take some time, now, to do this: we might want to get up and approach someone, or we may be sitting next to someone with whom we could begin to engage in this vital dialogic aspect of *teshuvah* – repentance and finding forgiveness.

There then emerged – after a moment or two of aching silence – a kind of dull, low growl of embarrassed discontent from the assembled gathering. I could just as well have been asking them to come forward naked and sacrifice a goat to Baal. I realised – my grandiosity not having quite extinguished my sensitivity to the gathering mood – that I might have misjudged things a little. I needed to do something to remedy the situation.

Undaunted by the frisson of disapproval that was rippling through the room, I got down from the reading desk at the front of the synagogue and went towards the Chairman of the community in order, I hoped, both to model what I was asking people to do, and to myself apologise for anything that I had done to upset him over the past year (there'd been a few things). As I approached him, the look of frozen horror that I saw etched on his face taught me two lessons that have stayed with me to this day. First, never underestimate the extent to which one's own religious enthusiasms may not be shared by others; and, second, that the emotional complexities around the theme of forgiveness may involve some of

1   Based on Mishnah Yoma 8:9

the hardest psychological, emotional and spiritual work that we are ever called on to do.

Judaism's understanding of forgiveness is rooted in the Hebrew Bible. The capacity for forgiveness is one of the major characteristics attributed to the Judaic God, with images of a forgiving God scattered throughout the scriptures. Jewish communities to this day recite one such Biblical text on *Yom Kippur*: 'The Eternal One, the Eternal One, a God of mercy and compassion, slow to anger, generous in love and truth, showing love to thousands, *forgiving* sin, wrong and failure, who pardons...' (Exodus 34:5–7). This is a key motif, repeated throughout the day, and acts both as a reminder to the atoning Jew that they are bound up in a relationship with a divine energy animated by recognisably human qualities – such as forgiveness – and that the human task and responsibility is to mirror these divine qualities. We can learn to forgive, and are enjoined to forgive, because we are in relationship, both millennial and yet personal, with a God who is 'forgiving'.

It may well be that the Hebrew Bible's pictures of 'God' are filled with imaginative anthropomorphised projections of a whole spectrum of human emotions and attributes (from compassion to hatred) – 'God' made in our image, as it were – but the power of such a self-constructed image of divinity transcends its origins within the Judaic imagination. The Biblical portrait of a forgiving God, now embedded in Jewish consciousness and liturgy, acts as a source of both comfort and encouragement: just as we can be forgiven, so we can find within ourselves the capacity (*imitato dei*) to forgive. This is part of our 'divine' potential. Such, at any rate, is the theory.

Almost every single one of the nearly 50 occasions in which the Hebrew Bible mentions the act of forgiving, it is God who is either doing the forgiving, or is asked to do the forgiving, or is mentioned in texts instructing the community how to seek forgiveness from God through ritual or cultic means. And yet the exception to this – and indeed the very first time the word 'forgive' appears in the Bible – is in an entirely person-to-person context. The Biblical prototype for forgiveness is what transpires between Joseph and his brothers in Egypt following the death of their father Jacob.

What does this text reveal about the psychodynamics of forgiveness?

> When Joseph's brothers saw that their father was dead, they said: 'What if Joseph still bears a grudge against us and pays us back for all the wrong that we did him?' So they sent this message to Joseph: 'Before his death your father left this instruction: "So shall you say to Joseph: 'Forgive, I urge you, the offense and guilt of your brothers who treated you so harshly.' Therefore please forgive the offense of the servants of the God of your father." And Joseph was in tears as they spoke to him. (Genesis 50:15–17)

Joseph – who, we recall, is described by the narrator as the highest authority in the land after Pharaoh – seeks to calm the nerves of his understandably fear-filled siblings. The memory of his betrayal by his brothers[2] has not disappeared, but he gives a 'religious' spin to the long-term consequences of his siblings' murderous intentions towards him: '...although you intended me harm, God intended it for good...the survival of many people'; and he follows it up with words of reassurance: 'And so, fear not, I will sustain you and your children' (verses 20–21). And the Biblical narrator brings this dramatic episode to a close with the comment: 'Thus he reassured them, speaking kindly to them [literally: speaking to their hearts]' (verse 21).

So, on the surface, this text – the first and only text in the Hebrew Bible that shows forgiveness being sought and enacted on an interpersonal level – seems straightforward: wrongdoing is acknowledged by the perpetrators; forgiveness is requested; forgiveness is offered through both reassurance and action. And yet a closer reading of the text reveals its deeply enigmatic quality. For the act of seeking forgiveness by the brothers is based on a lie. Cannily, the brothers cast their appeal to Joseph in the form of an instruction coming from their father: 'Our father Jacob has asked you to forgive us' is the message – but this is a fabrication. There is no textual basis for this claim in the preceding narrative. But it is psychologically astute – for they know (or they think they know) that Joseph's reverence for Jacob will likely sway his

---

2   Genesis 37

decision to forgive them. Yet how do we read Joseph's tears as they spin this tale? Is he genuinely moved by what he experiences as a heartfelt acknowledgement of wrong committed? Or is he in tears because he realises that the brothers haven't changed their devious natures and are attempting to manipulate him into forgiveness? The Biblical storytellers reveal their artfulness – and psychological acuity – by leaving this question unresolved. It's a question with a universal and timeless quality. How often might one be faced in life with this multi-faceted dilemma: how genuine, how wholehearted, are those seeking our forgiveness for hurt caused? How are we to judge? Does it matter what's in someone's heart? What are we to do with our not-knowing?

Whether Joseph believes them or not, whether the request for forgiveness is genuine or not, ambiguity is set aside and we are given a picture of the enactment by the injured party (Joseph) of the capacity to overcome any residual feelings of anger, hurt or grievance. From a Judaic perspective, this is the Biblical model for how to forgive: Joseph substitutes goodwill and protectiveness and the urge to preserve life for the kind of feelings that often dominate after wrong has been done – anger, the wish for revenge, the inability to let go of a residual sense of hurt or injustice.

How did Judaism develop and refine its understanding of forgiveness over the two millennia that followed the canonisation of the Hebrew scriptures?

The general attitude of early Judaism is summed up in the verse from the post-Biblical ethical work, the 'Wisdom of ben Sirach' (Ecclesiasticus): 'Forgive your neighbour their wrongdoing – so that your sins will be forgiven you when you pray'.[3] This attitude feeds into Rabbinic Judaism, where the distinction is made – as we saw in my opening remarks – between wrongdoing that is seen to be committed against God (failure to keep the Sabbath, the dietary laws, and so on – the rituals that the tradition prescribes to maintain the distinctive identity of the Jewish people) and wrongdoing committed against a fellow human being.

The former has to be dealt with between a person and their maker – forgiveness is an existential matter for the heart and soul

---

3   Ecclesiasticus 28:2

and is a subjective, psychological and spiritual activity involving prayer, inner reflectiveness and personal resolve to return to one's better self. The latter has to be enacted between oneself and whoever one has harmed – it has to be resolved on the human level.

One of the consequences of this is that the normative Judaic attitude to forgiveness shares out the responsibility: the person who has caused harm has to *seek* forgiveness, and the person who has been hurt has to *grant* forgiveness. And the rabbinic tradition, as recorded over time in the Talmud, sought to legislate for, and guide people through, both sides of this forgiveness equation. Thus we find a statement such as:

> Even if a person makes financial restitution to another whom he or she has harmed, they are not forgiven by God until they seek personal forgiveness from the one harmed. And that latter person, if they do not forgive the other, is called cruel/merciless.[4]

While highlighting the importance of forgiving those who have injured us in any way, the Talmudic rabbis were also keen to see these interpersonal relationships as being 'triangular', so to speak – in the sense that they always saw a divine dimension in play as well as a human one:

> If a person has received an injury, then even if the wrongdoer has not asked for their forgiveness, the receiver of the injury must nevertheless ask God to show the wrongdoer compassion, just as Job prayed for his friends…(Rabbi) Gamaliel said: Let this be a sign to you, that whenever you are compassionate, the Compassionate One will have compassion on you.[5]

More than 1500 years after these rabbinic discussions were written down and became foundational for Jewish thinking about questions of forgiveness, a mid-19th-century German compilation of Jewish laws – a kind of 'how to be Jewish without having to study all the texts of tradition' anthology – summarised the Jewish stance on forgiveness as follows:

---

4   Talmud: *Baba Kama* VIII: 7
5   Talmud, *Baba Kama*, IX: 29, 30

> If someone comes to you and asks for forgiveness, you must do
> so with a perfect heart, and not be cruel, for such an attitude is
> not characteristic of the Jewish way... It is customary for a Jew to
> be slow to anger and easily appeased, and when sinners ask for
> forgiveness we should do so wholeheartedly and with a willing
> soul. Even if you have been grievously wronged, you should not
> seek vengeance, nor bear a grudge against the other... If one
> doesn't let one's hatred pass away, one's prayers are not heard on
> Yom Kippur; but one who is magnanimous and forgives has all
> their own sins forgiven. (*Kitzur Shulchan Aruch* 131:4)

Again, what we have here is a theoretical stance: a religious
tradition can articulate an ethical perspective until it is blue in
the face but it doesn't mean that adherents of that tradition can
live out the rigorous demands such high-minded ideals place on
us. It may be worth noting that rabbinic realism also recognised
that someone may be repeatedly unable or unwilling to forgive
hurt done to them – in which case the seeker after forgiveness has
their own responsibility absolved after three honest attempts. Such
pragmatism is a way of balancing the ethical demands of a tradition
with ordinary human frailties and fallibilities.

Nevertheless, it can be sobering to encounter testimony of
individuals who have been able to respond to life events by offering
forgiveness in a manner congruent with the highest ideals of the
Jewish tradition. One such example is the testimony of Mathilde
Rathenau. She was the mother of Walter Rathenau, the German-
Jewish statesman who served as Foreign Minister during the
Weimar Republic and was assassinated in 1922 by a right-wing
terrorist group. To the mother of her son's murderer, she extended
the following words:

> In grief unspeakable, I give you my hand. You are the most pitiable
> of women; tell your son I forgive him in the name and spirit of the
> man he murdered; I forgive, even as God may forgive, if before an
> earthly judge he makes full confession of his guilt, and before a
> Heavenly One he repents. (Reform Synagogues of Great Britain
> 1985, p.728)

Such a stance is aligned with the rabbinic injunctions outlined above and with the down-to-earth humility of the ethical treatise Avot de-Rabbi Nathan (c.700–900 CE) which states simply and directly: 'Learn to receive suffering, and forgive those who harm you' (Montefiore and Loewe 1974, p.462). This same unvarnished piety is to be heard in the prayer of an unknown woman that was found on a piece of wrapping paper in Ravensbruck concentration camp at the end of the Second World War:

> O Lord, remember not only the men and women of goodwill but also those of ill will. But do not remember the suffering they have inflicted upon us; remember the fruits we brought thanks to this suffering, our comradeship, our loyalty, our humility, the courage, the generosity, the greatness of heart which has grown out of this; and when they come to judgment, let all the fruits that we have born be their forgiveness. (Reform Synagogues of Great Britain 1985, pp.505–506)

So much for the theoretical stance about forgiveness articulated by Jewish ethical teaching – that if a person has done wrong (hurt or injured another person in word or deed) it is their duty to acknowledge the wrong and ask for forgiveness; and that it is the duty of the injured party to offer forgiveness. This is the *halacha* – Jewish law. The dynamic of forgiveness is dependent on the person who has done wrong taking responsibility for what they have done and having the humility and the courage to ask for forgiveness; and it is the responsibility of the injured party (whatever they might feel about it) to offer forgiveness to the wrongdoer.

But how does this play out in everyday life?

Anyone who has ever been hurt in a relationship, anyone who has ever been let down, or abused, or betrayed, anyone who has suffered mockery or humiliation, anyone who has been wronged in a relationship – and this must include all of us, whether it is as a child with their schoolmates, or at work, or in business, or in friendships, or in a marriage – all of us know what it is to be the injured party.

All of us know the pain, the distress, when we have been wronged – by our peers, or by strangers, by colleagues, by the state, by our parents, or our children, or our partners. The hurt can be physical, emotional, mental or psychological. Or it can be all of these. This is the stuff of everyday life, the hurt we inflict and the hurt we receive, the hurt we perpetrate and the hurt we endure. We know it well. Sometimes we feel we know it too well. And we know too how hard it is – when we are feeling injured, when we've been bruised or damaged, when we have suffered through someone's actions, or lack of actions – we know how hard it is to forgive.

Why should we forgive, we say, when they haven't suffered too? Why should we forgive, when they haven't acknowledged our hurt? Why should we forgive, even if they have admitted the hurt they have caused? Why should we forgive, just because they ask us to? As if it's the easiest thing in the world. When forgiveness is one of the hardest things in the world – one of the hardest emotional, psychological, spiritual activities of the human heart and soul.

I still haven't forgiven some people, for some things. I know this. And I see myself as quite a forgiving person. But some hurts still stick stubbornly inside, and some angers and resentments, and I can't forgive – or at least I haven't managed to yet. And I don't think I'm alone in this recognition that to forgive is very hard work. So although Jewish teaching says it's our duty, if we are the injured party, to forgive, it doesn't tell us *how* we are supposed to do that. It doesn't offer a psychologically informed step-by-step programme on how to forgive. It leaves us to our own devices. It leaves us to struggle with our own limitations, our own small-mindedness, our own unyielding obstinacy.

Of course, it can be easier to forgive when someone who has done us wrong admits that they have. Faced with someone's tears, or words, or acts of contrition – in the immediacy of that moment, that living encounter, or in reflecting on it in the aftermath of such an encounter – something in us may soften, something in us may recognise our common humanity, that we are all capable of inflicting hurt. We use a word like 'heartfelt' to evoke the special quality of such moments – when a hurt that's been caused is truly regretted, and the injured party can allow the other's 'heartfelt' regret to penetrate their own hurt heart. It takes courage (and humility) to ask for forgiveness. And it takes a kind of courage (and humility) to forgo one's self-defensive *amour-propre* and allow somebody's act of contrition to dissolve our narcissistic hurt – there can be a sort of perverse pleasure and comfort in not allowing anyone in, and nursing our own wounds.

But, of course, scenarios where forgiveness is both offered and accepted don't always happen. Maybe the one who has caused harm or hurt just can't find it in themselves to ask for forgiveness – this probably happens more often than not. Or maybe they are no longer here to do it: sometimes people die before there's an opportunity for this kind of reconciliation. In either case, we might want to forgive, we might want to be released from old hurt, an old grievance, an old wound we still feel, but we just can't find it in us to forgive, or work out how to do it.

So then, perhaps, all we can do is *try to forgive ourselves*. Forgive ourselves for our inability to forgive others. Can we at least do that? Maybe that is the clue to being able to forgive someone else for the hurt or wrong they have done us. We have to be able to forgive ourselves – for being so weak, so sensitive, so fragile, so uncaring. We have to be able to forgive ourselves for our common, shared human frailties and inadequacies. We have to be able to forgive ourselves for all the times we fail to live up to our ideals, all the times we don't act from our generous and compassionate selves, for all the times we are mean-spirited and selfish and cruel. We have to be able to forgive ourselves for all the times we fail to live from our better selves.

And if we can do this work, this inner work – and it is psychological work and spiritual work, and it never ends – if we can do this work as best we can, then we might be able to begin to forgive others who have also failed to live out their better selves and have caused us the hurt and harm in the first place. The beginning of forgiving others is learning to forgive oneself.

The psychodynamics of forgiveness involve a tapestry of complex themes. *Seeking forgiveness* – so much shame to face, so much fear, so much risk of rejection, so much hurt to face about the hurt we have caused: how does anyone do it? *Forgiving others* – the hurt we bear may have been inflicted deliberately or accidentally, knowingly or unknowingly, we feel ourselves to be the injured party on so many occasions: how does anyone do it? *Forgiving oneself* – not casually, flippantly, defensively, but with as much compassion and moral seriousness as we can muster: again, how does anyone do it?

And yet, time and again, we do it, and must do it: for the world depends on it.

References

Ganzfried, S. (1864: translated 1961, Goldin, H.E.) *Kitzur Shulchan Aruch,* Code of Jewish Law: A Compilation of Jewish Laws and Customs. New York: Hebrew Publishing Company.

Montefiore, C.G. and Loewe, H. (1974) *A Rabbinic Anthology.* New York, NY: Schocken Books.

Reform Synagogues of Great Britain (1985) *Forms of Prayer for Jewish Worship, Volume III, Prayers for the High Holydays.* London: Reform Synagogues of Great Britain.

Chapter 2

FORGIVENESS AND CHRISTIANITY

Anthony Bash

Ask many a Tom, Dick, or Harriet in the street about the Christian view of forgiveness, and they are likely to say that Christianity is *the* religion of forgiveness and love, and that Jesus was the first to teach that to forgive, even the unrepentant, is morally very worthwhile. They might also add that when Jesus forgave the people who were killing him, he wonderfully modelled what he had taught about forgiveness. Some who do not have a Christian heritage might even know the words Jesus said as he was dying, 'Father, forgive them, for they know not what they do' (Luke 23:34).

And of course, to forgive does make good sense, for the alternatives are so much less attractive. Vengeance and retribution are self-evidently not good ways to settle wrongs. Neither is cutting off contact with those we think have wronged us, nor are nursing grudges and grievances. Being bitter about wrongs can leave people 'knotted up' and deeply unhappy. Conventional wisdom also suggests that lack of forgiveness can sometimes make people ill and depressed.

The practice of forgiveness is a hallmark of Christianity – Tom, Dick, and Harriet are, to this extent, right. However, what the New Testament documents say about forgiveness – when and how to forgive, and what forgiveness is, for example – is considerably more complicated and more nuanced than popular understanding would suggest.

The first point to make is that Christianity, despite what people typically think, did not 'invent' or 'discover' forgiveness or the idea that forgiving the unrepentant might be a virtue. There is widespread evidence that indicates people have always been forgivers according to the social and cultural norms of their day, even if they did not describe their actions by a word that in our culture and traditions corresponds to the word we use for 'forgiveness', and even if how they practised forgiveness might be different from the way we might practise it today. An example illustrates the point. The three Greek words for interpersonal forgiveness that we find in the New Testament do not occur in pre-Christian secular Greek literature as meaning 'forgive' and 'forgiveness'. In fact, in ancient Greek there is no word for 'forgive' and 'forgiveness' in the sense that we mean these things today. So, should we say that the ancient Greeks did not forgive those who wronged them? Not at all! They described their forgiving actions in ways that do not correspond with New Testament language and concepts, and they thought of forgiveness rather differently from the ways that those who wrote the New Testament did.

In the language and forms in which we understand forgiveness today, forgiveness grew out of Old Testament Jewish culture and practice. (Some may be surprised by this, as the faith of the Old Testament is sometimes parodied as being primarily vengeful and retributive.) For example, the second-century BC Jewish scribe, ben Sira of Jerusalem, borrowed the Greek language that was used of *God's* forgiveness in the Septuagint (the translation of the Hebrew Old Testament in Greek), and adopted it to refer by analogy to what we now call 'interpersonal forgiveness' (see Sirach 28:2). As we shall see, Jesus developed this way of looking at interpersonal forgiveness. He also expanded the range of people whom one should love (and so forgive) to include not only one's 'neighbour' (that is, those related to us by birth, culture, or nationhood – see Leviticus 19:17–18) but also all those who look to us for love and forgiveness (see, for example, Luke 10:25–37, the parable of the Good Samaritan).

So, what exactly is interpersonal forgiveness in the Christian tradition? If we start with the New Testament, we see that there are principally three words that express the pattern of interpersonal ethical behaviour called 'forgiveness' that Jesus so robustly developed.

Two of the words (*aphiemi*, a verb, and the related noun, *aphesis*) have both a Greek and a Jewish line of interpretation. As for the Greek line, the two words were already used in other contexts in secular Greek, as I have said. They were used in the context of letting something or someone go, giving up, leaving, and sometimes even permitting someone or something. They were also used for writing off or waiving a debt. The choice of these words to denote what people meant by interpersonal forgiveness suggests that interpersonal forgiveness is to let go of taking vengeance and retribution, as well as to let go of even the desire for vengeance and retribution. In modern-day terms, to forgive in this way will mean that those who have been wronged let go of the personal consequences – whether they are moral, legal, or psychological – of having been wronged. It also means that they no longer attribute the wrongdoing to the wrongdoer but a) release the memory of the wrongdoing from association with the wrongdoer, and b) treat wrongdoers as if they were discharged from moral culpability.

As for the Jewish line of interpretation, the two words were already in use to describe in Greek God's merciful response to human wrongdoing, and so they had come to be interpreted as meaning God forgave human sin. The way God's forgiveness was understood in the period of the Old Testament was by a variety of metaphors, such as by God putting sin behind God's back (Isaiah 38:17), casting sin into the sea (Micah 7:19), treading sin underfoot (Micah 7:19), removing it 'as far as the east is from the west' (Psalm 103:12), and blotting it out (Nehemiah 4:5). In other words, when God forgave, the wrong and its consequences were in some way detached from attribution to the wrongdoer, and the wrongdoer was thereby discharged from continuing moral accountability and culpability.

One implication of using ideas about God and what God did in this way was to make divine forgiveness the model, as much as it could be, for fleshing out the nature and scope of interpersonal forgiveness. (ben Sira had used one of these words in Sirach 28:2, for example.) More overtly and at a later time, see Colossians 3:13, where Paul writes to the members of the church at Colossae, 'As the

Lord has forgiven you, so you also must forgive one another': in other words, the form, scope, and meaning of interpersonal forgiveness were to be rooted in the pattern of Jewish understanding about divine forgiveness.

The other word commonly used for forgiveness in the New Testament is the verb *charizomai*. It means 'to give a gift' or 'to give freely'. Etymologically, the word is related to *charis*, which means 'grace' or 'gift'. *Charizomai* was used in secular Greek, and is commonly found in writings that honour people for their civic-minded beneficence. The word can also refer to cancelling a debt. Paul the Apostle adapted the word to refer to how people are to behave towards one another within Christian communities, and by it he meant that people were to be generous, long-suffering, and kind towards one another. (The word had not previously been used in quite this sense and context in either secular Greek literature or in the Septuagint.) When Paul uses the word in the context of communal relations, he means that people should forgive or pardon one another, and the word is usually translated that way. Both the etymology and Paul's use of the word bring out another idea of forgiveness: forgiveness is a gracious act of kindness, which may even be undeserved – an act of kindness that is much like the giving of a gift.

Now that we have completed this brief linguistic background summary, we can step back and say that the New Testament is the first sustained exploration in ancient literature of what it means for people to forgive and be forgiven. However, the New Testament does not say all that there is to say about forgiveness. There is even evidence within the New Testament of a degree of debate and perhaps even of disagreement on some points. The process of exploration about the nature and scope of forgiveness that the New Testament began continues today, judging by the volume of books and articles that are being published! See, for example, Chapter 6, where Stephen Cherry explores the idea of self-forgiveness, an aspect of forgiveness that the New Testament does not directly address. Also left unaddressed in the New Testament are questions such as whether groups can forgive or be forgiven, whether we can forgive the dead, and whether – and how – we can forgive unknown wrongdoers.

From what the New Testament does address, we can say, for example, that people are to forgive 'anyone' of 'anything' (Mark 11:25) and people must go on forgiving those who seek forgiveness (Matthew 18:21–22; Luke 17:3–4). Luke 11:4, Mark 11:25 and Matthew 6:12 link interpersonal forgiveness to divine forgiveness: Matthew 6:12, for example, is part of the Lord's Prayer and, in its traditional form, includes the words, 'Forgive us our trespasses [sins], as we forgive those who trespass [sin] against us.' The link is further explored in Matthew 18:21–35 (the parable of the Unforgiving Servant) and is probably best explained as meaning that it is impossible at least not to want to forgive others if one is a recipient of divine forgiveness, since to be a recipient of divine forgiveness is necessarily also to be transformed by it and to start to become a person who forgives in the way that Christians are to forgive.

When it comes to the writings of Paul the Apostle, Paul sees forgiveness as part of a compendium of virtues that help build communities. In Ephesians 4:32, for example, he urges the members of the church in Ephesus to be kind to one another, tender-hearted and forgiving towards each other, clearly understanding these virtues as different ways of describing how to build a loving community. The same pattern of thinking is evident in Colossians 3:12–13, where Paul seems to think of compassion, kindness, humility, meekness, patience, forbearance, love and forgiveness as different aspects of the same set of interpersonal and communal virtues.

As with any new ethical concept, it is relatively easy to set out broad principles but, if I may put it this way, 'the devil is in the detail'! This point has come sharply into focus in my mind as I was preparing to write this chapter, because a friend of mine who was talking about her own experiences of hurts, said to me, 'I just don't understand how people can suffer grievous wrongs, and so quickly say they have forgiven the person who wrongs them.' The rest of this chapter will, I hope, offer some reflections on and ways of thinking about her comment.

For many of us, forgiveness is a process that we weave in and out of, some days feeling more forgiving about a wrong, and on other days, feeling less forgiving. For most of us, forgiveness is not a once-and-for-all, irrevocable step. We may say to someone that we have forgiven them, but if we are honest we still have to go on forgiving them. In this sense, forgiving another person is like peeling off the layers of an onion: we may think we have forgiven, only to discover there is still more to forgive or that we need to forgive all over again.

It is also true that forgiveness is a spectrum of responses to wrongdoing. One can see evidence of what we might call 'thickly textured forgiveness', when the wrongdoer and victim have talked about the incident, and when perhaps an apology has been given and what can be put right has been put right. Perhaps also reconciliation and the restoration of the former relationship result. However, there are varieties of less thickly textured forgiveness – we might call these varieties examples of 'thin forgiveness' – where the forgiveness is alloyed with other responses. Such a case might be where the wrongdoer has died, and the victim has come to learn about some of the complexities and issues the wrongdoer faced that make the wrongdoer's action more explicable (but still wrong) and so more forgivable.

Given such a range of possible ways of forgiving, it might be better not to think of forgiveness as one type of response to wrongdoing whereby we say, 'This is forgiveness but that is not' but, rather, to recognise that forgiveness is the gift of the giver, and the giver sets the parameters of his or her gift of forgiveness and may label the gift as such. So long as there is, in the philosopher Ludwig Wittgenstein's phrase, some sort of 'family resemblance' with the general understanding of forgiveness, forgiveness is forgiveness, if someone thinks it to be forgiveness, whatever the niceties of the details of a particular act may be. We thereby avoid an absurd – and judgemental – approach to another's actions, such as by saying, 'What you have done is not to forgive, even though you think you have.'

In terms of the Christian tradition of forgiveness, there is considerable debate about whether to forgive unconditionally is an example of forgiveness in its most thickly textured form. (This is in part what my friend had in mind when she wondered how people can forgive quickly: she observed that after suffering a grievous wrong, people sometimes quickly forgive without apparently also engaging with the person who wronged them.)

In support of the supposed virtue of unconditional forgiveness, people point to what they understand to be the example of Jesus on the cross, and say, as I suggested above, that in Luke 23:34 Jesus forgave those who were killing him. In other words, to forgive unconditionally is to follow the example of Jesus, enormously difficult though it obviously is.

But did Jesus forgive unconditionally? Leaving aside the fact that Luke 23:34 is a disputed text (in many Bibles, it is placed in square brackets, indicating that its manuscript authenticity is to some extent doubted), a straightforward reading of the words indicates that Jesus prayed that God would forgive those who were killing him. Despite the popular view, the words are not a prayer of forgiveness on the part of Jesus. Rather, they are a prayer that God would forgive those who acted in ignorance both of Jesus' identity and status and of his innocence. The words do illustrate that Jesus himself loved his enemies and that he prayed for them, as he himself had taught that people should (Matthew 5:44) but, on any straightforward reading, the prayer does not indicate that he was thereby forgiving his unrepentant enemies.

We can go further. The pattern of forgiveness in the New Testament is that almost always repentance and remorse precede forgiveness, and where repentance and remorse do not appear to precede forgiveness, they are in fact implied. In other words, unconditional forgiveness is not the pattern of forgiveness in the New Testament. This is not surprising, since interpersonal forgiveness is modelled on divine forgiveness, and repentance and remorse always precede the gift of divine forgiveness. Of course, Christians should still pray for and love those who wrong them, even if the wrongdoers are not repentant. We should not underestimate how difficult this can be, or that in this case, as in many others, Jesus taught a radical and counter-intuitive ethic. But it is one step too far to say that Jesus taught and modelled that we are obliged to forgive the unrepentant.

There are sound reasons why forgiveness without antecedent repentance and remorse is undesirable:

- If a wrongdoer is not aware of the wrong that has been done, the wrongdoer may possibly repeat the wrong on another occasion or in a different situation. People often show continuity in their behaviour, and they may not even be aware of the hurt they cause by their actions. In other words, forgiveness without repentance denies wrongdoers the opportunity to learn from past mistakes. To give an everyday example, sometimes people may not realise that their language and behaviour are sexist or offensive: it may help them to change if they are helped to see that what they are saying and doing is inappropriate and unacceptable.

- To forgive unconditionally denies a wrongdoer the opportunity to put right a wrong. Some wrongdoers are appalled when they realise the wrong they have inadvertently caused, for example, and eagerly wish to 'clear the air' and to put right the wrong they have done when they have been made aware of it.

- To forgive unconditionally appears to make light of the fact that people are moral agents who are responsible for their actions. Being responsible and being accountable as a moral agent are part of the richness of being human. Simply to choose to overlook the fact of a wrong and so not to hold a wrongdoer to account does a disservice to a wrongdoer because it does not give due place to the attributes and responsibilities that characterise an adult human being who is also, incidentally, a wrongdoer. For example, some of us may know people who, often long after an event, discover that they have done wrong or caused offence, and who then say, 'Why did no one treat me like an adult and tell me?'

- To forgive unconditionally may be to deny victims the opportunity to be heard, and to speak out about how they have been violated. After a wrongdoing, it matters that victims stand up to those who have violated them and name both the wrong and its effects on them. An important and interesting book that explores this idea is *Ethical Loneliness: The Injustice of Not Being Heard* by Jill Stauffer (2015).

- Following on from the last point, part of being able to move on and forgive a wrong is for victims to know their response to the wrong has been affirmed and validated. It also matters to victims to know that their anger is not an eccentric quirk of a maladaptive personality! Thus, if victims forgive unconditionally, they may suffer not one but two blows: the first is that they were violated because of the wrong itself, and the second is that they have added to the violation (whether voluntarily or, as we shall see below, by societal pressure) by forgiving without also having validation of how they feel and without receiving justice. (I am not necessarily referring to justice as administered by judicial institutions but justice in the sense of knowing, after having been wronged, that one's outrage, hurt and bewilderment have been affirmed, understood and engaged with by dispassionate onlookers.)

- To forgive unconditionally may have the indirect effect of buttressing systemic evil and injustice, as some political and social frameworks appear implicitly to promote the supposed moral virtue of unconditional forgiveness. The (probably) unintended effect can be to leave the deviant behaviour unchallenged and so for forgiveness to be a (perhaps unintended) tool of oppression, control and domination. For example, many women's groups have recently been pointing out that those who suffer domestic abuse sometimes consider that they should forgive their abusers because it is 'right' to do so: such actions obviously can have the incidental effect of leaving the abuser and the abuser's deviant behaviour unchallenged and undealt with. They can also leave abusers still thinking that their behaviour, which in former times may have been normative, is acceptable in modern societies.

- Perhaps surprisingly, to forgive unconditionally denies victims the opportunity to learn from those who have wronged them, since right and wrong are not always as simple as people think them to be, and they are often not as one-sided as people assume. This latter point is powerfully illustrated in the New Testament in the story of the woman who had been caught in an act of adultery (John 8:1–11).

True, according to the Old Testament, the woman had sinned (and for this sin faced a death sentence); also true was the fact that her accusers had themselves sinned. So, Jesus said to the woman's accusers, 'Let the one who is without guilt [from sin] throw the first stone [to execute the woman]' (John 8:7). Unsurprisingly, since each of the woman's accusers had sinned, they were shamed when confronted with their own double-standards and self-righteousness. As a result, none of them was willing or able to take part in executing the woman.

Of course, we may choose to forgive the unrepentant because we wish to, and it is not necessarily wrong to choose to do this. There is even evidence that sometimes, when forgiveness precedes repentance, a wrongdoer is so moved that the wrongdoer then repents. From the world of literature, we have the example of Bishop Myriel in Victor Hugo's novel, *Les Misérables*, (1862): Myriel forgave Jean Valjean for stealing some of the Bishop's silverware, thereby moving Jean Valjean to repentance and a changed life. But the point I want to press is that to forgive in this way is not mandatory, or even morally better; on some occasions, for the reasons I have set out, it may even be less helpful than offering forgiveness after repentance.

It is also important to acknowledge that we cannot always tell whether a person's repentance is genuine. Those of us who have had contact with children will know that children are often quick to say 'sorry' but often rather less quick in the future to model a change of behaviour! Jeffrey Murphy quotes an unnamed Hollywood mogul saying of sincerity, 'Sincerity is the most precious thing in the world. When you have learned to fake it, you've got it made' (Murphy 2012, p.155). The same is true of repentance.

True repentance – for all the difficulty of telling whether it is false or genuine – should lead to changed thoughts and behaviour, as well as changed feelings. I suggest true repentance is characterised by the following descriptors. The first is that wrongdoers connect with and relate to the hurt and suffering they have caused. Part of this will be to recognise that they have violated and disrupted the social and psychological well-being of their victims. In other words, wrongdoers need to *empathise* with their victims. Second, wrongdoers need to experience a degree of *guilt* and *shame* on account of their actions, and to be prepared voluntarily to make appropriate *restitution* and *reparation*. Last, wrongdoers need to show evidence of *moral re-formation*, having renounced and repudiated their former ways of thinking and acting. In other words, repentance marks a thoroughgoing change of thoughts, behaviour and feelings that is likely to lead to a long-term change of lifestyle.

You may recall that I said earlier that interpersonal forgiveness is, to some extent, modelled on the pattern of divine forgiveness. We have seen, for example, that just as God forgives only after repentance and remorse, so human beings seem best suited to forgive after repentance and remorse.

However, in four important respects, divine forgiveness does not work well as a model for interpersonal forgiveness, and it is important to clarify where and how this is so, for we often conflate the two models and end up confused.

First, interpersonal forgiveness concerns two parties which in this chapter I have usually referred to as 'the wrongdoer' and 'the victim'. When it comes to divine forgiveness, there is a wrongdoer – a human being whose actions from a divine perspective are wrong – but not a victim, for there is not an obvious way that we can regard God as a 'victim' of human wrongdoing. Various attempts have been made to say how God might be regarded as a 'victim' but I am unpersuaded by those attempts, and I regard them as little more than trying to square a circle!

Second, in terms of person-to-person actions, we are faced with what Hannah Arendt in *The Human Condition* (1958) has called 'the predicament of irreversibility'. To put it simply, an act once done cannot be undone. God may in some way be able to 'wipe the slate clean' but with human beings we cannot do that. Forgiveness, when offered by one person to another, does not and cannot reverse the fact that a moral wrong has been committed, or the fact of the pain, hurt and suffering caused by the wrongdoing. The best that forgiveness can do is to heal the relational consequences caused by the wrongdoing. This is, of course, important, but is a limitation on the nature and form of Christian forgiveness.

Next, divine forgiveness results in reconciliation between the human wrongdoer and God. Interpersonal forgiveness sometimes also results in reconciliation between the wrongdoer and the victim, but not always, and not necessarily. After a wrongdoing, it may be wise to heal the relational rupture that the wrongdoing caused but not revert to the former pattern of the relationship. For example, a person who has been physically abused by a wrongdoer may decide that to return to the company or presence of the wrongdoer – even a deeply repentant wrongdoer – would be unwise and put the former victim at continuing risk.

Last, and very importantly, the Bible insists that divine forgiveness is always just, whereas interpersonal forgiveness, by its very nature, cannot be just, because it involves the victim waiving the right to retribution and treating the wrongdoer as if the wrongdoer were discharged from moral culpability.

To my mind, we cannot both forgive a wrongdoer and take the wrongdoer to court in the knowledge that another, a judge, will impose retribution on them in the form of a judicial sentence of punishment or damages.

So, is a victim who chooses to forgive always left without justice? I think not, because genuine repentance, which should almost always precede the gift of forgiveness, in effect offers the same, or even better, outcomes that one hopes would result from a court of law. Look back at what I said about repentance: wrongdoers should empathise with their victims, and acknowledge guilt and shame about the wrongs that were perpetrated. Victims should receive reparation and restitution, and wrongdoers should demonstrate moral reformation.

I suggest that a narrative of Christian forgiveness with repentance offers processes and ways to deal with wrongs to engender moral change that are *more* effective than anything that might come through judicial processes. For at the heart of Christian forgiveness with repentance is the fact that both the victim and wrongdoer, unlike always in a court of law, are volunteers: there will be a victim who voluntarily forgives a wrongdoer out of mercy and love, and a wrongdoer who voluntarily repents and chooses a better way to live in the future. And I write this as a former solicitor now turned theologian who is fully convinced that this view can be robustly defended!

Further reading

I have written two books that explore further the questions raised in this chapter. They are *Just Forgiveness* (SPCK 2011) and *Forgiveness: A Theology* (Cascade 2015). Both books are written for the general reader, who has no specialist knowledge.

Thanks to Matthias Bash for reading and commenting on a draft of this chapter.

References

Arendt, H. (1958) *The Human Condition*. London and Chicago, IL: University of Chicago Press.

Murphy, J.G. (2012) *Punishment and the Moral Emotions: Essays in Law, Morality, and Religion*. Oxford and New York, NY: Oxford University Press.

Stauffer, J. (2015) *Ethical Loneliness: The Injustice of Not Being Heard*. New York, NY: Columbia University Press.

Chapter 3

FORGIVENESS IN ISLAM
From Prophetic Practice to Divine Principle

Reza Shah-Kazemi

One of the great unsung heroes of our times is the former vice-President of Bosnia, Rusmir Mahmutćehajić. He is a hero not so much for what he has done – though by any standards, his achievements, political and scholarly, are remarkable; rather, he is a hero for what he did not do. He did not cry for vengeance against the Serbs in response to the atrocities committed by Serbian militia against the Muslims of Bosnia in the genocide of the 1990s, when the unspeakable evil of concentration camps returned to Europe. Instead, he called upon his fellow Muslims to forgive their erstwhile enemies. First, his stark statement of the war crimes:

> More than a thousand of their masdjids [mosques] have been destroyed, over a hundred and fifty thousand people killed, over fifty thousand women and girls raped, and more than a million people expelled from their homes. The dark forces of human evil have touched every aspect of their existence – hence the danger of their becoming so radicalised by suffering that they take on the nature of the perpetrators. (Mahmutćehajić 2000, 144)

But Mahmutćehajić does not take on the nature of the 'dark forces'; instead, he invokes the following verses of the Koran:

Repel [evil] with that which is most beautiful in goodness, and
then [it can happen that] your enemy will become a bosom friend.
But none can respond thus except those who exercise patient self-
restraint; and none can respond thus except those who are granted
tremendous grace (41:34–35).

Mahmutćehajić was not a lone merciful voice amid outraged cries
for revenge. On the contrary, his was simply the most powerful
voice expressing a widespread spirit of reconciliation amongst
the Bosnian Muslims. We can also cite the then Grand Mufti of
Bosnia, Mustafa Cerić, who was asked (after he had given a speech
in London, May 1994) whether it was going to be possible for the
Bosnian Muslims to live in peace with their Serbian neighbours.
He replied: 'We have to live with them, even if we do not want to,
because of what the Koran teaches us'.

We see here the tension between the all too human desire
for revenge—going hand in hand with a desire for retributive
justice—and, opposing this, a noble sentiment of forgiveness and
reconciliation, generated by belief in the Koranic Revelation. Now,
it is true that the Koran does uphold the Biblical principle of 'an eye
for an eye'; for the sake of both deterrence and retributive justice,
perpetrators of crimes must, in principle, be punished. This is
necessary for the sake of the collectivity. But the needs of society
do not prevent the individual, as a victim of injustice, forgoing the
right to retribution, and forgiving one's enemy. After re-affirming
the Biblical principle of proportionate retaliation, the Koran adds:
But whoever forgoes this, as an act of charity, it will be considered
as an atonement for him (5:44–45). Similarly: And the requital of
an injury is an injury like it; but whoever forgives, and brings about
peace, his reward is with God … those who are patient and who
forgive—[such virtues] go to the heart of the matter (42: 40-43).

One observes a fine balance between the requirements of
justice and the prerogatives of forgiveness. On the plane of social
order, the rights of justice—and hence proportionate retaliation—
must be upheld; but there is a higher plane, where the spirit of
forgiveness prevails: it is this spirit which takes one to the 'heart of
the matter', for, according to a well-known 'divine saying' (hadith
qudsi: a statement by God, transmitted by the Prophet, but which is

not in the Koran): 'My mercy prevails over My wrath'. In every case of manslaughter brought to the Prophet for judgement, he urged the family of the victim to forgo the punishment and to forgive the murderer (Brown 2016, p.13). In so doing, he was following the injunction of the Koran: Let them forgive and pardon: do you not wish that God should forgive you? God is indeed All-Forgiving, All-Merciful (24:22).

History provides us with countless examples (see Shah-Kazemi 2006) of Muslim leaders choosing to forgive rather than avenge, and thereby following in the footsteps of the Prophet. Muhammad means more to Muslims than the phrase 'role model' can convey. His extraordinary life as an orphan, a shepherd, a merchant, persecuted prophet, banished exile, a commander-in-chief, a judge, and finally, head of state; not to mention his multiple family roles, as father, a husband, a widower, a grandfather—all of these modalities of being and complex relationships serve to construct the multi-dimensional paradigmatic 'crystal', through which the Light of divine wisdom is refracted into kaleidescopic rays of guidance in all aspects of life. His character is considered the quintessence of all the virtues, his words, deeds and conduct (referred to as the prophetic Sunnah) becoming thus so many keys opening up every dimension of one's life to divine beauty. Innumerable details have been recorded of the Prophet's acts and sayings in all of the important situations which he found himself in. Consequently, the Muslim today can distill an all-encompassing moral viaticum by which to traverse the complexities of life; doing so not only by adhering to the precepts of the Prophet, but also— we believe—with the active, loving and ever-accessible assistance of the spirit of the Prophet himself.

Of all the incidents of forgiveness and forbearance that one can find in the richly recorded details of the Prophet's life, his conduct at the bloodless conquest of Mecca in 630 is particularly noteworthy. The Prophet had given a guarantee that no person would be harmed, but one of his lieutenants, Sa'd ibn Ubada, called out to Abu Sufyan, leader of the Quraysh of Mecca: 'O Abu Sufyan, this is the day of slaughter! The day when the inviolable shall be violated! The day of God's abasement of Quraysh.' Abu Sufyan rushed frantically to the Prophet, asking the Prophet if he had revoked the amnesty that he had promised, and pleading with him: 'I adjure thee by God, on behalf of thy people, for thou art of all men the greatest in filial piety, the most merciful, the most beneficent.' Abu Sufyan was not engaging in hyperbolic last-ditch flattery: his description of the Prophet was entirely accurate, according to all the accounts of the time. Muhammad was renowned for precisely these qualities of mercy and compassion, as was acknowledged, however reluctantly, even by his bitterest enemies. 'This is the day of mercy,' the Prophet replied, 'the day on which God hath exalted Quraysh' (Lings 1983, pp.297–8). And he cited the words ascribed by the Koran to Joseph, when he forgave his brothers: There will be no retribution against you today; may God forgive you. He is the most merciful of the merciful (12: 92).

Stanley Lane-Poole (1987, p.29) gives us the following apt description of the forgiveness that defines this turning point of Islamic history:

> He freely forgave the Quraish all the years of sorrow and cruel scorn in which they had afflicted him, and gave an amnesty to the whole population of Mekka. Four criminals whom justice condemned made up Muhammad's proscription list when he entered as a conqueror to the city of his bitterest enemies. The army followed his example, and entered quietly and peaceably; no house was robbed, no woman insulted … Through all the annals of conquest there is no triumphant entry comparable to this one.

The Quraysh were understandably fearful of retribution from the Muslims, given the long years of persecution to which they had subjected the Muslims in the first phase of the Prophet's mission, from 610 (the first revelations of the Koran) to 622 (the Hijra or 'flight' from Mecca to Yathrib—later to be called 'Medina'). During these twelve years the Prophet and his small band of followers were ridiculed, insulted, subjected to blockade, tortured, and some were martyred—and finally banished altogether. The Prophet's resistance was entirely non-violent.The response throughout this ordeal was always to 'turn the other cheek'. And, it is well recorded that during these long years of persecution, the Quraysh were acutely aware of the need to keep the visiting pilgrims to the Ka'ba, as well as trading caravans, as far away from Muhammad as possible lest they be attracted by the radiance of his personality—the impeccability of which they were all forced to acknowledge: prior to his mission, he was known in Mecca by the epithet al-amin, 'the trustworthy'. Even if they now interpreted his noble aura as a bewitching charm or, at best, a merely natural charisma, they knew that the unimpeachable character of the man himself was the most convincing proof of the truth of his claim to be a prophet.

The Koran describes the Prophet as being endowed with a tremendous character (68:4). And the character traits for which he was famous, both before and after the revelation of the Koran, were his mercy, compassion, and gentleness; these qualities were complemented by an implacable sense of fairness, justice and propriety. In particular, one trait of the Prophet's character, his gentleness, which rather poorly translates the Arabic word, hilm, was (and remains, one might say) the key to understanding the success of Islam, from the human point of view. Hilm is a quality composed of mildness, serenity and that imperturbable composure born of complete self-mastery, generating a far-sighted wisdom infused with a sense both of justice and compassion. The basis for our claim that this prophetic gentleness was a key to the success of Islam is the following verse of the Koran: Through the mercy of God, you dealt gently with people. Had you been harsh and heart-hearted, they would have fled from you. So pardon them, and ask forgiveness for them, and consult them in their affairs (3:159).

One of the consequences of the Prophet's gentleness and forgiveness at the conquest of Mecca was that many bitter enemies overnight became trustworthy allies. The Prophet's conduct at this turning point in history embodied the spirit of the following verse of the Koran: The good deed and the evil deed are not alike. Repel the evil deed with one which is better, then lo! He, between whom and thee there was enmity [will become] as though he were a bosom friend (41:34).

Let us consider the quality of prophetic forgiveness within the context of the emulation of the Prophet, which each Muslim considers a fundamental duty of his faith. What is to emulated, first and foremost, is the Prophet's love of God, which is at the root of the beauty of his soul; and from this beauty of soul flow all the essential virtues. The underlying principle at work, relating our love of God both to our emulation of the Prophet and to the practice of forgiveness, is expressed succinctly in the following verse of the Koran. The Prophet is told to say to the Muslims: If you love God, then follow me; God will love you and forgive you your sins. God is All-Forgiving, All-Merciful (3:31).

The Koran describes the divine Mercy in a manner which is as inspiring as it is overwhelming: God's love is infinite and thus His sustenance is given to us beyond all reckoning (2: 212), indeed, beyond anything 'deserved' by us. It is very important to note the way in which divine mercy calibrates divine justice: Whoever comes [before God] with a good deed will receive ten like it; but whoever comes [before God] with an evil deed will only be requited with its like; and no injustice will be done to them (6:160).

However grave be the sin, God's mercy outweighs it:

O My slaves who have transgressed against your own souls: despair not of the mercy of God. Truly God forgives all sins. Verily, He is the Forgiving, the Merciful (39:53).

God's mercy is absolute, which means that He not only forgives sins, but absolutely obliterates them. God is repeatedly described in the Koran not only as the 'The All-Forgiving' (al-Ghafur, al-Ghaffar, al-Tawwab, etc.) but also as 'The Effacer [of sin]' (al-'Afu). O you who believe, if you are mindful of God, He will grant you discernment, and efface your sins, and forgive you. And God is of infinite grace (8:29).

One of the most important pasages in this context is the following:

...whoso engages in polytheism, commits murder or commits adultery, the punishment will be doubled for him on the Day of Judgement, and he will abide therein disdained – except the one who repents and believes and performs righteous acts; as for such, God will transform their ugly acts into beautiful ones. And God is ever Forgiving, Merciful. And whoever repents and acts righteously, he verily repents to God with true repentance (25:69–71).

Once the repentance of the sinner is sincere, and the sin is not repeated, God's forgiveness is total, which means that the sin is absolutely effaced from the slate of the repentant sinner's conscience. He is absolved, objectively, from punishment in the Hereafter; and his liberated, subjectively, from the psychological and emotional repercussions of the sin in this life: the terrifying ghosts of regurgitated guilt. Needless to say, the repentant sinner is to do whatever possible to make reparation in relation to those who have suffered as a result of his sin. He is thereby 'born again', enabled to resume life in society within a fully rejuvenated moral and civic paradigm – the paradigm of the Sunnah. The Sunnah is understood and assimilated as the perfect expression of the primordial human norm – an intrinsic purity of soul which is not only each person's birth-right, but which is more 'real' than any of the sinful actions which may outwardly contradict and besmirch this inmost substance of the human spirit. This primordial nature of the human soul is called the fitrah, a word which is related to the divine Name, al-Fatir, one of the several names meaning 'Creator', and it is to this primordial human nature that we now turn our attention, in relation to the subtle teachings contained in the Koranic story of Joseph and his brothers.

The 'spiritual psychology' of forgiveness

Let us return to the words of Joseph, cited by the Prophet from the Koran when he forgave the Quraysh at the peaceful conquest of Mecca, and examine them in context. Joseph tells his brothers that he will not punish them for their evil act against him; and makes it clear that his act of forgiveness derives from, and indeed manifests, the merciful nature of God: There will be no retribution against you today; may God forgive you. He is the most merciful of the merciful (12:92). Joseph's act of forgiveness is not only connected to his knowledge of God's essential nature as forgiving and merciful; it is also the consequence of his perception of what one might call the psychological 'mechanics' of evil. He perceives evil not simply on the surface, in terms of its human enactment; rather, he sees, with the eye of the heart, the cosmic root of evil and the way it is insinuated into human intentionality. He refers to the monstrous act of his brothers in terms of the 'dissension' instigated by Satan, avoiding the ascription of the act to them directly. He says the following, after his parents and brothers prostrate to him, fulfilling his dream as a youth:

> ... this is the fulfillment of my vision, my Lord has made it come true. He has been gracious to me. He brought me out of prison and brought you out of the desert after satan had created dissension between me and my brothers (12:100).

Joseph takes us to a spiritual vantage point from which it is easy to liberate ourselves from the desire for revenge against those who may have wronged us. For he sees, on the one hand, the intrinsic purity of the soul's nature, the fitrah; and, on the other, the extrinsic source of its corruption. As regards the fitrah, Joseph knows that human nature, as fashioned by God, is the incorruptible core of the human spirit: at 30:30, after mention is made of the fitrah, the Koran says: nothing can change the creation of God. That is the eternally established religion. But most people are ignorant. In other words, this fitrah constitutes at once the divine foundation and spiritual quintessence of all possible religious forms: this eternal 'religion' is constituted by the human spirit; it thus precedes, ontologically, all subsequent 'religions', whose very diversity demonstrates their relativity vis-à-vis the uniqueness of 'the' religion. So say 'the eternally established religion' is to say religion as such, as distinct from such and such a religion. The vision that arises out of this description of the fitrah is one in which the fundamental nature of the humanity is intuited as an incorruptible core of love and knowledge of God, an underlying spiritual quintessence with which the subsequent forms of religious belief and systems of morality must resonate if they are to be salvific. Conversely, sinfulness is seen in this light as arising not out of the fitrah as such, but out of a forgetfulness of one's true nature, and this forgetfulness renders the soul susceptible to evil which comes, not from within, but from something utterly alien to one's God-given nature.

Here, it is important to understand that, in terms of spiritual psychology, the devil (al-shaytan) is not simply the form taken by the cosmic force of evil upon contact with human beings, remaining totally alien to the soul that it influences. There are also doors in the soul which can be opened to the devil through forgetfulness of one's true nature; these doors are openings to the whole host of vices that flow from forgetfulness. Once these doors are opened, the devil is, as it were, invited into the soul; and the soul begins to identify itself with the vices instigated and insinuated by the devil. These doors remain locked by vigilant virtue, prayer, and its quintessence: the remembrance of God. This constant awareness of God (taqwa: a word which is translated by 'piety', but whose root meaning is 'protection') goes hand in hand with both fear and love of God, and one remains faithful to the integral state of the fitrah. One remains true to oneself, according to the creative intention of God. 'Truly God made the human being according to His own form (sura)' the Prophet tells us; and it is also related that he specified the qualitative nature of this divine 'form': 'Truly God made the human being according to the form of al-Rahman'. We will return to this theme in a moment.

Continuing with the notion of the 'mechanics' of evil: in the chapter entitled 'The Resurrection' (al-Qiyama; no.75), the opening verses are oaths taken by God: Nay, I swear by the Day of Resurrection. Nay, I swear by the self-accusing soul (75:1-2). The implication is clear: what happens on the Day of Resurrection – posthumous judgement – is prefigured and anticipated in this world by the judgement of the soul by the soul itself, here and now. 'Take yourself to account', says the Prophet, 'before you are taken to account'. In this world, the soul 'accuses' itself of its own transgressions in order to rectify itself, and thus save itself from a hellish recompense after death. Another set of verses allude to the process of posthumous judgement in terms which evoke the Hindu principle of karma. On the Day of Judgement, we are told, each soul will be given its 'book', wide open, and will be told: Read your book. Your own soul suffices on this day as your judge (17:13). This is because, on that 'Day', the soul will see things in the light of a spiritual conscience no longer veiled by worldly attachments and egotistic illusions; it will see clearly what its actions merit in the way of punishment or reward. Returning to the chapter, 'The Resurrection', we read, at verses 13–15:

On that Day the human being will be told what it has committed and what it has omitted. But no! The human being has insight into his own soul. Even though he puts forward his excuses.

The Koran refers to various types of soul, which can be understood as levels or degrees of spiritual development. The lowest is what Joseph refers to: al-nafs al-ammarah bi al-su', 'the soul commanding evil'; this is the fallen soul in its unregenerate and unrepentant state, in which innate conscience, moral and spiritual, has been smothered by forgetfulness, worldliness and egotism, and then all the vices which are generated thereby. In this state, the insinuations and seductions of the devil dominate the soul, and it thus 'commands' evil: the doors of the soul are flung open to the cosmic force of evil, the 'devil', and this results in evil action. The second degree of the soul, as just noted, is referred to as al-nafs al-lawwama, the 'self-accusing' soul: the conscience has awoken, and the struggle against evil ensues. The third and final degree is referred to as al-nafs al-mutma'inna, the soul at peace (89:27), wherein victory over the adversary has been achieved, through the grace of God responding to the efforts of the soul. The soul in this state has returned to its pre-lapsarian condition, its true celestial nature: Return unto thy Lord, God says to this soul at peace, with gladness that is thine in Him and His in thee. Enter thou among my slaves. Enter thou My Paradise (89: 28–30; translation by Lings (2007, p.188).

This return to Paradise—for the saint, a return which is actualised spiritually in this world already—is brought about through mercy, not through the merit of human action. The Prophet told his followers that not one of them could enter Paradise through their actions. 'Not even you, O Messenger of God?' 'Not even me—it is only through being whelmed by God's mercy that I can enter Paradise'. Divine mercy is thus the omega of the human cycle; but it is also its alpha, because forgiveness lies at the very core of the Fall from Eden, as this is depicted in the Koran. In contrast to the Biblical notion of the Fall, and original sin, the Koranic account of the Fall places all the accent upon the immediacy of Adam's repentance, and the equal immediacy of God's forgiveness. After the primal act of disobedience, Adam and Eve repent (see, e.g., 7:23), and this meets with acceptance by God:

> Then Adam received words of mercy from his Lord, and He
> relented towards him. Truly, He is the Relenting, the Merciful. We
> said: 'Get down from here, altogether; but when guidance comes
> to you from Me, as it assuredly will, whoever follows My guidance
> shall not fear, neither shall they grieve' (2:37–38).

Instead of being saddled with Adam's original sin, the nature of
post-lapsarian man is marked by a predisposition to repentance.
The ancestral 'memory', impressed by the Koranic revelation upon
our spiritual imagination, is therefore one of repentance following
sin, on our part; and forgiveness arising out of mercy, on the
part of God. Whence the appropriateness for the Muslim psyche
of the saying, 'man repents, God relents'. In Arabic both of these
words, repent and relent, are expressed by the same Arabic root,
taba, literally: 'to turn'. The repentant sinner 'turns' to God seeking
forgiveness, and God 'turns' to man bestowing forgiveness. Hence
we find that one of the names of God referring to His forgiveness
is al-Tawwab, the One who is perpetually 'turning' to man with
mercy, compassion and forgiveness.

Maintaining contact with the fitrah, becomes increasingly
difficult in our post-Edenic world. It requires not only the inner
struggle referred to by the Prophet as the greatest jihad, it also
needs divine mercy. Joseph makes this point clearly when he is
finally exonerated of all charges in the presence of the Pharaoh. I
do not exonerate myself, he says, for truly the soul commands evil,
unless my Lord has mercy (12:53).

Prophetic forgiveness: reflection of Divine Mercy

The Prophet, as mentioned above, is the role-model par excellence,
or rather: the 'beautiful role-model' (uswa hasana: 33:21), the
notion of beauty being inseparable from that of virtue (ihsan),
the two words sharing the same root (hasuna: 'to be beautiful').
The whole purpose of the prophetic mission, according to a well-
known saying of the Prophet himself, was to teach people how to
attain beauty of soul, nobility of character: 'I was only raised up [as
a prophet] for the sake of completing the most noble character-
traits'. This statement can be seen as a commentary on the Koran's

description of the Prophet as a mercy for all the universes (21:107). The sum of all the essential virtues is that beauty of soul which reflects the 'mercy' (rahma) of God; that mercy by which God's very Essence is described: God has inscribed mercy upon His very Self (6:54); that mercy from which nothing in existence can escape: My mercy encompasses all things (7:156). Let us recall that al-Rahman and al-Rahim are the two 'Names of Mercy' which inaugurate every chapter of the Koran (except one) and consecrate every single action of the pious Muslim: Bismillah al-Rahman al-Rahim: In the Name of God, [Lovingly] Beneficent, [Lovingly] Merciful. These two Divine Names evoke the pulsation of divine love, a pulsation which is both creative and attractive, manifesting and reintegrating. According to both the theologians and the mystics of Islam, God creates and reveals as al-Rahman, and He saves and redeems as al-Rahim. Therefore, rahma is the alpha and omega of existence.

What is therefore seen, first and foremost, in the beauty of the prophetic character is a reflection of the Divine Self, whose Essence is absolute goodness, beauty, love, mercy and compassion – all of these qualities being evoked by the notion of rahma, a word related to the word for womb, rahim. 'I have derived my name, al-Rahman, from the word rahim', God declares, in a hadith qudsi. And the Prophet himself helps us to see the maternal love which is implied by rahma. When, at the fall of Mecca, a woman lost her baby and then found it, clutching it to her breast with immense joy and relief, the Prophet and his companions who witnessed the scene were deeply moved. The Prophet then imparted a crucial evocation of the meaning and the nature of rahma. He said that God has more rahma for us than this mother has for her baby.

We are given here a wonderful teaching on the inner reality and deepest root of compassion, mercy and forgiveness: these qualities flow spontaneously from an organic, all-encompassing 'maternal' love, stemming from what God is by nature, and not manifesting some arbitrary decision on His part, something He may or may not will. Through His infinite love for us, God manifests mercy, compassion and forgiveness; and, out of gratitude to Him for being what He is by nature and essence, we cannot but manifest our love for Him.

In the chapter entitled 'Women', the opening verse reads:

> O mankind! Do your duty to your Lord, Who created you from a single soul, and from it created its spouse, and from the two of them spread a multitude of men and women. So do your duty to God, in Whom you claim your rights, and do your duty to the wombs (4: 1).

It is intriguing that the Koran uses the idea of taqwa – piety, revernetial awe, recollectedness in the presence of God, duty to God – not only in relation to God but also in relation to 'wombs'. One of the meanings here – an exoteric or legal meaning – is to honour the ties of kinship; but a deeper meaning relates to the spiritual symbolism of the womb, and what has been said above. One readily appreciates why the Prophet referred to God as al-Rahman when he said: 'The heart of the believer is the throne of al-Rahman'. The closer we come to the reality of the human heart, the closer we come to the pulsation of God's loving compassion and mercy, creating and redeeming. So, even if it is true that the concept of unity, tawhid, dominates the content of Islamic thought, it is mercy, rahma, that governs the heart of Islamic faith. Mercy is to unity what rays are to the sun: the oneness of God reveals its most fundamental nature through the rays of love, mercy, compassion and forgiveness, by which the entire universe is illuminated and penetrated, encompassed and consummated.

References

Brown, J. A. C. (2016) 'Sin, Forgiveness and Reconciliation: A Muslim Perspective' in Lucinder Mosher and David Marshall (eds), *Sin, Forgiveness and Reconciliation: Christian and Muslim Perspectives*. Washington D.C.: Georgetown University Press.

Lane-Poole, S. (1987) *The Speeches and Table Talk of the Prophet Muhammad*. Delhi.

Lings, M. (1983) *Muhammad—His Life According to the Earliest Sources*. London: Islamic Texts Society, and George Allen & Unwin.

Idem. (2007) *The Holy Qur'an: Translations of Selected Verses*. Cambridge: The Royal Aal al-Bayt Institute for Islamic Thought & The Islamic Texts Society.

Mahmutćehajić, R. (2000) *Bosnia the Good—Tolerance and Tradition* (tr. Marina Bowder). Budapest and New York: Central European University Press.

Shah-Kazemi, R. (2006) *The Spirit of Tolerance in Islam*. London: I.B. Tauris.

Chapter 4

FORGIVENESS IN THE BUDDHIST TRADITION

Vajragupta

Of the hundreds of hours of TV I watched when I was young, just a few scraps and fragments have stayed with me. One of these was a programme I watched about 'restorative justice' back in the 1980s. That is a long time ago now, but my memory is of a group of women entering a prison room, fearful and apprehensive, keeping close together for comfort and safety. They sat down one side of a table in the middle of the room. Then several men in prison uniform came in. They entered one by one, also frightened, appearing lost, not knowing where to look, and they sat along the opposite side of the table. Women who had been victims of rape and men convicted of rape were being brought face to face. The atmosphere was taut to snapping point, the fear and tension almost unbearable – even through the thick glass of the TV screen.

One by one the women told their stories, what had happened to them and how it still haunted them and blighted their lives. They were ordinary women from all walks of life and as they talked they grew more confident, more open and forthright, and more able to look the men in their faces.

The men sat stony-faced at first, but they had chosen to be there and they were willing to listen, to really listen. Some stared at the table, some began to weep, some began to look up at the women, allowing them to see their shame and their tear-streaked faces.

Then some of the men spoke, expressing gratitude to the women for telling their stories. They too were ordinary men from a variety of backgrounds and they too told their stories, of how their lives had gone so wrong, and how they now lived with the awful gravity of what they had done. By now the women were also weeping, looking at the men differently, with less fear and the possibility of forgiveness. The tension had broken. It was still painful to watch, even from the safe distance of my living room. There was so much pain and grief, yet also glimpses of compassion and understanding, glimmers of light and beauty where there had been so much darkness.

This obviously made 'great TV'; it was strong, emotional, compelling viewing. But it was more than that. We had witnessed something extraordinary, a profound spiritual breakthrough. That was why it stayed in my mind all these years and sprang back into consciousness when I started writing this chapter on Buddhism and forgiveness. I will return to this story at the end of the chapter and to why such stories of reconciliation and forgiveness are so inspiring and moving.

To write a Buddhist perspective on forgiveness brings certain challenges. 'Forgiveness' is an English word with particular meanings, connotations and associations in our culture – Christian, pre-Christian and secular. Some of those meanings might be quite subtle and sub-conscious. We may need to unravel them and see them more clearly in order to understand what a different tradition such as Buddhism might have to say. There are words such as 'karma' that have no exact equivalent in English (or other European languages), and there are words like 'forgiveness' that have no exact equivalent in the Buddhist tradition. On the one hand, we need to be careful, not bringing in unconscious assumptions from one side or the other, so that nothing important or significant is 'lost in translation'. On the other hand, and on the plus side, making these cross-cultural comparisons might throw new light on what a concept such as 'forgiveness' really means.

The Buddhist word that is nearest in meaning to our word 'forgiveness' is the word *khanti*,[1] which literally means something like 'unaffected by' or 'able to withstand'. It is usually translated as 'patience', 'forbearance', 'tolerance' and also as 'forgiveness'.

---

1   *Khanti* is Pali, the Sanskrit is *kshanti*.

Khanti is seen as a beautiful and high ideal, a highly positive and desirable ethical quality. It is one of the 'perfections' practised by someone intent on gaining Enlightenment out of compassion for all living beings.[2] It is not a grim, grit-your-teeth, grin-and-bear-it stoicism. It is a warm and concerned kindness in the face of difficulty or emnity. But nor is it saccharine-sweet, naive, over-accommodating, sacrificing of your own needs or preferences for the sake of keeping everything 'nice' and avoiding conflict. *Khanti* entails robustness; one is emotionally resilient enough to remain patient, to face difficulty squarely and truthfully, to stay engaged in its midst, and to try and be helpful.

All this gives us a clue as to what forgiveness is. It is to forbear, even when a wrong has been done to you, even though it may be painful. It is not to downplay that wrong, or to deny the feeling of pain. But you don't let those feelings take you into a state of ill-will or hatred, of wanting to inflict pain back, of wanting revenge. (Interestingly, in the etymology of the English word 'forgiveness' there is a parallel with this. The 'for' that is the prefix of the word, denotes 'abstention' or 'renunciation'. So to 'for-give' is to 'abstain from giving' – to not return-in-kind, to hold back from taking revenge.)

To forgive is to let someone off the consequences of their action in terms of our own personal response or reaction to it. We forgive and forget. The slate is wiped clean. We will only be able to do this if we view the person with *metta* (loving-kindness). Often when someone is inconsiderate, or downright hostile to us, it is painful and we (understandably) want to push away and minimise that pain. It is reasonable enough to want to protect ourselves from more pain, but what also often happens is that our ego feels diminished or slighted and we feel a need to restore and reinforce our sense of self. So we 'push away' the perceived cause of that pain. We may do this 'externally' – we react with a few sharp, unkind, dismissive words to the person concerned. And we do it 'internally' – our mind kicks into overdrive, re-playing the painful incident

2   In the traditions dating back to early Buddhism, ten *Paramis* (perfections) are often listed; in Mahayana (later) Buddhism there are six. *Khanti* is included in both sets.

again and again, trying to think of the irrefutable put-down we wish we had thought of at the time.

We are trying to push away the perceived cause of the pain, but – perversely – in doing this our mind becomes contracted and focused around it. We can't get the incident out of our heads, our thoughts circle round it endlessly, and it looms larger. The Buddhist word for this is *papanca* – which means something like 'spreading out', 'proliferation' or even 'amplification'. Through thoughts and stories that proliferate in our minds, we amplify what it was that person did that we didn't like; we see that and only that about them. Our view of them becomes limited, narrow, even distorted.

We can end up in a state of aversion which is just as painful, if not more so, than the original incident. Our ego is locked around that pain in a way that perpetuates and enlarges it. All this makes it more likely that when we meet that person again (or when we encounter a similar situation) all those feelings and stories and interpretations will be re-activated. We are then likely to react to the person in a way that keeps the whole cycle going. (They too may have their head full of stories and interpretations, which will condition how they perceive and respond to us…)

However, if we can stay in touch with some *metta*, then we don't go into such a powerful overdrive of negative interpretation. We acknowledge that the incident was painful. Perhaps we felt humiliated in front of other people. Maybe it was someone who we had been trying to help who hurt us and we feel used and taken for granted. We acknowledge all those feelings and give ourselves *metta* or kindness. And we try to think kindly of the other person. Perhaps we look at their conditioning and the pressures they are under in their life, the various factors that might have led them to behave as they do. Maybe we try to see their positive qualities, to see them as a more rounded human being, in order to counteract the tendency of our aversive mind to focus only on the negative. Or perhaps we reflect on how, if we are honest, we might have also contributed to what happened, and how we might have dealt with the situation more helpfully.

Above all, we are trying not to 'fix' that person, not to identify them solely with the action they did, but to see them as more than that, as a multi-faceted human being with potential for good and bad, as someone who can change for the worse but also for the better. If we can do that, then we can forgive them.

Of course, it is much easier to forgive on some occasions than others. If the way we were wronged was relatively trivial – a colleague who, on a bad day, is grumpy and complaining, or a friend who hasn't returned that book they borrowed – we can usually throw off our irritation. If the person is someone with whom we are familiar then we know in our own experience that there is more to them than negative speech or a forgetful, inconsiderate act, and so, again, it is relatively easy to take a larger view of them and forgive. If someone has made a sincere apology it helps us to see them differently, for our minds not to contract around the way we were wronged, not to identify them with just that action, and to let it go.

This is why, if it is us who has done some wrong or harm to someone, it is important to apologise if we can. Acknowledging the pain or inconvenience we have caused and saying we are sorry may really help that person move on. The apology may be uncomfortable to give, but it will release us from our sense of having done wrong, and it may help release the other person from the sense of having been wronged. To apologise where appropriate is an act of generosity and consideration.

At other times forgiveness is much more difficult and challenging. Some things that human beings do to other human beings might seem impossible to forgive. If what has been done to us (or someone we love) is more serious and weighty, if there has been no apology and one even fears the same thing might happen again, or if the person who committed a crime against us isn't known to us and is still free and at large – how can we forgive in these kinds of circumstances? If we try to imagine what it would be like to be the mother whose young daughter has been murdered by terrorists, or to be a dispossessed young man living in a city bombed to smithereens by a powerful state, how can we expect to forgive?

These are dark and difficult questions and there are, of course, no easy answers. I do not know how I would respond in those kinds of situations. But I do know the pain would be intense and that raging forces of fear and hatred would be unleashed in me; my mind would be full of furious voices of revenge. And yet I also know that, in the words of the Buddha, 'hatreds never cease through hatred, they only cease through love'.[3] I know that the best thing to do would be to have that internal struggle with myself, to forbear, to feel the pain but not give in to hatred, to try to contain and resist that desire for revenge. To give in to it would only worsen my pain and perpetuate the tragic cycle of hate and violence.

In the Buddhist tradition, there is a meditation practice known as the *metta-bhavana* – which means 'the cultivation or nurturing of loving-kindness'. It is designed to help us develop more positive emotion and stronger responses of friendliness and kindness to anyone we meet. It is not so easy to explain a meditation in a book; if you wanted to learn this meditation it would be best to find a class or a teacher who could lead you through it. But, essentially, the practice is done in five stages – in the first stage we cultivate *metta* for ourselves, in the second stage for a good friend, then someone who is 'neutral' to us (we don't have strong positive or negative feelings for them), then someone we find difficult (where negative feelings may predominate), and then finally radiating out *metta* to all beings, all over the world.

In each stage, we choose a relevant person and we bring them to mind, to try and get a sense of them and their lives. We acknowledge any feelings or thoughts that arise in us, and we try to encourage and cultivate a sense of well-wishing towards that person. We try to nurture a kind, helpful, understanding attitude towards them; we try and imagine them at their very best and wish that they may experience themselves like that. I have known many people over the years who have found this meditation practice deeply transformative. Often this has been especially in respect of the fourth stage – dealing with painful feelings towards a 'difficult' person. Through meditating in this way, they have been able to forgive and let go, sometimes after years of pain. They have finally been able to dig themselves out of painful, limiting and entrenched attitudes towards someone, and release the ill-will that accompanied that. They are, finally, able to set themselves free. It may have taken years of patient practice before they were able to do this, but it was worth it in the end.

---

3   *Dhammapada,* chapter 1, verse 5.

There are three last points I would like to make about forgiveness from the Buddhist point of view.

First, although we can forgive and 'wipe the slate clean' in terms of our own attitude to someone, this doesn't take away other consequences of what they have done, including the karmic effect of their action. Central to Buddhism is the notion of karma – that through anything we do, say, or even think, we are creating particular tendencies, habits or tracks in the mind that shape our character and therefore influence our future actions, words and thoughts. The principle of karma describes how we are creating a moral personality for ourselves, at every moment of our lives, in everything that we think and do, large or small, positive or negative.

That character we develop influences our whole life; it colours the whole way we experience the world. For example, if I am generous, I tend to develop a more easy-going, abundant, generous personality. That means it becomes easier for me to be generous in the future. It also means that it is quite likely I will be popular and well liked and that people will be generous back to me. However, if I get into a habit of being stingy, this tends to reinforce a penny-pinching, sceptical attitude where I always question if someone really needs what they are asking for. I tend to feel less abundant and it becomes harder to be generous in the future. And this may mean I am less popular and fewer acts of generosity come my way in life. In this way, the principle of karma describes how ethical actions tend to produce happiness and unethical actions tend to produce unhappiness.

In real life, it often doesn't seem as clear as this; it is not always so black and white, because not everything that happens to us is the result of karma. There are all sorts of conditions and influences at work in the world and karma is only one among them.[4] The generous person may still get their house burgled and the stingy person might win the lottery. Nevertheless, it is likely that a

---

4   This is an important point because often one comes across popular explanations of karma in which *everything* that happens to you is a result of your karma. But this is not the Buddha's teaching. In Buddhism, there are different 'levels' of cause and effect at work. To the physical, biological and psychological levels of causality described by science, Buddhism would add a karmic, or ethical, level of causality.

generous person will be better able to bear their loss because of their generous attitude to life, and the miser won't find happiness through winning a large sum of money.

Karma is not the punishment or reward of an outside agent; it is just how our thoughts shape our mind, which then shapes future experience. Only I can change my mind, change how I think. Only I can resolve to act differently in the future and also undertake good, ethically skilful acts that counteract negative karma. So, although you might forgive me, and not yourself wish for any further negative consequences to accrue to me, there are still ethical consequences for me that only I can take responsibility for and change. Only I can start to 'wipe the slate clean' from the karmic point of view. (However, it is also the case that if you forgive me, it might encourage and support me to take that ethical responsibility – it might help me to believe that it is possible for me to change.)

Sometimes in devotional rituals a Buddhist might ask the Buddha to forgive his or her faults. But this has a different significance to what a ritual of confession and forgiveness means in a theistic religion. The Buddha isn't a creator God, but an Enlightened being; we don't need the Buddha's forgiveness because we've disobeyed his commandments or gone against his wishes. As stated above, no one (not even a Buddha) can wipe away our karma, only we can. But acknowledging what we have done may still help us to put it behind us, to feel able to start afresh and try again. The significance of confessing to the Buddha is more 'psychological' than 'theological'. It is a way of acknowledging our faults and failings to one who is wise and compassionate, and in the context of our own aspiration to change and develop more wisdom and compassion for ourselves. It is a way of inspiring ourselves, so that we feel it is possible for us to really change.

The second point I would like to make is that forgiveness is not being a door mat. Although we are trying to forgive and not give way to hatred, there may also be situations that we need to stand up to, injustices that we need to challenge. Forgiving someone is not in contradiction to pointing out to them the harm they have done and urging them to stop. Forgiveness makes us more able to confront injustice and respond with fortitude and determination, rather than giving in to despair and frustrated rage.

In the case of a serious crime we may still believe that the perpetrator needs to be caught and put behind bars for the sake of other people's protection (and perhaps for their own protection). But that would be our motive – to avoid further harm – rather than wanting to inflict punishment and revenge. We would want them to have the best chance of facing up to what they had done and of trying to change for the better, although we shouldn't be naive about how difficult that may be. Many perpetrators of serious crimes live the rest of their lives in denial; what they have done is too painful for them to contemplate, or own up to. But there is always the possibility of change. This is why I would expect Buddhists to want the criminal justice system to be as reformative as possible and also to be opposed to the death penalty, even for the most awful crimes.[5]

My third and last point is that sometimes we need to forgive ourselves. You may have noticed that in my description of the *metta-bhavana* meditation, the first stage was to nurture kindness, well wishing and a helpful attitude towards oneself. Sometimes, in the heat of the moment, or under the pressure of difficult circumstances, we do or say things that we later bitterly regret. We need to be able to understand and forgive ourselves, and see that we can change and act differently in the future. The *metta-bhavana* practice can help with this too. We may need to distinguish feelings of 'regret' from 'guilt'. The latter involves a negative self-view; it is where our self-image congeals around something we have done in a way that makes it harder to change and move on. Regret says, 'I wish I hadn't done that, I will try to act differently in the future'. Guilt says, 'I'm bad, useless and worthless because of those things I do'. Regret may be painful, but it helps us take responsibility for our actions. Guilt, however, is unhelpful and spiritually undermining.

This subject of forgiveness takes us into dark and difficult areas of human life. Forgiveness may not be easy; it is to love where there is no obvious reason to love. Forgiveness requires being willing to

---

5   There is a famous story of the Buddha fearlessly encountering a mass murderer
     called Angulimala. He tries to attack the Buddha, but the Buddha persuades him
     to give up his evil ways. Angulimala totally changes his life and even becomes a
     monk. The Buddhist prison chaplaincy organisation in the UK is named after
     Angulimala.

bear pain; it is to forbear for the sake of a greater good. Forgiveness may not always take away that pain, at least not immediately. But it stops us being trapped and defined by it, and this will tend to lessen and soften the pain over time. We don't rigidly define people solely by their past actions, or define ourselves by what was done to us. This is ultimately liberating. Forgiveness is light in the darkness, an act of courage and generosity that is noble and beautiful. To forgive is to refuse to be limited by worldly circumstances, by what has happened to us, and to allow a bigger love and compassion to break through. In other words, it is a deep and powerful spiritual transformation – for the forgiver and possibly also for those forgiven. That is why that TV programme I saw all those years ago stayed so clearly in my mind, and why it was so profoundly inspiring and moving.

Chapter 5

OUT OF THE DEPTHS
Offenders and Forgiveness

Gwen Adshead and Jesse Butler-Meadows

*When we forgive evil we do not excuse it, we do not tolerate
it, we do not smother it. We look the evil full in the face, call
it what it is, let its horror shock and stun and enrage us, and
only then do we forgive it*

Lewis B. Smedes, *Forgive & Forget:
Healing the Hurts We Don't Deserve*

Introduction

Offenders come in many forms and guises and not all of them are
in prisons or in secure psychiatric hospitals. In this chapter, we will
reflect on what we are learning about forgiveness from our work
as psychiatrists working with people who have hurt others while
mentally ill. We work in a secure mental health service where men
and women may be sent by the courts for treatment instead of
being sent to prison. Depending on the type of offence and the
impact on the community, they may spend years in secure care,
often longer than if they had gone to prison; and during those years
they are expected to engage in therapy to discuss their offences and
their response to them.

It is a privilege to be witness to this process, and this chapter is
based on therapeutic conversations we have been part of. We are
grateful to the patients for their agreement to the use of material

from those conversations as part of this chapter; no identifiable materials are presented here and names are changed to protect the innocent and guilty alike. We are also grateful to Erwin James, who has written about his experience of life after serious violence, who shared his experience at a workshop on forgiveness at our clinic, and whose work has been an inspiration.

Miserable offenders: remorse and forgiveness

As always when one examines a complex human experience involving both thoughts and feelings, one becomes aware of a tension between a mental experience as a state and as a process. Forgiveness seems to be experienced as a state of mind and yet there is another aspect that involves a conscious decision-making process that one engages in to a greater or lesser degree. Similarly, there is a tension between forgiveness as an individual experience, and as a relational one between people. 'Forgiveness' seems to have an active sense to it that implies a way of relating towards others, not a single mental event.

This theme is explored elsewhere in this book in greater detail and with wiser analysis. In our chapter, we will assume that forgiveness is a relational process for the forgiver and the forgiven. We also assume that remorse and forgiveness are linked concepts in some way; with some form of connection between the two. Offenders are unlikely to grasp or engage in thinking about forgiveness unless they are also exploring remorse and regret, so we will also discuss this issue briefly, drawing on Murray Cox's rich and comprehensive work, *Remorse and Reparation* (1999).

Historically, the Ministry of Justice required offenders to show remorse for their offences as evidence of a reduction in their risk to the public. While this is now less explicitly required, there remains an expectation for offenders to express genuine remorse and repentance for their crimes. Remorse is also a complex psychological experience, combining both anxiety and guilt, and it may be that offenders sometimes hope to obtain forgiveness in the external world to ease painful internal feelings of remorse and guilt. It may be difficult for offenders to articulate such complex feelings, or to know how to begin to put these experiences into words.

Forgiveness presents a similarly difficult conceptual challenge for offenders to articulate. In our experience, offenders are aware that they have done their victims both harm and wrong, in the sense that their victim is physically injured (thus harmed) but also 'wronged' by being treated as merely a means to an end, or an object to bear the brunt of an offender's feelings. However, when they are first detected and arrested, offenders are often frightened and stunned by what has happened, and they are usually advised to say nothing and certainly not to admit their guilt. As the trial process wears on, denial and avoidance of responsibility may be a central part of any legal defence strategy, which makes it difficult to take on board and accept the reality of the harm and wrong done. It is only after conviction that the process of acceptance and reflection can really start (Adshead 1998).

Their victims are both present and absent for offenders in secure care. At one level, their victims are ever-present in terms of ongoing risk assessments and the implicit requirement to demonstrate the 'right' attitude of remorse and regret. At another level, it becomes impossible for the offender to dwell on the experience of the victim at all times. As a consequence, the victim slips out of sight until the offender is reminded. In secure psychiatric care offenders are under constant scrutiny for evidence of risky attitudes and lack of remorse as evidence of risk. Consequently, offenders find themselves aware of having to say the 'right' thing at all times: 'If I could meet my victim again, I'd shake him by the hand and I would know that he forgives me because he loves me.'

Shame and forgiveness

An important aspect of living with the identity of offender is being socially excluded from the community, where previously one had taken membership and admittance for granted. They inevitably join a community of the excluded, together with people with whom they feel no bond: one man offered group therapy said, 'I don't want to be in a group with people like me.' This poignant comment is a reminder of the powerful effect of shame on social identity, and the loss of a sense of being 'seen' securely and with dignity by others. Those who bring death to a community will be excluded and shunned into a new way of relating to others: a position of shame, guilt and embarrassment. In this new position of shame and guilt, it can seem impossible to be allowed to look others in the eye: the offender is expected to look down and stay down, not to expect to be treated normally.

Offenders are aware that they are simultaneously held in mind and rejected by others; for example, a group therapy session began with a discussion about a story printed in the *The People* newspaper about a group member. (Readers may like to reflect on how they might feel if all their 'offences' were printed in a national newspaper for others to examine.) The therapists wondered aloud whether group members might have a more general concern about what 'people' thought of them, especially victims and relatives of victims who might also be related to the group members.

Social exclusion and a sense of shame makes asking for forgiveness seem impossible. Forgiveness becomes especially complex when the perpetrator and victim are members of the same family group, so that the offender is both a destroyer of an attachment and one who mourns the loss of it. In a therapy group for people who had killed family members, the group members were acutely aware that their family members faced a real dilemma in how to relate to them. They could see how their family members might hate and fear them, but at the same time, they wanted their family members to know that they were mentally ill at the time and to accept that they were not monsters. Contact with family members was complex for many group members, and the therapists found it hard to know what to say or what to think in response.

The sense of being forgiven may bring, instead of relief, an intensification of guilt and shame. Those offenders who are deeply unhappy may experience pain if others are kind to them because it does not fit with their view of themselves as 'bad' and also serves in some way to distance them from the others who have the ability to do such good. It may stir up a kind of envy of those who have the capacity for kindness, which then intensifies the feelings of being 'bad'. In one case known to us, a man who had tried to kill his family was visited by a surviving family member. Nearly all the professionals involved were amazed by this, and they were also appalled: what they found so awful was what they imagined the offender might feel. There was much speculation about whether the visitor was trying to punish the offender with kindness; that they were unaware or not thinking about the pain they might inflict on the offender. And the professionals were not wrong; the offender suffered greatly from these visits, but also clung to them as evidence that he was not completely lost to his former life and attachments, that he was not entirely 'beyond the pale'.

Forgiveness and suicide

Most readers will know that the phrase 'beyond the pale' comes from historical accounts of communities who used markers (pales) to delineate the boundaries of the community. Those beyond the pale had been expelled and were excluded from the community forever. In this context, it is impossible not to make the associative leap to the pale rider on a pale horse, and Shakespeare's image of death's pale flag.

For people who have committed what have been called 'horrendous evils' (Adams 2000), there may be a real question about whether their lives are worth living. Suicide is a constant theme for those whose identities have now been fixed as 'offenders', especially as particularly 'horrible' offenders. In a very short space of time, even 30 seconds of madness, two lives may have been destroyed forever with no going back. The experience of forgiveness is only about the future, about whether they dare to dream of living normally. Even where there is a kind of forgiveness available, it seems and feels provisional, like a float that may help a man keep his head above water but provides no guarantee that he won't drown.

Forgiveness and redemption

Few of the offenders we have met say that they expected to be forgiven, and they seem to know that they cannot expect forgiveness from others, although they hope for it. In this sense, they have an awareness that there is a process of forgiving for the offended that takes time and is painful. Just as they have to take time to come to terms with the reality of what they have done, and how this has fundamentally altered their relationship to the world, so they can come to appreciate that the offended might take a long time to come to terms with what has been done to them.

In a recent talk to patients in a secure unit, Erwin James described how a man who had been close to one of his victims came to see him in prison and had commented that James's victim 'would be proud of what he had achieved'. James then went on to comment how conflicted he felt about receiving forgiveness; how he both wanted forgiveness but felt that he could not ask for it, because it was 'the victim's prerogative' to give forgiveness.

So offenders can and do understand that forgiveness is a type of gift that is unique in terms of human giving, in that it comes sometimes unexpectedly, out of pure generosity, with no duty or ritual attached. Forgiveness is less like a birthday or Christmas gift than a sacrifice – that which makes something sacred. This theme of 'salvaging the sacred' is explored in depth and great beauty by Marian Partington (2012) in her book *If You Sit Very Still* about the aftermath of her sister's murder. Partington describes how her engagement with forgiveness was and is crucial to the transformation of meaningless to meaningful suffering.

Forgiveness, then, can transform a relationship between the offender and the offended. Given as a free gift, forgiveness is able to reach out and invite the offender to reconnect to the social world that they have been excluded from, and from which they exclude themselves. Partington's account of the transformation of something profane and damaged into something sacred and humanly important finds an echo in Dan McAdams's work on 'redemptive narratives' after negative events. McAdams suggests that there are some people who can redeem their lives after disastrous turns in the road (McAdams *et al.* 2001). This process involves the development of a story that reflects on what is past, what is lost and how to live in the present with that experience. A 'redemptive narrative' is one like Marian Partington's which reflects actively on all aspects of experience and gives voice to both the old and new identities.

Martha Ferrito and her colleagues explored this idea of redemption in a series of interviews with homicide perpetrators (Ferrito *et al.* 2012). The researchers asked them to talk about what they made of their experience and how they saw the future in terms of 'recovery'. What has emerged from this work, and related discussions (Adshead, Ferrito and Bose 2015), is the importance of identity after homicide; that coming to terms with the offence entails a process of relating to the identity of being an offender. To be forgiven by others is to be offered a way to relate not only to others but to oneself, and this is crucial to the task of developing a new way of living with the offender identity.

But not everyone can engage with forgiveness, or accept it. There is a painful section in Partington's book when she reaches out to her sister's murderer to offer forgiveness and is rejected. It is hard to imagine a state of mind that would reject such kindness, but then it is hard to imagine a state of mind that gave rise to such cruelty. It is not only hard but terrifying to think of the psychological effort it must take to maintain such a cruel state of mind day in, day out.

Forgiveness and mental health

Most offenders who have any insight struggle with guilt and shame and often articulate a sense that they have no right to be forgiven or to forgive themselves. An inability to forgive oneself is likely to be associated with psychological pain and depression, which may be so severe that it impairs any process of recovery and rehabilitation.

The forensic mental health system may generate a paradox in relation to offenders. Offenders in secure psychiatric settings may be encouraged to forgive themselves on the grounds that they were mentally ill at the time of the offence, and therefore cannot (and should not) take either full responsibility for the offence or the self-condemnation that goes with responsibility. Although for many offenders this psychological stance has a concrete reality in law in terms of legal defences set out at trial, nevertheless such a stance may sit uneasily with the psychological process of acceptance of the offender identity. It may not make sense for offenders to be told not to feel guilty (because their mental illness contributed to the offence) when they both feel guilty and are (in some physical sense, at least) guilty. Even more paradoxically, mental health professionals may take up incoherent positions regarding guilt and responsibility: they may tell offenders they were not really responsible because they were mentally ill, but if an offender then begins cheerfully to say that they are not to blame because they were ill, the offender may be accused of lacking remorse!

Perhaps the key issue here is 'articulation': not just the expression of emotional experience but also some sense of separating a complex experience into different parts and by reflection reworking and reconnecting the parts into a new whole. As therapists, we are aware of how people tell a story of themselves when they start in therapy, and how that story has to change as they develop a new understanding of themselves. In relation to offences, this could be thought of as the process of dismantling a 'cover story' (Adshead 2011) and building a new story that can include an appreciation of the reality of actions taken and choices made. Murray Cox called this process a '*scala integrata*', an integrated scale/a gradual progression (Cox 1986) but it might be better described as a '*Via Dolorosa*': a slow stumbling walk to and past a moment of dreadful truth when a human life came to an end.

Conclusion

Forgiveness is crucial to life after violence, and those who are forgiven can have an opportunity to lead a new life in some sort of connection. But the process of thinking about forgiveness and accepting it is neither simple nor painless.

We end our chapter with some quotations from a discussion of recovery and forgiveness that took place in a secure unit for offenders with mental illness, all of whom had committed acts of grave violence. This group was led by Erwin James (2003), who has written extensively about his experience of life after offending. These quotes hint at the complexity of the emotional labour of forgiveness:

> I'll never forgive myself for what I have done…it's an open wound that I can't heal.

> I'm not sure about forgiveness…it's a bit too convenient…sorry seems pathetic after what I've done.

References

Adams, M.M. (2000) *Horrendous Evils and the Goodness of God.* Ithaca, NY: Cornell University Press.

Adshead, G. (1998) 'The heart and its reasons: constructing explanations for offending behaviour.' *The Journal of Forensic Psychiatry,* 9(2), 231–236.

Adshead, G. (2011) 'The life sentence: using a narrative approach in group psychotherapy with offenders.' *Group Analysis,* 44(2), 175–195.

Adshead, G., Ferrito, M. and Bose, S. (2015) 'Recovery after homicide narrative shifts in therapy with homicide perpetrators.' *Criminal Justice and Behavior,* 42(1), 70–81.

Cox, M. (1986) 'The "holding function" of dynamic psychotherapy in a custodial setting: a review.' *Journal of the Royal Society of Medicine,* 79(3), 162–164.

Cox, M. (1999) *Remorse and Reparation* (Vol. 7). London: Jessica Kingsley Publishers.

Ferrito, M., Vetere, A., Adshead, G. and Moore, E. (2012) 'Life after homicide: accounts of recovery and redemption of offender patients in a high security hospital – a qualitative study.' *Journal of Forensic Psychiatry & Psychology,* 23(3), 327–344.

James, E. (2003) *A Life Inside: A Prisoner's Notebook.* London: Atlantic Books.

McAdams, D.P., Reynolds, J., Lewis, M., Patten, A.H. and Bowman, P.J. (2001) 'When bad things turn good and good things turn bad: sequences of redemption and contamination in life narrative and their relation to psychosocial adaptation in midlife adults and in students.' *Personality and Social Psychology Bulletin,* 27(4), 474–485.

Partington, M. (2012) *If You Sit Very Still.* London: Jessica Kingsley Publishers.

Chapter 6

USES AND ABUSES OF SELF-FORGIVENESS

Stephen Cherry

As a phrase, 'self-forgiveness' has a marmite-like quality, arousing emotional responses from those who love it and those who hate it. In this chapter I will try to remain dispassionate, while showing that these responses reveal something about the incommensurable way in which different disciplines consider the whole realm of forgiveness. More interesting than this, however, will be some of the areas where self-forgiveness is presented and understood in a way which is both more pragmatic and less polemical. Consideration of such begins to open up some ways in which 'forgiveness', when understood in a non-technical and relatively 'wide-angled' way, can be both a value and a practice that assists personal and professional functionality (or, as Freud would call it, 'love and work') in circumstances where mistakes, failings and faults are inevitable, and yet where it is difficult to make allowance for them without sacrificing either high standards of performance or principles of justice.

The forgiveness family

In my own writing about forgiveness I have found it helpful to suggest that we might think about the 'forgiveness family'. The point of this is to clarify that while we can speak of interpersonal forgiveness, the forgiveness of God and self-forgiveness quite sensibly, these 'forgivenesses', while they have some common features, also differ from each other in significant ways.

When it comes to interpersonal forgiveness it is often said that only the victim can forgive, but many acts of intentional harm have more than one victim, and to make an obvious point explicit, if there is more than one victim it may be that any two victims are not of one heart and mind when it comes to forgiving the perpetrator. What does this mean for the perpetrator – are they forgiven or not?

When it comes to the forgiveness of God, however, no such ambiguity – or rather plurality – can exist. God either forgives or does not forgive. God does not have a sibling who may be more or less generous or mean in forgiving. However, God's forgiveness is unlike interpersonal forgiveness in a number of ways. God is not the direct victim of unjust hurt and harm when, say, a child is abused or a teenager stabbed or an office worker bullied to the point of breakdown. A theologian might argue that, nonetheless, God is offended because all such actions are sins and sins are *de facto* offences against God, and that we could therefore think of them as quasi-injuries. We can concede the first point – a sin is indeed an offence against God. But is a 'quasi-injury' the same as an actual injury? Is God our *victim* when we sin?

I would argue not. When a person is unjustly hurt one of the things that happens is that they are empowered to give or withhold forgiveness, to take primary responsibility for the emotional tone of any ongoing relationship with the offender. If you have hurt someone you have no right to demand that they ignore it, or forgive you, or just 'get over it'. Of course, people often do just this because they are inclined to continue the relationship while acquiescing in the abuse of power that led to the offence in the first place. But this does not make it right, good or healthy. And part of the point of the language and practice of interpersonal forgiveness is that its lack signals the need for some relational work that addresses the injustice and establishes things on an equitable basis for the future.

God's forgiveness is not like this. God is not empowered by our repentance to become forgiving. Rather it is in God's nature to forgive (by token of being merciful) and God's forgiveness is not just the re-ordering of a particular relationship, but the pardoning and absolving of all the sins of the sinner. Penitents may present a list of sins to the priest in the confessional, but they are met by just one absolution.

Self-forgiveness is different because the self is neither another or God. The self cannot be its own victim in the same way that another can be its victim. Nor does the self have the divine perspective, which means that it is not aware of every level of sinfulness and at the same time able to regard the whole person with a uniquely powerful gaze of forgiving love.

However, the self is in some ways like another and in other ways like God. It is like God in that its perspective is unique. The self has self-knowledge, which is notoriously both better and worse than the perspective that another might have on it. But, unlike God, the self is often mistaken about itself. Self-knowledge is famously difficult to achieve, and by its nature it is impossible to calibrate, especially negative self-knowledge. I may consider myself the most mean-spirited person on the planet. Friends may disagree, but they will not know the depths of malice of which my imagination is capable. Truly we can never know how bad, or for that matter good, we really are. As someone has said, self-delusion is almost inevitable.

Faced with the complexity of the 'forgiveness family', many are inclined to organise it. My own theological temptation is to promote the forgiveness of God to the position of great ancestor of the tribe. The ethicist, however, will take interpersonal forgiveness as the paradigm. Those who come at forgiveness from a psychological perspective, especially some forms of psychotherapy, will want to begin with self-forgiveness. 'Unless you can forgive yourself you will never forgive anyone else' is a frequently heard saying. Whether or not it is true is open to question, but it clarifies that for the psychotherapist it is often self-forgiveness that is primary.

Simply to note this difference in perspective and priority is helpful and edifying. My model of forgiveness as a family, with divine forgiveness as the progenitor, is challenged by the ethical and psychological perspectives. Maybe the word 'family' is too loaded anyway. Perhaps I should think of a 'forgiveness cluster' and represent it by an equilateral triangle that can be approached from any direction. Or perhaps I should think of it as a constellation of stars.

Self-forgiveness or self-acceptance

Before coming to the positive aspects of self-forgiveness let me clarify why it is a dubious concept both from the theological and ethical perspective.

As a Christian priest interested in forgiveness, I have learned to pay attention when I hear the phrase 'I can't forgive myself'. My response to this tends to be affirmative. 'Well no, you probably can't: forgiveness properly belongs not to you but to the person or people you have hurt or to God against whom you have sinned.'

For this reason, I was encouraged by a review article about self-forgiveness published in the *Journal of Religion and Health* in 2011, which deconstructed the idea and concluded that 'self-acceptance is a more accurate and useful term for the process and benefits attributed to self-forgiveness'. Making the distinction between self-forgiveness and self-acceptance is helpful in a number of ways. First, because it accepts that there is indeed a problem here – that problem being, as I understand it, that the self is at irreconcilable odds with itself. It finds that in the aftermath of having done something culpable and hurtful, it can get no peace.

It is naive, to say that the source of this peace must lie either in the offended other or in God, and to blank off the possibility of any intrapersonal reconciliation. This is because sometimes people have trouble in accepting the forgiveness of others or God. Despite it being manifestly 'on offer', it is resisted. The proffered forgiveness does not seem to get to the heart of the troubled self; it does not get to the source and origin of the ongoing recriminations. The theologian Paul Tillich used to rail against this sort of resistance in the pulpit, '*Simply accept the fact that you are accepted!*' (Tillch 1962, p.63) This is a plea that makes an exasperated sort of sense. Unfortunately, however, the problem here is not whether or not the person on the receiving end is behaving rationally, but that something is blocking or inhibiting their capacity to accept the gift of forgiveness offered by another or God.

Inability to accept the forgiveness of others is not the only problem that requires something that might be called 'self-forgiveness' as the answer. The other may be absent (you might have murdered them) and you may not believe in God, leaving self-forgiveness as the only way out of a living hell. Such a living hell might be experienced with or without the imposition of punishment. Some might never be able to forgive themselves even after being punished because no punishment could be severe enough. Another arena where self-forgiveness might be invoked is one where knowledge of the offence to be forgiven is private. These are situations where people speak of having 'let myself down' or had the experience that they have failed not by an objective or legal or even divine standard, but have offended against their own personal moral code or values. People in such situations who decline to excuse themselves ('I was having bad day', or 'that was not the real me', or 'no one else really noticed') are troubled by the trap in which they find themselves. Unless they can, as it were, stand aside from their own self-disappointing failure or fault, they are stuck either with endless recrimination and shame or with accepting that they do not live up to their own standards. Such a person would be inclined to feel a fraud or hypocrite – a 'phoney' to use the word so often used of disappointing others in J.D. Salinger's *Catcher in the Rye*.

The reality of all this is unarguable – but is it close enough to either interpersonal forgiveness or divine forgiveness to warrant the name 'forgiveness'? This is a question that is of great interest to theologians and ethicists. But it is of little or no interest to a psychotherapist because it is the paradigm through which they see forgiveness.

Those who value self-forgiveness as a category, as opposed to those who see it as a category error, will be familiar and adept with the self-hyphen formulation. Self-regard, self-esteem, self-respect will be understood as sensible and non-problematic. Self-forgiveness will be seen to belong to this cluster of reflective concepts. It will be understood as the product of a period of work in which the self comes to the view that investing time and energy in self-recrimination, or even self-hatred, is unproductive and unhealthy; it is better to drop the subject and re-respect the self – after all, we are all more than the sum of our most heinous mistakes or most despicable desires. The self's orientation towards the self needs to move on from this negative, punitive stance not only for the subject's sake but for the good of relationships and the benefit of the community and society of which this person is a member; self-disgust or self-hatred is anti-social and narcissistic – a curving in of the self on the self.

So – is it better to call this sort of personal development self-acceptance or self-forgiveness? The strident ethicist may howl for justice's sake and say that it is only the victim can forgive, and the theologian will remind us of the divine prerogative and power to pardon and deliver from all sin. There is a good reason, however, to prefer the phrase 'self-forgiveness' over 'self-acceptance'. The power of the word 'forgiveness' does not reside primarily in any particular claim about who can forgive; that is simply a romantic limitation of the concept. The truth is that forgiveness is plural and operates at many levels in parallel, in series, and in subtly similar and different ways. The power of forgiveness, rather, is that unlike 'acceptance', it is a moral word: it creates the space for two actions: a 'stop' and a 'start', or as the theologian Miroslav Volf has put it, 'exclusion' and 'embrace'. Forgiveness is based, in other words, on both 'judgement' and 'mercy' and is a product of the inter- and intrapersonal tension between the two over a period of time: this ongoing yet ultimately resolved tension is the 'healing agony' in the title of my book (Cherry 2012).

The reason that self-forgiveness is better than self-acceptance as a term is that 'self-forgiveness' admits in its vocabulary that something that cannot be ignored is wrong and that it needs to be put right. Of course, 'self-forgiveness' might not be good, integral or sincere; it might be cheap, hypocritical, unwise and unhelpful. But the same could be said of what passes for interpersonal forgiveness. But the existence of such sham forgiveness, in which something else, such as condonation or excuse, is passed off as forgiveness, does not mean that there can be no genuine interpersonal forgiveness.

My argument is that it is much the same with self-forgiveness. Thinking and speaking in terms of it can add to the richness of our understanding of what the word 'forgiveness' points to when used in different contexts by people of different intellectual and professional tribes and guilds, and for different purposes. There is not, I suggest, one perfect paradigm of forgiveness to which all others must approximate if they are to be called 'forgiveness'. Rather, the reality is that after unjust hurt there are a variety of responses at different levels, some of which count as 'forgiveness' because they make space both for justice and mercy and because they operate not at the level of impersonal movement of the state but take into account, and focus on, the human and subjective elements, both, interpersonal or intrapersonal. Thus I do accept a clear distinction between forgiveness and pardon, but also want to suggest that the phrase self-forgiveness is a legitimate and helpful use of the word 'forgiveness' and something better than mere 'self-acceptance', though forgiveness always includes some acceptance .

Use and abuse of self-forgiveness

In the remainder of this chapter I want to focus more specifically on the use and abuse of self-forgiveness.

Self-forgiveness, if entered into as an *alternative* to other forms of forgiveness, would seem to be an abuse of the concept. In this regard, however, it is not especially different to divine forgiveness – or at least the seeking of divine forgiveness. I have heard stories from prison of perpetrators wanting to tell their victims that, 'It's all right now, God has forgiven me'. It's a relatively small step to imagine someone saying, 'It's okay, I've forgiven myself'. Whatever self-forgiveness is, it can't be an alternative to other forms of forgiveness.

It may, however, be an alternative to divine forgiveness, although it sometimes is. The atheist cannot invoke divine forgiveness, but may well want to keep the possibility of self-forgiveness alive alongside other forms of forgiveness. A theologian may look at this with concern, possibly even disdain, and denigrate this arrogation to the self of the authority of God. But just because some see it as a sophisticated and advanced development of the human desire for the forgiveness of God, which properly supersedes and overrides that desire, and theological reflection judges this hubristic and complacent, doesn't mean that there is not a positive form of self-forgiveness.

Moving on to appropriate uses of self-forgiveness we come to the territory of 'mistakes'. It is the most common word I have found in different types of literature on this subject: technical psychological and psychotherapeutic writing, self-help books and also ethical reflections. There seem to be two forms of argument regarding self-forgiveness and mistakes. One is that self-forgiveness is appropriate and helpful when people are too hard on themselves in the light of having made a mistake. The other is that self-forgiveness is a necessary concept, which takes the form of a virtue in allowing practitioners to cope with the reality of mistake-making where the professional culture is perfectionist.

In her book *Forgiving Yourself*, Beverly Flanigan develops the approach she set out in her first book, *Forgiving the Unforgivable*, to the specifics of forgiving yourself. She identifies four phases[1] in self-forgiveness:

- Phase 1 Confronting yourself

- Phase 2 Holding yourself responsible

- Phase 3 Confessing your flaws

- Phase 4 Transformation.

She speaks of the necessity of 'accomplishing' each phase, 'to free yourself from self-imposed captivity' and emphasises that the process will be a 'struggle'. She suggests that there will be variety in the ways in which progress will be made: for some it is the struggle of personal work, others may need professional therapy and for yet others she suggests that, 'God's grace is key'. She is not at all prescriptive: 'no approach is right for everyone' (Flanigan 1996, p.59).

One could say that Flanigan's first two phases are about honesty and accountability. If our main frame of reference for forgiveness is interpersonal forgiveness, however, this is not the normal place for thinking in terms of forgiveness to begin. Interpersonal forgiveness stories begin in an episode of unjust hurt. Self-forgiveness, however,

---

1   'The word "phase" here is used to help readers organise concepts. It is not meant as a scientific, or maturational, concept that implies an inviolable, sequential ordering of phenomena, one falling before or after another in a specific, predictable order. Phase is used as an overarching idea that gives guidance to people who are attempting to forgive themselves so that they can see the "big picture" and any tasks that need to be accomplished to make self-forgiveness complete' (Flanigan 1996, p.59)

begins not in the event itself but in the recollection or, as Flanigan puts it, in the 'self-confrontation'.

Her third phase is where the person who seeks self-forgiveness confesses their flaws. This is perhaps a surprising development for those who thought that self-forgiveness was entirely conducted in the inner workings of the self. What is interesting about Flanigan's method is that the confession is not necessarily made to the one who has suffered at your hands, or to a priest or another religious figure – though she does discuss this second option. The important thing for confession is the listening capacity of the confessor and that there is a shared understanding of confidentiality. Coming from a religious perspective she views bad experiences in the past as perhaps the most serious inhibitors of confession in pursuit of self-forgiveness. It is inevitable that some people have bad experiences of confession, but it is ironic as well as honest and sad to note that these create their own need for healing.

Flanigan's final step is 'transformation' which is, she insists, not just merely 'change'; it is the word for what happens when people 'recreate themselves'. Here she interestingly contrasts the transformation that happens in someone who is able to forgive others with that of those able to forgive themselves. We are concerned with the second list. Self-forgiveness involves transformation:

- from: struggling to admit mistakes, limits and wrongdoings...to: becoming insightful regarding personal flaws and understanding that no one is perfect

- from: guilt or self-hatred and regret...to: positive use of the past for the future

- from: being unaware of personal flaws and mistakes...to: being aware and able to confess them to others

- from: being unaware of interpersonal or spiritual connectedness...to: being connected at either or both levels.

(Adapted from Flanigan 1996)

Flanigan takes a moral tone which would, I think, please those who have ethical considerations in mind as they approach forgiveness. She writes that in the fourth phase 'it is important to know that *you cannot forgive yourself until you commit yourself to personal change*' (Flanigan 1996, p.148, emphasis original). And she goes on to consider apology, restitution and purification rites. It is interesting and important to note that these come *after* the process of self-forgiveness. Clearly she does not view self-forgiveness as an alternative to other forms of forgiveness, but something that might make it possible to embark on that 'generous and creative venture of trust'.

Self-forgiveness as virtue in medical practitioners

Our second case study of self-forgiveness comes from an exploration of what the 'virtue' of self-forgiveness might mean in medical practice, specifically in what the author calls 'doctoring'. Jeffrey Blustein (2009) recognises that the paradigm case of 'forgiveness' is interpersonal, of perpetrator by victim, but is not against its 'reflexive application', suggesting that it is no more of an oxymoron than 'self-taught'. He goes on to set his reflections in the context of the perfectionist culture of contemporary medicine: 'Physicians are not permitted to make mistakes since mistakes have grave consequences; physicians should not acknowledge uncertainty to patients since an admission of medical fallibility will alarm them...' There is nothing wrong with physicians striving for excellence, the problem is that they have to learnt how to deal constructively with 'their perceived limitations, shortcomings and lapses' (Bluestein 2009, p.88).

Blustein hopes that a virtue of self-forgiveness will help practitioners 'distinguish between those situations when self-reproach is reasonable and those when it is not' (p.89). In fact, he sees dealing with unmoveable self-reproach or debilitating self-blame as the work of self-forgiveness. Of course, one way to deal with these things is to come to condone the actions for which we reproach ourselves. This is not more appropriate in self-forgiveness than it is when we are challenged to forgive others.

Blustein helpfully describes self-forgiveness as 'a matter of overcoming the self-reproach that accompanies a diminished sense of self-worth', the context being that self-worth is diminished for good reason (p.90). By self-reproach he means emotions such as 'guilt, shame, self-loathing, and self-contempt' (p.91). The argument is that while it is reasonable and appropriate to feel bad having made a mistake, it is not good to let that feeling of badness, whatever form it takes, get out of hand. One way he explores this is by suggesting that it is by self-forgiveness that we may legitimately restore our self-respect. The point here is that while our self-esteem will rightly take an irreparable dent when we discover that we have made a harmful and costly mistake, our self-respect should not be based on a fantasy version of ourselves – the perfect professional who never gets anything wrong and makes no mistakes. Rather, the good physician, for instance, is one who feels multiform pangs of regret when a mistake comes to light but is not terminally incapacitated by them. Self-forgiveness doesn't aim to eliminate self-reproach, but it does need to moderate it. The vital thing, however, is that, as with inter-personal forgiveness, the process is first to recognize responsibility for what has gone wrong, and second to limit the recrimination.

Blustein considers two ways in which self-forgiveness might go wrong, for instance if one is too easy on oneself. He is able to line up ethicists and theologians who are concerned that the prospect and work of self-forgiveness may be a substitute for seeking forgiveness from those harmed, and become thereby 'a self-confirmation of a state of estrangement' and not, therefore, 'forgiveness' in any meaningful sense. He does, however, think that self-forgiveness is a legitimate option in circumstances where an offender has done real work of adjustment and repentance and had a genuine change of heart but the offended will not respond to apology. It is hard to define this clearly, so Blustein does so negatively, 'when the wronged party is justified in not forgiving the wronging party, the latter is not justified in forgiving himself' (p.96).

Another problem of self-forgiveness is the situation where the offended rightly forgives, but the offender will not forgive themselves. Blustein describes this as a situation where someone is 'controlled and debilitated' by self-reproach. Such a person has a chronically and irreversibly diminished self-respect. Blustein is not especially concerned with this because in his view the matter is largely of theoretical interest. Those coming from a psychotherapeutic perspective may, however, see this as a common and fundamental issue.

In an illuminating section, Blustein asks what the benefits of the virtue of self-forgiveness are for the person who possesses it. Crucially he sees it as delivering more than inner peace. It allows a person to live well; for him, self-forgiveness is properly and helpfully re-moralising. However, these benefits only come if self-forgiveness is done properly, and in clarifying this Blustein makes it clear that he does not see self-forgiveness merely as a change of internal attitude to an aspect of one's own past.

> ...the benefits [of self-forgiveness] must be secured as a result of examining oneself realistically and honestly, taking responsibility for what one has done and been, confessing and seeking forgiveness for one's wrongdoings and flaws, and resolving to prevent repetition and to improve. The person who does not take responsibility, or who takes responsibility only half-heartedly – not just on particular occasions but so repeatedly that we can say it is characteristic of her not to do so – does not show respect for the victims of her wrongdoing and does not have the virtue of self-forgiveness. (2009, p.101)

Blustein emphasises that while self-forgiveness benefits its possessor, it is not entirely self-regarding. He believes that if we cannot forgive ourselves we will be unlikely to relate well to the mistakes and faults of others.

As I have mentioned, Blustein's focus is on the medical profession, and his concern is to clarify an aspect of the character of a good doctor. As he explores the role that the virtue of self-forgiveness can play in helping the doctor cope with the death of patients and the reality that mistakes are made, he emphasises that self-forgiveness involves keeping away from questions of blame by focusing on questions of responsibility. He also returns to a point he makes early on, which is that appropriate self-forgiveness is necessary if the doctor–patient relationship is to be one where trust grows and flourishes. He sees this as not only appropriate and good but vital to the whole business of doctoring.

Conclusion

Although when judged from the perspective of either interpersonal forgiveness or divine forgiveness, self-forgiveness can seem a vain or vapid category more appropriately rendered self-acceptance, the phrase does in fact have ethical, psychological, theological and practical worth. It refers not to a cheap alternative to other forms of forgiveness, but to a necessary *adjunct* in some cases, and in others a necessary *preliminary* to other forms of forgiveness. Moreover, self-forgiveness, whether construed as 'work' as it is by Flanigan, or 'virtue' as Blustein sees it, is valuable because it calms sensitive minds and gives them peace, but also because it re-moralises people making them more open and therefore trustworthy.

The term 'self-forgiveness' can easily be abused, but this abuse should not prevent us recognising and seeking to understand and articulate in ever more nuanced and practical ways its nature and value in human affairs.

References

Blustein, J. (2009) 'Doctoring and Self-Forgiveness.' in Rebecca Walker and Philip J. Ivanhoe (eds) *Working Virtue: Virtue Ethics and Contemporary Moral Problems.* Oxford: Oxford University Press.

Cherry, S. (2012) *Healing Agony: Re-Imagining Forgiveness.* London: Continuum.

Flanigan, B. (1996) *Forgiving Yourself.* New York, NY: Macmillan.

Tillich,P. (1962) The Shakings of the Foundations. London: Penguin.

Vitz, P. C. and Meade, J. M. (2011) 'Self-Forgiveness in Psychology and Psychotherapy: A Critique.' *Journal of Religion and Health, 50,* 20, 248–263.

Chapter 7

ON FORGIVENESS AND MEDICAL HARM

Deborah Bowman

Introduction

Many years ago, I interviewed doctors about their mistakes for my PhD. I had become interested in the subject when I spoke to a medical friend about loyalty in the profession and whether it could be as much vice as virtue, sometimes leading to tribalism that compromised the interests of patients. She had explained that, for her, the stakes in medicine are so overwhelmingly high and the fear of mistakes so great that perhaps it did mean she was more forgiving of her colleagues than might be common among other professional groups. She went on to tell me that such generosity was hard to achieve when faced with forgiving oneself after contributing to medical harm. I knew then that I had found a subject by which I would remain fascinated, even through the long years of juggling a full-time job and young family with the demands of a PhD.

That fascination has endured throughout my career. Nothing could have prepared me for the memorable stories and the intense emotions that I heard during my fieldwork. Since then, I have continued to explore harm in medicine and to think about forgiveness and what it might mean in relation to medical harm. In this chapter, I share that thinking and consider what we mean by forgiveness when harm has resulted from medical care.

Who or what is being forgiven when harm has occurred in medical settings? Is it within the gift of anyone involved to forgive, or does the value of forgiveness derive from its source (which must be recognised as credible)? Is forgiveness an inherent good: a virtue that needs no further explanation and in respect of which there need be no further demonstrable value or positive consequence? Might the pursuit of forgiveness be problematic or even harmful? What might be the conditions of, and for, forgiveness and what difference does the preposition make in this question? How can our understanding of, and approach to, forgiveness capture the complexity, uncertainty and inherent fallibility of medical care?

In exploring these questions, I draw on over 20 years of working as an academic in medical ethics and in providing clinical ethics support to staff and patients in the NHS. I also revisit some of the stories I heard when I was doing my PhD. Those stories reveal much about how we yearn for and negotiate forgiveness, how we recognise its power, our resistance to insincere or unearned forgiveness and the unpredictable and painful responses of people following harm in medicine. I also invited my Twitter followers and Facebook friends to tell me what forgiveness means to them and I was overwhelmed by the responses, which were honest, raw and thought provoking. I am grateful to everyone who spoke to me with openness, courage and generosity.

Defining and experiencing forgiveness in healthcare

In her ground-breaking book on medical harm, ethics and forgiveness, Nancy Berlinger (2005) identifies two senses in which the word 'forgiveness' is used. First, it denotes an act of pardon or absolution leading to reconciliation with the person considered to be responsible for the harm. The second, perhaps less common meaning, is to waive or discharge any outstanding obligation or to let another off from a responsibility, debt or duty, but without the need for reconciliation. These distinct meanings matter and determine what we think, feel and do when we consider forgiveness and medical harm. And all three of those verbs – think, feel and do – are important when we are discussing forgiveness. No one can forgive or be forgiven without attending to thought, emotion and action. How does the health system negotiate these two different definitions of forgiveness when harm has occurred?

Forgiveness as an act of mercy and reconciliation

The first approach whereby pardon or absolution is granted and reconciliation between the parties may follow underpins many of the approaches to forgiveness in healthcare. Professional bodies and their respective codes of conduct require individual clinicians to disclose and apologise where harm has occurred. The moral significance of honesty has been further emphasised by the statutory duty of candour, which requires healthcare organisations to be open and transparent, including in circumstances when care goes wrong. These expectations of honesty emphasise what might be considered steps towards forgiveness in Berlinger's first sense. It is an approach that requires individual and organisational accountability, apologies, explanations and, where possible, some element of restorative justice. It is an approach that reflects a body of evidence which shows that for many people, the primary concern when a medical error or clinical harm has occurred is to receive an apology and to prevent it from happening to others (Vincent *et al.* 1994; Kraman and Hamm 1999; Vincent and Coulter 2002). The desire for acknowledgement and a wish to ensure that there is no recurrence was evident too in the replies I received from people on social media when I asked about forgiveness.

When patients, doctors and families come together to talk honestly about what has happened it can be transformative. One doctor told me about a patient who had lost a child following a medical error (for which he was partly responsible) and described the relationship that they were able to rebuild after those painful conversations:

> I think the main thing with her was she wanted to know if it would happen again, or as far as possible, you know, there's nothing to do to bring back the dead baby obviously. And I spent a long time talking to her and she was actually about to sue the hospital because she'd come across a brick wall of, 'No, the notes were lost, the consultant wasn't there, he couldn't talk to her, whatever,' and in the end I said, 'Look, I'll phone up the consultant and speak to him [the other doctor involved].' So, I said, 'Please, all she [the patient] wants to do is talk it through. She knows you can't – you know, it's happened.' And they (sic) said fine, we'll see her, and had

a long talk with the consultant as well, and as a result, you know, nothing could bring the baby back. It was a disaster that happened, it was looked at in depth, and, you know, scanning techniques and all sorts of, you know, there was a lot of hospital stuff that was reviewed. And she didn't sue anybody, and she remained my patient, and, you know, she's moved away now, but, you know, we had a good relationship for another ten years after that. And I think that was – it was horrible, but it was such a good lesson for me, in that I think that most people – I mean people are obviously angry, upset, distressed – all these things when it happens. To be open about communication and actually, I know it's a question of how you say it, and so on. But I mean that was just – it was, you know, I felt awful because I knew I'd missed it. (Doctor 13)

Many of the relational aspects of responding to medical harm, including some of the ways in which complaints, disputes and potential legal actions are managed, such as conciliation and mediation, seem to be working towards forgiveness in Berlinger's first sense. The goal is, if not reconciliation, at least an acceptance and the facility to rebuild a relationship with healthcare professionals in general, although maybe not the specific individuals who were involved. It is not difficult to see why this is an appealing approach. All of us will become ill and will need to depend on the care of professionals at some stage in our lives. The inherent vulnerability of the human condition requires us to find a way that we can trust our doctors, nurses and caregivers. Without being able to believe again in the reliability of healthcare professionals and the institutions within which they work, we are abandoned to a future where care prompts only suspicion and fear.

The problems of reconciliation

Yet, might this first approach to forgiveness, in its emphasis on choosing to pardon another and working towards reconciliation, be problematic or even harmful? What if a patient or family member does not want to hear apologies and explanations? Why should someone whose life has been irrevocably altered by medical harm engage with the individual or organisation that caused that loss and distress? Given that organisations have prescribed timescales for investigations and processes, what might it mean to involve someone in efforts at reconciliation prematurely or at a time that has been determined not by their interests, wishes and needs, but by institutional requirements? Does the expectation of professional bodies and the statutory duty of candour risk compromising the sincerity of any apology and explanation? If so, can forgiveness follow when the impulse to reconcile has been externally rather than internally driven?

These questions warrant thought and attention, yet are not often considered within the monolithic systems of healthcare and its regulation. Forgiveness that involves pardon and seeks reconciliation must be a voluntary and sincere act. It can neither be forced nor insisted on. To expect or to seek such forgiveness is to ask a great deal of someone and may cause further harm. To do so because a hospital system or process requires or expects it is insensitive and seems to misunderstand the nature of forgiveness. It risks further damage and suggests a response that does not prioritise the needs and wishes of those who have been harmed.

The psychoanalyst, Coline Covington (2016) demonstrates, drawing on case studies, the ways in which expecting or even focusing on forgiveness can be damaging. She proposes that individual or societal pressure to forgive may contribute to those who are already hurt, denying the enormity of their loss and distress as a way of 'converting shame and suffering into something commendable' (Covington 2016, p.138). She further considers forgiveness as a form of social control, particularly when meetings are convened for the purpose, noting that 'forgiveness is an act of individual choice and not something that can be determined by or imposed on groups' (Covington 2016, p.139).

Covington is not alone in noting the potential limits and problems of forgiveness, particularly when it is controlled or determined by an external agency, agenda or process. Smith, who also considers forgiveness from the perspective of a psychoanalyst, describes the tendency of some analysts to emphasise, or even impose, forgiveness on their patients as 'an act of aggression on the analyst's part' (Smith 2008, p.934). Holloway, too, observes, when considering the South African Truth Commission, that forgiveness cannot be compelled or expected merely because a forum has been created in which it is desired. He notes, 'We only add to the trauma if we try to urge or hurry people into a forgiveness they are humanly incapable of offering' (Holloway 2002, p.53). Yet, he also believes in the value of forgiveness and the devastating impact for those who cannot forgive:

> We cannot order people to forgive, but we can recognise that their inability to forgive may have the tragic effect of binding them to the past and condemning them to a life-sentence of bitterness… The inability or refusal to forgive, though it may be morally appropriate, always extends the reign of the original sin into the future, so that it can end up dominating a whole life or the life of a whole people. (Holloway 2002, p.54)

In the healthcare system where harm is the antithesis of what is intended and sought, attending to the process by which forgiveness is sought matters. While critical incident procedures, complaints investigations, dispute resolution and even litigation necessarily have prescribed stages, formats and timescales, it is vital to consider whether those structures help or hinder the harmed. It may be a difficult question for the NHS and its staff to face, but could it be that, in some cases, the very procedures intended to help and to facilitate forgiveness exacerbate damage and cause greater harm?

Is there a way of providing space within the health service that acknowledges the complexity of forgiveness after medical harm? That it may be a life's work? That it may never happen? That remediation is often impossible? That one's relationship to forgiveness will be part of the unpredictable ebb and flow of emotions that follow loss, distress, hurt and injury? If forgiveness cannot be 'stage managed', is it possible to create conditions where forgiveness is freely given, meaningful and responsive to the needs of the people involved? In the next section, I discuss responsibility and fallibility and the ways in which each informs how forgiveness is conceptualised following medical harm, by both patients and doctors alike.

Responsibility, fallibility and forgiveness

The first element of forgiveness that is often cited as important is accepting responsibility. Yet the relationship between responsibility and forgiveness is complex for both parties following medical harm. To forgive in the sense of mercy and reconciliation usually depends on specificity, i.e. on the knowledge that someone erred or that an act went awry. Explanations are part of that specificity – offering a narrative that accounts for the harm. There is often an assumption of, or search for, causality: because of x, harm y occurred. Blame may or may not be part of how that narrative is presented and heard, but most families and patients will want to understand whether someone's act or omission led or contributed to the harm that ensued. Such a step sounds simple and yet the nature of clinical practice is such that it can be difficult to know 'what happened' and whether anyone is or should be considered responsible. Medicine is a complex, high-stakes and uncertain business practised by fallible human beings often in resource-constrained and pressurised environments. As Marianne Paget notes 'medicine is an unfolding activity. The now of mistakes collides with the then of acting with uncertain knowledge' (Paget 1988, p.48). Moreover, the capacity to make good may be limited and the stakes are arguably higher than in most other professional endeavours. Medicine is inherently risky and imbued with fallibility. While efforts are made to mitigate both risk and fallibility, those efforts can never be entirely successful.

Uncertainty in medicine further complicates the discernment and explanation of harm. When doctors talk about harm, a recurrent theme is whether, given the uncertainty of a clinical presentation or problem, they could only have known they had erred in hindsight. The effect of hindsight bias pervades the management of harm, yet it is infrequently acknowledged. Such complexities and uncertainty lead to categorising medical harm. Terms such as 'slips', 'lapses' and 'violations' are invoked to distinguish perceived degrees of responsibility and, by implication, culpability. This doctor's description of what she calls a 'genuine mistake' is an example:

> I missed a congenital cataract in a child once, and that probably wasn't the best thing. But I had actually done what I should have done to test for it, and, in retrospect, thinking back on it, I don't

think I'd have picked it up. I mean, I was aware of what I should've done, I'd done it, and I'd missed it. And I think that's going to happen, and I think that had I not been aware of what I should've been testing for or looking for in that baby check, then I would say I was not competent. But I think that was just a genuine mistake. (Doctor 10)

Considerable attention has been afforded to the 'what' of defining error or harm, although it remains contested. Less attention has been given to the 'who' in defining medical harm and that too matters, particularly when considering forgiveness. Sociologists and ethnographers have produced rich accounts of medical talk and the negotiation of professional norms by and among clinicians.

Since Charles Bosk's seminal study of American surgeons and their mistakes (1976), much has been written about the ways in which doctors navigate and determine the relative significance of, and appropriate response to, medical harm. This doctor described how he considered the relative importance of harm:

It's the consequences for the patient, the consequences for you personally, how far they challenge your sense of the doctor you want to be, and how far you think, 'well, that happens'. So, are they unusual or are they common? Are they minor? Are they major? Um – are they a lapse in care; are they a 'significant event'? (Doctor 17)

The process of naming is illustrated by the multiplicity of factors embedded in the excerpt above. Outcomes matter, as might be expected in a positivist discipline like medicine. Frequency of occurrence is relevant to this doctor. He acknowledges that medicine carries 'inherent' risk by the statement 'well, that happens'. His nomenclature distinguishing between a 'lapse' and a 'significant event' is intriguing. Finally, this doctor does not question that it is his prerogative to define whether an episode constitutes a 'lapse' or a 'significant event'. The medical perspective on significance is exclusive.

Yet, medical harm is experienced by people other than the clinician. Without openness towards and attention to those non-professional experiences, perceptions and responses, it is unlikely that there can be space for forgiveness. Responsibility denotes accountability for the harm, but it must also attend to perspectives other than the professional. There must be an approach that recognises that the narrative about harm is not solely at the discretion of an individual professional or an organisation, but is dispersed and divergent. It is as important to consider who defines medical harm as it is to determine what constitutes medical harm when thinking about forgiveness and responsibility.

There is a further consideration when reflecting on the notion of responsibility in relation to forgiveness after medical harm, namely the relationship between individuals and systems. The last 20 years have seen a shift in the rhetoric of medical accountability whereby individual responsibility, and sometimes blame, have been replaced by greater attention to systems, data gathering and collective education. Reviews of medical harm and failures of care will commonly consider the chain of events rather than single acts or omissions. Root cause analysis and no-fault reporting systems are encouraged, albeit with variable impact. The emphasis of policy discourse is less on bad apples, but on orchard husbandry.

Alongside this shift in approach towards understanding and responding to medical harm, the UK system of healthcare is increasingly pressured, with resources more constrained and the context within which care is provided potentially compromised. These changes are beyond the control of individual clinicians, except in so far as they can express their views in the ballot box with the rest of the electorate, yet these systemic variables influence the quality of their work and, sometimes, contribute to harm. One doctor described how he believed policy allowed for misattribution of responsibility for medical harm:

> Of course, it's never the government's fault. It's never because the systems are at fault. It's never because they're [the government] not putting enough money into it. It's the doctor's fault. We're the ones making them [mistakes], right? That's what they want the public to believe. And that might sound a bit paranoid, but that's how I honestly believe the situation to be. It's a very convenient way of deflecting blame from yourselves. (Doctor 9)

Does our conception of forgiveness need to extend beyond the individual and human–human interaction to include systems, policies, organisational culture and procedures? Is that even possible? When I asked my followers on Twitter to tell me what forgiveness meant to them, most cited 'taking responsibility' as central. Yet, what does it mean to take responsibility when harm has arisen in a complex, uncertain, contested, fallible and imperfect context? What might the implications be for forgiveness?

Once again, we grapple with the complexity of forgiveness: taking responsibility is an oft-cited expectation or pre-requisite for those who have been harmed to consider forgiveness. Yet, the pressurised system within which healthcare is provided, the plurality of the healthcare team, the inherent uncertainty in medicine and the unavoidable, untameable fallibility of the human beings who work as clinicians render the attribution of responsibility fraught and challenging. Of course, no one who has been harmed should be further burdened with details of the complex context within which the harm has occurred, but these are considerations that should be more widely explored and discussed. The possibility, shape and boundaries of responsibility in relation to medical harm are integral to creating the conditions for forgiveness, not only for patients and families, but as the next section discusses, for professionals too.

Doctors and forgiveness

The pursuit of forgiveness is seductive, but difficult when it comes to a professional forgiving him or herself. Whether it is forgiveness in the sense of pardon and reconciliation or in the sense of discharging or letting go, many doctors find it challenging to consider forgiveness following medical harm. Professionals have been called the 'second victims' of medical error (Wu 2000; Seys *et al.* 2012). The impact on clinicians is well documented and includes serious mental health problems, including suicidal ideation, incapacitating emotional reactions, avoidance and, for some, leaving medicine. That is not to suggest that doctors are unique in their struggle to forgive themselves. As Holloway notes:

the hardest place to start [with forgiveness] is in the struggle with our own guilt…most of us seem to be quite good at forgiving or understanding human weakness in people we love, at sticking with our friends through the painful consequences of their mistakes. It is much more difficult to apply the same generosity to ourselves. (Holloway 2002, p.49)

During many of the interviews, visible emotion was evident when doctors were describing their mistakes. For these interviewees, the experience had remained upsetting even years later. One doctor compared his reaction to grief:

It's a bit like grief reaction, I suppose. You go through a kind of shock phase and this feeling of 'Oh God, what happened?', and then there's the kind of intense anger and sadness about what's happened, and then I think you move on to the useful time, which is when you actually start and, you know, look at the process and look what happened. It doesn't go away though, never. It never leaves me. Even after all this time. I even dream – you know – dream about it, sometimes. (Doctor 18)

Another described the isolation following medical harm; an experience that she believed could only be understood by another doctor:

I was really upset. Really, really upset. And my partner was very supportive. But that wasn't enough, actually. And it was only when I came to work on Monday and talked to a colleague here, who said, you know, if you talk me through it… That was really, really important. So I think – I think peer support is absolutely crucial, actually. (Doctor 4)

The doctors described feelings of self-doubt, disappointment, self-blame, shame, emotional turmoil, anguish, sadness, anxiety and fear. The emotional legacy of the harm lingered and, for some, led them to question whether they could continue to practise medicine. One doctor described how she mis-prescribed a potent sedative to a taxi driver:

So now – so if he had mowed down loads of people I would not be sitting here today. Because potentially it would be a huge cock-up.

Potentially, if it had gone to court that he had been prescribed a major tranquilliser, someone would have had a hard job defending me. But it didn't. That didn't happen. And he was changed over, and no harm came out of it. But it was – it made me realise how close you can come… I wouldn't be sitting here not because – I think – I don't think I'd be struck off, I think – I'd – I'd be found at fault, I'm sure of that. But I don't think I'd be able to continue if a major disaster had happened, I just don't think I could continue to work… I could see myself giving up medicine…say if he'd killed a kid or something. (Doctor 8)

Several doctors described the difficulty of moving on from harm and regaining professional confidence. The doctors rarely confided in anyone who wasn't medically trained about their error, including family. Only other clinicians offered the optimal combination of emotional support, awareness of healthcare practice, advice and information. Although the interviewees reported varying degrees of support, the overriding conclusion was that little could restore a doctor's emotional stability and professional confidence after harm other than time. One doctor memorably expressed how he filed away a mistake so he could function while also recognising the intense pain caused to the family whose child was harmed by his mistake:

It was such an empty and unsupported time [visibly upset]. I think er – I look back, and I think to be honest if I look at it, even now, years on – well, it probably is – it's a little bit – it's a little bit hermetically sealed and put away now, to be honest, for the sake of being able to move on [tearful]. I thought, you know, 'I've cocked up here and I really shouldn't be doing medicine'. And the impact on me – well, it was nothing compared with the impact it had on the family, was it? (Doctor 3)

Forgiveness, medical harm and learning

Many clinicians and patients emphasise the importance of learning from medical harm and error. Taking responsibility is considered a moral act that is evidenced by demonstrable learning with the intention that others will be prevented from either causing or experiencing future harm. In the last 20 years, the emphasis has shifted from individual learning to systemic and collective learning via initiatives at systems level such as anonymised reporting databases, confidential inquiries and organisational audits.

Evangelism about the value of education after harm has led some to challenge the notion that medical error is axiomatically 'wrong'. Buetow, for example, distinguishes between desirable and undesirable errors, considering that those that 'facilitate learning and innovation' can be desirable (Buetow 2005, p.55). However, Buetow is silent on who should determine whether an error is considered desirable or undesirable, and how patients might feel about unwittingly contributing to a desirable error database, even if it was educational. One interviewee, a GP, fascinatingly used the word 'learning' as a synonym for 'mistakes':

> And one of the characteristics of general practice is that it's going on behind closed doors all the time, isn't it? So you can quietly carry on making your mistakes, or making your – er – learning – er without that necessarily being directly observed. (Doctor 3)

Without exception, willingness to learn from medical harm was considered essential both by the doctors I interviewed and the patients who have since spoken to me about medical harm. Learning makes devastating loss and painful harm purposeful. It allows meaning and perhaps even order to emerge from chaos and distress. The priority afforded to learning from harm is reflected in policy.

Since Sir Liam Donaldson, the then Chief Medical Officer, promised to make the NHS an 'organisation with a memory' nearly 20 years ago, the ideal of 'forgiving and remembering' (Bosk 1976, 2000) has dominated.

In a profession that demands calm and decisiveness, it is perhaps not surprising that being seen to 'do something' by learning from harm is so highly valued. Yet the hopes of professionals and patients alike for the potential of learning from harm are often idealistic, seeking guarantees that similar harm cannot recur. That the same doctors who had spoken to me about the inherent uncertainty and inevitable risks of medicine could be emphatic that they could prevent future mistakes reveals a strong faith in the redemptive power of learning. How comforting to believe that those same human beings 'learn' so effectively from error and harm that they are guaranteed to be eliminated in future. Learning from error becomes essential to living with the uncertainty and risk of medicine. No wonder it is wholeheartedly, albeit unrealistically, embraced.

The notion that future harm can be avoided has seduced policy makers, academics, professional organisations and patients alike for decades. How much more attractive the idea must be to those who are struggling to live with medical harm. If medicine itself has been misrepresented as a perfect and mature science, claims of learning from harm may also be contributing to unreasonable expectations on the part of both doctors and patients. The doctors whom I interviewed often described telling patients that learning had occurred from harm. This is a laudable approach, acknowledging implicitly work suggesting that most patients seek an apology, an explanation and assurance that such an event will not happen to anyone else. Yet there is an element of idealism that is at odds with the uncertain and risky nature of medicine. Sharing learning is often cited as an example of meeting patient expectations after error (Manser and Staender 2005). But little is said about the potential for creating greater and unrealistic patient expectations by offering assurances that the error will 'never happen again'. The errors and harms described by my interviewees were all susceptible to recurrence and, elsewhere in our conversations, the doctors themselves acknowledged the ever-present potential for repeating their mistakes.

The implications for forgiveness are considerable. In one sense, attention to systems and learning potentially removes some of the impediments to forgiveness. It is a demonstrable commitment to sharing information and to improving the system and experience of healthcare for all those who provide and receive it. Our collective understanding of human factors, systems errors and medical harm has improved exponentially. The emphasis on sharing knowledge and experience seeks to vitiate the individual shame that can follow for a professional who has made a mistake leading, some suggest, to a culture of understanding rather than blame. However, there may also be some barriers to, or problematic effects on, forgiveness.

If, as I have argued, we overstate the redemptive effectiveness of learning and neglect the complex truths of medical harm and error, we risk a second breach of trust. We are offering a solution that is well intentioned, but ultimately flawed. When the doctor errs again or when the patient reads about another person who has been harmed in the same way, that belief in learning is found to be illusory. Forgiveness is, in many ways, about hope: the possibility of a future that acknowledges loss and damage but is not dominated or determined by its painful legacy. Yet sustainable hope is realistic. It depends on a capacity to face that which is also difficult and that which we would rather deny. It is about finding the possibility of a future while knowing that chance, uncertainty and failure will inevitably be part of our experiences. It is about finding a way to connect again, even with the knowledge of the imperfection that imbues medicine, healthcare and our world at large. That takes an honest appraisal of healthcare and medical harm. It requires us to accept that there is a contested, complex, uncomfortable and uncertain character to medical care that is constant and defining. That acceptance is, it is suggested, more likely to make meaningful forgiveness – of self and others – possible and sustainable.

Forgiveness and medical harm: concluding thoughts

If, as Nancy Berlinger suggests, there are two ways to define forgiveness – as mercy or pardon, or as discharging or waiving an obligation – it does not make the challenge of exploring forgiveness after medical harm any easier. The excerpts from the doctors who participated in my research and the diverse responses of people when I said I was writing this chapter, demonstrate the knotty, individual, nuanced, pluralistic and complex nature of forgiveness in relation to medical harm.

One striking theme in those responses was the assumption by the majority that I would be advocating forgiveness or even claiming it as a moral imperative. Some seemed angry with me for asking about forgiveness, assuming a normative claim rather than a genuinely open question; others appeared defensive and explained at length why forgiveness was not appropriate or possible for them. That assumption and its impact fascinated me: whatever our individual perceptions of, and relationship to, forgiveness, it has a capacity to discomfort. It is that realisation that unlocked, for me, what might be an ethical approach to forgiveness that has seemed, for most of my career, to be a dauntingly difficult subject.

Forgiveness has immense power, both to transform and to unsettle. It is a shifting, unpredictable and complex presence in our lives. It is both an idea and an ideal. Forgiveness may be simultaneously comforting and disturbing, constant and changing, desirable and repellent.

Forgiveness after medical harm can neither be forced nor its timing constrained. It may be possible and beneficial for some, but not for others – doctors and patients alike. Forgiveness follows a breach of trust, inadvertent or otherwise, when harm has occurred in an environment where care was the expectation. As such, honesty is essential. Such honesty will involve facing and accepting that which is difficult and painful about the limits of medicine and those who practise it. It depends on a willingness to attend to how people and medicine are, rather than how we wish they were.

Such emotional labour is demanding and sometimes overwhelming. Any system, policy, procedure or practice that does not acknowledge the complexity, significance and power of forgiveness is doomed.

Perhaps all we can ask is that we have a healthcare environment where people can find the space to explore forgiveness with openness, patience and responsiveness, but without any pressure or expectation of outcome. That would be enough. That would be transformative.

References

Berlinger, N. (2005) *After Harm: Medical Error and the Ethics of Forgiveness*. Baltimore, MA: Johns Hopkins University Press.

Bosk, C. (1976) *Forgive and Remember: Managing Medical Failure*. Chicago, IL: University of Chicago Press.

Bosk, C. (2000) 'Understanding Harm.' *Hastings Center Report* July-August, 44–45.

Buetow, S. (2005) 'Why the need to reduce medical errors is not obvious.' *Journal of Evaluation in Clinical Practice*, 11(1), 53–57.

Covington, C. (2016) *Everyday Evils: A Psychoanalytic View of Evil and Morality*. London: Routledge.

Holloway, R. (2002) *On Forgiveness: How Can We Forgive the Unforgivable?* (Canons). London: Canongate Books.

Kraman, SS. and Hamm, G. (1999) 'Risk Management: Extreme Honesty May Be the Best Policy.' *Ann Intern Med*, 131, 963–967.

Manser, T. and Staender, S. (2005) 'Aftermath of an adverse event: supporting healthcare professionals to meet patient expectations through open disclosure.' *Acta Anaesthesiologica Scandinavica*, 49(6), 728–734.

Paget, M. (1988) *The Unity of Mistakes: A Phenomenological Interpretation of Medical Work*. Philadelphia, PA: Temple University Press.

Seys, D., Wu, A.W., Van Gerven, E., Vleugels, A. *et al.* (2012) 'Health care professionals as second victims after adverse events: a systematic review.' *Evaluation and the Health Professions*, 36(2), 135–162.

Smith, H. (2008) 'Leaps of faith: is forgiveness a useful concept?' *International Journal of Psychoanalysis*, 89, 919–936.

Vincent, C., Young, M. and Phillips, A. (1994) 'Why Do People Sue Doctors? A Study of Patients and Relatives Taking Legal Action.' Lancet, 343, 1609–1613.

Vincent, C., Coulter, A. (2002) Patient Safety: What About the Patient? *Qual Saf Health Care*, 11, 76–80.

Wu, A. (2000) 'Medical error: the second victim.' *British Medical Journal*, 320, 72.

Chapter 8

RESTORATIVE JUSTICE AND FORGIVENESS

Marian Liebmann

When I was director of Mediation UK, I received many phone calls from journalists, often starting with, 'I'm looking to do a piece on your amazing work in the criminal justice system – the idea is to get the victim to meet the offender and forgive him, isn't it?' I would take a deep breath and say, 'Not quite.' This common assumption raises the following questions: why do people often make this assumption? Is there any truth in it? And what is the relationship between forgiveness and restorative justice?

Restorative justice

Before we can reflect on the relationship between forgiveness and restorative justice, it is important to understand what restorative justice is. One definition is:

> Restorative justice works to resolve conflict and repair harm. It encourages those who have caused harm to acknowledge the impact of what they have done and gives them an opportunity to make reparation. It offers those who have suffered harm the opportunity to have their harm or loss acknowledged and amends made. (Restorative Justice Consortium, 2006)

Some practitioners point out that only rarely can victims of crime be really restored to their previous condition. Even if goods are returned or insurance claimed or wounds healed, there are still likely to be emotional scars for the victim. The hope is that, rather than aim to simply restore what has been lost, a dialogue between victim and offender can transform the crime into something different, so that the experience can be a healing one for all concerned. This is sometimes known as transformative justice. This is demonstrated by the principles of restorative justice:

- Victim support and healing are priorities.

- Offenders take responsibility for what they have done.

- There is dialogue to achieve understanding.

- There is an attempt to put right the harm done.

- Offenders look at how to avoid future offending.

- The community helps to reintegrate both victim and offender.

These principles characterise the aims of restorative justice in transforming the harm done and prioritising the healing of the victim.

Howard Zehr (2002) compared and contrasted retributive and restorative justice – retributive justice being concerned mainly with meting out retribution or punishment to the offender, restorative justice mainly with putting things right for everyone, especially the victim. Some of the values of restorative justice identified by Zehr are: dialogue, mutuality, healing, repair, repentance, responsibility, honesty and sincerity. He suggests six key questions to help analyse how restorative an intervention or model is:

1. Does the model address harms, needs and causes?

2. Is it adequately victim orientated?

3. Are offenders encouraged to take responsibility?

4. Are all relevant stakeholders involved?

5. Is there an opportunity for dialogue and participatory decision making?

6. Is the model respectful to all parties?

Zehr's evaluative questions stop short of identifying forgiveness as a measure of how restorative an intervention has been. Likewise, the values do not require reconciliation in order for such a process or model to be successful. Rather, these questions draw out the principles outlined above that restorative justice must be adequately victim orientated, the offenders must take responsibility and there is opportunity for dialogue and participatory decision making. These questions also relate to a wider sphere and the effectiveness of restorative justice is assessed in context beyond that of interpersonal relationships.

Restorative justice includes many processes, such as conflict mediation, victim–offender mediation, restorative conferencing, family group conferencing, sentencing circles and victim–offender groups. It can be used to divert cases from arrest or court procedures, or be undertaken after sentence has been passed. It has a long history in traditional societies and was 'rediscovered' in the 1970s in many countries. For a brief history, see Liebmann (2007). In 2002, the United Nations Commission on Crime Prevention and Criminal Justice passed a resolution recommending restorative justice programmes; this gave encouragement to countries around the world to take up restorative justice (United Nations Commission on Crime Prevention and Criminal Justice 2002), and now most countries are involved, to a greater or lesser extent.

In many places the police have become firm advocates, as they see a way of serving victims of crime and rescuing young offenders from a life of crime. People with a law background see that legal processes often make matters worse and welcome the opportunities in restorative justice to sort things out on a human level. Even people with 'tough' views on crime see that restorative justice involves offenders taking responsibility for their crimes and doing something to put things right, something that does not often happen in the retributive system. They see this as 'more just' than offenders taking punishment without any thought for the victim.

Restorative justice and forgiveness

From these principles and values, it may be possible to identify some areas in which forgiveness can be part of restorative justice.

Many people understand forgiveness in terms of overcoming and restoring a broken relationship after a hurtful event. The motivation behind forgiving may be to transform both the person who is forgiving so that they might be released from their anger and hurt, and to provide a break from the cycle of vengeance or retribution, which might enable the offender to be transformed too.

One reason why people may make the assumption that the aim of restorative justice is forgiveness can be traced to its history. Many of the first people to become involved in this field did so for religious reasons (for example, Mennonites, Quakers and others), because the concepts of reconciliation, redemption and forgiveness found a practical expression. Indeed, it was a Mennonite probation officer who instigated the first recorded victim–offender mediation in recent times in the west. In May 1974 Mark Yantzi took two young men to apologise to 22 victims in Kitchener, Ontario, whose houses they had vandalised (Zehr 1990).

Desmond Tutu, Archbishop of Capetown, was one of the architects of the South African Truth and Reconciliation Commission. His well-known book *No Future without Forgiveness* (1999) has many examples of people who were able to forgive the perpetrators, despite grave injuries. Here is one story:

> A car bomb planted in the centre of Pretoria by the ANC near the headquarters of the South African Air Force (SAAF) resulted in 21 deaths and 219 injured people. The perpetrators applied for amnesty, and one of the injured people, Neville Clarence, who had worked for the SAAF and had been blinded by the bomb blast, attended the hearing. The main perpetrator, Aboobaker Ismail, apologised for causing the civilian casualties. Neville Clarence did not oppose the amnesty, but went up to Mr Ismail and shook his hand. He told him he forgave him even though he had lost his sight, and said he wanted them to join forces to work for the common good of all. This picture was shown on TV and in the newspapers as an example of what the TRC was all about. (Tutu 1999, p.120)

However, it does not follow that forgiveness is necessarily a religious concept, nor that a religious motivation to become involved in restorative justice comes from a religious obligation or imperative to forgive. Although there are authors who argue that forgiveness is a foundational concept of restorative justice (Kohen 2009), most authors and practitioners believe that forgiveness is a possible outcome, not an aim:

> Forgiveness or reconciliation is not a primary principle or focus of restorative justice. It is true that restorative justice does provide a context where either might happen. Indeed, some degree of forgiveness or even reconciliation does occur much more frequently than in an adversarial setting of the criminal justice system. However, this is a choice that is entirely up to the participants. There should be no pressure to choose to forgive or to seek reconciliation. (Zehr 2002, p.8)

Joanna Shapland's article 'Forgiveness and restorative justice: is it necessary? Is it helpful?' (2016) found that few victims mentioned forgiveness as an outcome of their experience of restorative justice (for serious offences). She postulated that, while some could forgive the offenders, in the sense of wishing them well for the future, they could not forgive the offence as it was too great.

Andrew Rigby, founding director of the Centre for the Study of Forgiveness and Reconciliation (Coventry University), writes that the conditions that facilitate interpersonal forgiveness are:

- Acknowledgement/confession/apology

- Expressions of repentance and the promise not to repeat the wrong

- Offers to make amends/undertake reparation.

(Rigby 2006)

These conditions are part of restorative processes, so that they can pave the way and make forgiveness more likely, although they can never prescribe it. Rigby's conditions that facilitate interpersonal forgiveness share a similarity with Zehr's values of restorative justice: dialogue, mutuality, healing, repair, repentance, responsibility, honesty and sincerity. So it is not surprising that restorative approaches to justice are often linked to examples of forgiveness.

Declan Roche writes (2003, p.120):

> It is a mistake for restorative justice practitioners to become preoccupied with trying to achieve reparation or forgiveness or reconciliation, as these things should not – and cannot – be forced by convenors... Convenors should focus on the more modest objective of ensuring that participants are able to participate effectively... When a convenor ensures a victim is able to speak and be heard, that victim will be more inclined to forgive than one pressured to do so.

For participants in restorative approaches to justice, forgiveness can mean different things and play different roles in the process. In Rwanda, the *Gacaca* process (a community process involving victims, perpetrators and the whole community) tried to provide a way for victims and perpetrators to come to terms with the effects of the genocide. This was particularly important because perpetrators often returned to their communities, where the victims also still lived. However, the victims did not all feel the same – here are two contrasting examples:

- 'How can I forgive you when you can return to your land and family and live your life as before, whereas I have lost my land and all my family – my husband and my four children? I have nothing.'

- 'How can I not forgive you when we are both sinners in the sight of God?'

The first woman was finally able to forgive when she and the perpetrator became part of a project in which perpetrators helped to build houses for victims, and she was able to move into a new house that he had helped to build (Hinson 2009; Singh 2012). Here the *Gacaca* process was an essential step in the first woman's journey to forgiveness, through dialogue and reparation; we might say that the *Gacaca* process provided the conditions that facilitated forgiveness. In the second instance, a religious attitude about the condition of the victim and the offender as sinners may have facilitated the *Gacaca* process itself.

Criminal justice stories: victims

Murder: immediate forgiveness

For Gee Walker, whose son was murdered in a racially motivated attack, her forgiveness was not at odds with the traditional justice system, but was about her family living by what they believed.

> Outside the court, Mrs Walker, with her daughter Dominique, who had gone to school with Taylor, said: 'Do I forgive them? At the point of death Jesus said, "I forgive them because they don't know what they do".
>
> 'I've got to forgive them. I still forgive them. My family and I still stand by what we believe: forgiveness.' She said that she had never been in doubt about the verdict.
>
> 'It's been real hard going, but I feel justice has been done. I'm sure they will get the maximum sentence.' (Bunyan 2005)

Several years later murderers, Taylor and Barton, requested a face-to-face meeting as part of a restorative justice programme. Gee was keen to take part: 'I saw these boys from a very young age and I'd like to know, why? I'd like to get inside their minds as killers, for them to tell me what happened, and why they did it. What went wrong in their lives? When did they make that transition from innocence to evil? I hope they would answer me that.' However, Dominique was against the idea: 'Taylor is only asking for this as it will look good for him. I'm not willing to play his game. Meeting us is something to do for a couple of hours to escape prison lockdown and the monotony. I don't want to hear anything either of them have to say.' (Traynor 2015)

Murder: forgiveness 'not on the table'

For others, forgiveness is not a simple matter. For many people, even after mediation, forgiveness is simply 'not on the table'. Suzanne requested a meeting with her stepfather, who had stabbed and killed her mother during an argument. She said afterwards:

> I've put that chapter to rest… I've done everything I can do, no need to see him again… I don't fear him, I don't see him as a demon any more…but forgiveness was not on the table.

It doesn't follow that, because forgiveness was not on the table for Suzanne, the meeting with her stepfather was not a success. Her words indicate that it provided some closure for her; the meeting addressed some of Suzanne's needs.

Murder: journey towards forgiveness

Lesley Moreland, whose daughter was stabbed to death with nearly 100 injuries, felt she needed to meet the perpetrator (Andrew) to understand what had happened, before she could begin to come to terms with it. It took four years to arrange the meeting, in a prison. She was relieved that Andrew had been able to talk and give an account that tallied with the information she already had.

She wrote about forgiveness at several different stages of her journey. At the time of the meeting, she was clear that, although she found the meeting beneficial, and Andrew had said that he was sorry, she had not been able to forgive him. She felt that it wasn't her place, that only her daughter could do so – so that any forgiveness from Lesley would be a betrayal of her daughter. She was upset by her inability to forgive, as there seemed to be a 'religious imperative' to do so. But she didn't bear Andrew any ill will, and the meeting had enabled her to see him as a person rather than 'just a murderer' (Moreland 2001).

Some years later she saw Archbishop Desmond Tutu interviewed in a television programme. This gave her a new way of looking at forgiveness, and she wrote to Andrew, as she knew he would soon be released:

Dear Andrew Steel

You will probably be surprised to hear from me. I have been thinking of you particularly this year when, if all had gone well, you would have completed your sentence. The Victims Contact Officer has told us that you will be applying again to the Parole Board in December.

It has taken me a long time to think about whether or not to contact you again. I recently saw a programme when Archbishop Desmond Tutu was interviewed. He said, 'Forgiveness is when you have been hurt, and you have the right to pay back, but you don't use that right and you gain the possibility of that person making a new beginning.' I can agree with that statement and so am writing to you to offer you my forgiveness for taking Ruth's life.

I hope your new application goes well for you and that you are able to work towards your release and have a fulfilling life when you are released.

Yours sincerely

Lesley Moreland

(Moreland 2006)

I interviewed Lesley Moreland again in 2015. She had not had any further contact with Andrew, but had kept in touch with the victim liaison officer, so she knew that Andrew had been released. She still did not bear him any ill will, and she hoped he was getting the help he needed to lead a non-violent and constructive life. She reflected that forgiveness was not something people should be expected to do, but that they should have the opportunity to stand back and process their feelings, which may be quite changeable over time (Moreland 2015).

Burglary: limited forgiveness

While restorative processes should not include the expectation of forgiveness or reconciliation, there are cases where a meeting between victim and offender plays a central role in the possibility of forgiveness. Amanda and David's house was burgled during the day and turned over, with things pulled out of cupboards and many things taken, including jewellery (a wedding ring and a favourite necklace). Their car was also stolen (later recovered) and antique boxes were damaged. Most annoying to Amanda was the theft of her new computer that resulted in the loss of a book chapter and (ironically) an article about a centre that supported people with drug and alcohol addictions. The police did not have evidence to convict the main culprit, but arrested Joanna, his accomplice. Facilitators from the pre-court pilot project asked Amanda and

David if they were interested in meeting the offender, and they agreed – they wanted to convey the impact of the burglary on them and also prevent it happening to anyone else. Joanna agreed to the meeting, which took place in prison and lasted three hours.

Amanda and David told how they had been affected and Joanna cried when she heard, especially when she heard the topic of the lost articles, as she had a drugs problem herself. Amanda and David felt a lot of sympathy for her, especially when they heard that she had been the victim of domestic violence. They encouraged her to make the most of herself and find a new life. The final agreement reflected this. The meeting finished with hugs, and Joanna and Amanda exchanged letters for some time after their meeting.

Amanda and David felt they could forgive Joanna as the meeting had helped them see her as a vulnerable person who had had a difficult life. They felt this understanding helped them towards forgiving her. It was more difficult to forgive the main burglar, as there was no such understanding available – and they were also angry with him for mistreating Joanna. The opportunity for sincere and honest dialogue through the meeting enabled a transformation in the relationship and attitude towards Joanna, which was not possible towards the main culprit.

Vandalism of church: forgiveness as 'second chance'

The success of a restorative process in a community is dependent on the presence, honesty and sincerity of the participants. Two young men, Mark and Tony, aged 18 and 19, caused thousands of pounds of damage to a church on a deprived housing estate. They agreed to meet the churchwarden and her husband (a licensed lay minister), Stephanie and Chris. There had been two break-ins within five days. The church had been turned upside down, with pews thrown around, doors kicked in, safes attacked and other furniture smashed on the floor. Groups using the church, including the Brownies, had to cancel their meetings. Stephanie had the task of organising the massive clearing-up process. The hardest part for her was the damage to the community using the church.

Both young men had agreed to come to the meeting, but only Mark turned up (with his mother for support), which was disappointing for Stephanie and Chris, although they felt that maybe Mark was able to be more forthcoming on his own. Tony said he would meet the victims after the court case instead, but did not keep his word. The meeting took place in a community venue in another area of the city to be on neutral ground. Mark was asked to speak first, and was clearly very nervous; his mother became tearful and upset, and needed some 'time out'. Stephanie and Chris told how devastated they had been, and how hurt the community had been. But they did not want the young men to go to prison, rather they wanted them to put something back into the community through community service.

Mark seemed to them to be genuinely sorry, and this enabled them to forgive him. For Stephanie, this was linked to giving people a second chance and having an equal relationship. For Chris, this meant putting aside hurt and resentment to look at the offender as an individual with their own needs. He reflected that forgiveness was often connected with perceiving the offender as contrite, but this was not always the case, citing Colin and Wendy Parry, who set up the Tim Parry Johnathan Ball Peace Centre in Warrington in 1993 after an IRA bomb had killed their son Tim and another child Johnathan. The bombers were never caught, and Chris remembered that Colin and Wendy forgave the IRA bombers without even knowing who they were. They both found it much harder to forgive Tony, as he had not turned up and participated in their meeting, and had made no effort to make amends – his behaviour at court also suggested to them that he was not sorry.

Arson: forgiveness withdrawn

Mark and Tony also set fire to and totally destroyed Craig's car. He relied on his car for work. He was devastated and although he was able to claim on his car insurance, he was left with a debt of three to four thousand pounds when he bought another car – which he could ill afford, with three young children. He had also lost the contents of the car and several days' work.

Craig also attended the restorative meeting described above, together with his partner. He was very anxious before the meeting, and this increased when he recognised Mark's mother – they were all from the same community. As the meeting progressed, Craig felt sorry for Mark, and believed his promises to change, so was prepared to forgive him. But his views altered when he saw Mark in the locality behaving as before, drinking and smoking cannabis, and when the case went to court, he recounted seeing Tony 'smirking'. He felt the two young men had 'got away with it' and had no intention to reform. It was made harder by the fact that their families and his drank in the same local pub. The saga was compounded by the fact that the court had paid no attention to his needs – there was no compensation order towards his severe financial losses. He said, 'While the innocent struggle, the guilty get off with it all.' Clearly Craig could not forgive Mark and Tony for their actions in this case.

Criminal justice stories: offenders

For some offenders, meetings with victims' families are transformative. Kevin, a lifer who murdered a woman in a house where he was working as a plasterer, spent 14 years in prison. At one point his probation officer spoke to the victim's husband, who said he had no objection to Kevin being released, if he sorted himself out. Kevin was overwhelmed by this – he had expected to be hunted down and shot as soon as he was released from prison. He said:

> It felt like seeing God. How can one man have so much compassion when I've ruined his life? It changed my life. It spurred me on to do the work of sorting myself out (which was very hard), in memory of my victim. I had previously thought I was such scum that I should just rot in hell and not bother to try. In psychodrama sessions, I worked on apologising to him, but it seemed wrong because it was so insignificant. After a lot of work, I saw that in the end the only way forward was to forgive myself and try to live a better life.

Although forgiveness is not mentioned by the victim's husband, this interaction with the offender played a key role in the offender's rehabilitation.

In 2001 Vi and Ray Donovan's son Christopher was kicked to death by three teenage boys (aged 15, 16 and 19) for no reason. They were convicted of murder and given life sentences with a minimum of nine to ten years to serve. Vi and Ray found it very hard to forgive them, despite their Christian faith. But in 2011, 2012 and 2013 they met the three young men after they had been released from the custodial part of their sentence. The meetings were facilitated by a mediation service, and were very intense occasions.

Vi and Ray wrote:

> When we met all three offenders and told them what it was like for us and the things we went through and are still going through and told them about the ripple effect and how it affected everyone in our family to the community, it made them realise the amount of people that were affected by their actions. Then to hear them say sorry made us both feel like a ton of coal was taken off our back. We felt free for the first time because we got all we ever wanted. We got answers to our questions and the truth. Now we hope we can leave those questions in the past and move on into the future.

For Vi and Ray, the restorative approach was valuable because the victims were given a voice and the process was victim centred: 'For the first time, you are not a sheet of A4 paper in a court room; and for the first time, they see you as a human being.'

One of the offenders wrote:

> Being part of the restorative justice process and meeting Ray and Vi Donovan was more powerful than any victim-awareness course and something that I will remember and no doubt influence the rest of my life. It also gave me the opportunity to apologise to them for their loss and give some background to my own experience and what I have done since. When Ray and Vi told me they forgave me it meant everything. It meant that they understood that what happened to Christopher was an incident that never should have occurred. Hearing them give me permission to have the best life

that I can made me feel human again. (Donovan and Donovan 2014)

In this case, for the offender it was more than just being forgiven that made a difference, it was hearing the voice of the victim in the face-to-face meeting. Forgiveness that is intrapersonal (just within the victim) is unable to be transformative in the way that this meeting was for the offender. The offender went on to write 'Meeting Ray and Vi has helped me to accept that I owe it to myself too. When I committed this offence, I was lost with no direction or purpose. That is no longer the case.'

Conclusion

It can be seen that forgiveness means different things to different people. For some it is a religious decision, whoever the perpetrators are. For others, it is related to the ways in which those who have harmed them face up to their responsibility to put things right if possible, and especially not to continue behaviour likely to lead to others being harmed.

Restorative justice is more about understanding and dialogue, having questions answered, victims being able to put things behind them, and offenders having the opportunity to learn about the harm they have caused, to apologise and try to put things right. For some people this may lead to forgiveness, for others it is simply 'not on the table'. For some people it is extremely important, for others of no great matter.

There is a danger in expecting people to forgive, especially if it comes from a 'religious imperative', as it can lead to victims feeling guilty if they cannot forgive. Different religions may have different views and moral codes about forgiveness. In addition, different cultures may be more or less inclined towards forgiving people who have done wrong and harmed others.

Although restorative justice does not have forgiveness as its aim, and it is wrong to assume that it is about forgiveness, nevertheless it can provide processes which pave the way for forgiveness to take place, and this can be important for many victims and offenders.

Note

Some parts of this chapter have been based on previously published work (*Restorative Justice: How It Works* by Marian Liebmann (2007)) with the publisher's permission.

References

Bunyan, N. (2005) 'I forgive you, mother tells racist thugs who killed son.' *Daily Telegraph*, www.telegraph.co.uk/news/uknews/1504443/I-forgive-you-mother-tellsracist-thugs-who-killed-son.html, accessed 29/12/2017.

Donovan, R. and Donovan, V. (2014) *Understanding Restorative Justice*. Sutton: Chris Donovan Trust.

Hinson, L.W. (2009) *As We Forgive*. DVD, available at: www.asweforgivemovie.com.

Kohen, A. 'The personal and the political: forgiveness and reconciliation in restorative justice.' (2009) *Critical Review of International Social and Political Philosophy*, 12:3. Faculty Publications, Political Science Paper 34. Available at: http://digitalcommons.unl.edu/poliscifacpub/34.

Liebmann, M. (2007) *Restorative Justice: How It Works*. London: Jessica Kingsley Publishers.

Moreland, L. (2001) *An Ordinary Murder*. London: Aurum Press.

Moreland, L. (2006) Personal communication.

Moreland, L. (2015) Personal communication.

Restorative Justice. (2006) Leaflet. London: RJC.

Rigby, A. (2006) Email 23.3.06, checked 11.8.15.

Roche, D. (2003) *Accountability in Restorative Justice*. Oxford: Oxford University Press.

Shapland, J. (2016) 'Forgiveness and restorative justice: is it necessary? Is it helpful?' *Oxford Journal of Law and Religion*, 0, 1–19.

Singh, L. (2012) *Beyond Right and Wrong: Stories of Justice and Forgiveness*. New York: Article19 Films. Available at: www.beyondrightandwrongthemovie.org.

Traynor, L. (2015) 'Murdered Anthony Walker's mum condemns early release bid of Premier League star's killer brother.' *Daily Mirror*, www.mirror.co.uk/news/uk-news/murdered-anthony-walkers-mum-condemns-6099386, accessed 29/12/2017.

Tutu, D. (1999) *No Future without Forgiveness*. London: Rider.

United Nations Commission on Crime Prevention and Criminal Justice (2002) *Basic principles on the use of restorative justice programmes in criminal matters*. Vienna: United Nations. Available at: www.unodc.org/pdf/crime/commissions/11comm/5e.pdf.

Zehr, H. (1990) *Changing Lenses*. Scottsdale PA and Waterloo, Ontario: Herald Press.

Zehr, H. (2002) *The Little Book of Restorative Justice*. Intercourse, PA: Good Books.

Chapter 9

UNDERSTANDING REVENGE
An Invitation to Let Go

Robin Shohet

Revenge carries with it the illusion that one's own suffering can be alleviated and one's own losses recovered if the enemy is made to suffer.

Tomas Bohm and Suzanne Kaplan, Revenge

Tout comprendre c'est tout pardonner (to understand all is to forgive all)

Introduction: the importance of understanding revenge

In this chapter I will outline what I consider the attractions of revenge and what advantages it seems to confer. By understanding the pull towards it, we may understand ourselves and others better, and see why although true forgiveness is an act of release, we don't easily manage to free ourselves.

Nearly 20 years ago a friend asked me to write a book with him on revenge. We collected stories from Northern Ireland, Israel/ Palestine involving couples who divorced acrimoniously, or family feuds. I drew on my own history and my inability to let go. While not overtly vengeful, I was certainly full of vengeful thoughts. I ran workshops on revenge, showing how prevalent it was. There was much laughter as we recognised we were all 'at it' in gross or subtle ways. Gossiping, put downs, 'forgetting', being late, not doing the dishes, sulking, withholding, refusing to acknowledge someone, envy, infidelity, being a failure, being a success even. None of these in themselves is necessarily vengeful, but all could be seen through the eyes of revenge in certain contexts.

The book was never written because in the end we decided to run a conference on forgiveness. Through exploring revenge, we came to see it as a dead end. In the Chinese saying, 'He who plots revenge should dig two graves' there is a strong indication of how it rebounds on the avenger. We discovered that revenge was a way of attempting to restore power, which did not ultimately work. Being obsessed with revenge keeps people tied to both the wound and the person who has done the wounding.

This dead end was predicted by a computer simulation that we came across in our research. It showed that the biggest threat to human survival did not come from global warming, population explosion or dwindling resources, but from the inability to forgive, to let go. Instead, the desire to revenge would lead to an escalation of conflict that would, on a global level, be uncontainable as increasingly powerful weapons became available.

Studying revenge was on many levels a rewarding process. On a personal level, I accessed parts of myself that were not fully conscious. Working on a therapeutic level with individuals, couples and families, I saw how it played itself out, and I could help people move beyond it. And I understood more about what appeared to be senseless events on the world stage.

There are studies which show that forgiveness benefits health. But advocates of forgiveness can sometimes underestimate the pull of revenge. It can give short-term benefits, such as regaining power, affirming a sense of justice, improving one's self worth ('I didn't lie down and take it'). It stops us feeling such uncomfortable emotions as grief, helplessness and shame. To go beyond revenge we have to be willing to feel the pain, and none of us does this readily. Like any avoidance of pain using drugs or alcohol, the wish to avenge can become an addiction, an obsession which ties the person both to the wound and the person who wounded them. The focus on getting even is a defence against feeling pain. Below are some of the pulls I have identified, which are often not fully conscious.

Building an identity: social pressure

One of the biggest pulls, I think, is that revenge can give a sense of identity. In the *Count of Monte Cristo*, Dante says, 'Don't take away my hatred. It is all I have.' In my therapeutic work, I have seen that the forming of an identity around revenge is one of the most powerful reasons for holding on to it.

Fighting for a cause can give life purpose, involve a sense of camaraderie and belonging, and provide an opportunity to claim the moral high ground fighting against the oppressors. There will be social pressures to do this – you could be seen as opting out of the cause if you don't take up arms.

When my colleague and I were studying revenge, he went to Israel/Palestine and interviewed a Palestinian family. For many years on the mantelpiece was a key of the house they had been evicted from, a symbol that demanded revenge as the sons joined the first Intifada. One day, the mother took it down and threw it away. She said, 'If keeping that key means my sons are killed or imprisoned, then I don't want it anymore.' The family and the other sons were released from the pressure to avenge the loss of their family home. This stopped the revenge being passed down to the next generation – a common reason for revenge where people feel compelled to avenge their ancestors.

To let go of revenge can result in isolation from one's family or community. There are many instances where family members who have forgiven the killers of a relative have been shunned, seen as betrayers by their family. In this way, letting go of revenge can cut us off from people who have been important to us, so the incentive to avenge is socially reinforced.

In contrast to this, at the conference on forgiveness that I helped to organise we played a video of an organisation in Sierra Leone called Fambul Tok (which means family talk). Sierra Leone had come out of an 11-year brutal civil war and people who had fought on opposite sides came back to their native villages, perhaps having killed or raped members of the other side's families. How were they to live together? Fambul Tok helped to create dialogue through ritual round a village fire where each side could listen to the other supported by the whole village. Just as there had been social pressure to fight and avenge, now there was pressure to forgive because the village needed cooperation to survive.

Victim consciousness

As well as building an identity around our wounds – and closely connected to this – there are the advantages of being a victim. A friend of mine was involved in a minor accident when someone ran into the back of his car. It was reported to the insurance company but there was no injury to him. For a whole month he was rung up by solicitors asking him if he would like to claim for his whiplash. In other words, it now pays handsomely to present yourself as a victim, and we can even see a hierarchy of victimhood. More victims, more rewards.

The framing of seeing ourselves as victims is beautifully described in Arthur Miller's play *Broken Glass* (written in 1994). The psychiatrist says:

> I'll tell you a secret. I have all kinds coming into my office and there's not one of them who one way or another is not persecuted. Yes, *everyone's* persecuted. The poor by the rich, the rich by the poor, the black by the white, the white by the black, the men by the women, the women by the men, the Catholics by the Protestants, the Protestants by the Catholics and of course all of them by the Jews. Everyone's persecuted...and what's amazing is you can't find *anyone* who is persecuting anyone.

The identification with the victim is very strong, and my experience is that behind all victim consciousness is a wish to punish. This is very clear when we look at stories of people who have transcended this need to avenge. In Marina Cantacuzino's book, *The Forgiveness Project* (2015), we see those who have forgiven support leniency for their attackers, recognising that their acts were unacceptable but still willing to recognise their humanity. What you see in all accounts of forgiveness is that the forgivers no longer see themselves as victims and lose the desire to punish.

The pull to victim consciousness is excellently described in Jill Hall's book the *Reluctant Adult* (1993). She maintains that victims cannot forgive because they have defined themselves in a way that stops them moving on. She says the pull to victim consciousness is so strong because it feeds off the wounded child within.

The need to be right

The 13th-century poet and Islamic scholar Rumi wrote, 'Out beyond right and wrong is a field. I'll meet you there'. I have found the need to be right to be a very powerful dynamic in human interaction. If we examine revenge, it comes from a feeling of having been wronged. If there is no feeling of being wronged, there will be no pull to revenge. People who have eschewed revenge very often have come to a place of deep acceptance of what is. They can condemn what has happened, but accept that the only thing that can now change is their attitude towards it. And the need to be in the right and hold on to the wound, in the short term gives a sense of self righteousness, but in the long term robs us of the deep peace that can come with acceptance.

That sense of I am right, or my cause is right, can be used to commit all sorts of acts. And from my own experience and working with clients, I have found underneath this need to be right is a very deep feeling of being in the wrong, or not good enough. And the pull to be in the right offers a moment (or some cases a lifetime) of relief from all that self-talk that everyone has where we beat ourselves up mercilessly.

> We make everything that's uncertain, certain. Religion has gone from a belief in faith and mystery to certainty. I'm right. You are wrong. The most dangerous thing in life is to believe truth has one face. (Brene Brown quoted in Cantacuzino 2015, p.16)

Justification: describing it as justice

Because of the need to feel right, we may justify wishes to avenge as being justice. In this way, we can avoid guilty feelings on a personal and societal level as we treat others inhumanely because they 'deserve it'. Later, I will mention restorative justice, which seems very effective, but our penal system, while advocating justice, might be a form of institutional revenge. Those who have threatened us deserve punishment. Rehabilitation or restorative justice are seen as soft, perhaps because they do not cater to our vengeful feelings. As Bohm and Kaplan (2011, p.17) say, 'Revenge can fuse with the system's way of functioning and thus conceal itself from clear view.'

In other words, certain structures in society can legitimise behaviour so we do not see it for what it is. At its most extreme, killing Jews, gypsies and homosexuals was an act of patriotism. And here I am raising the possibility that punishment could be institutionalised revenge, but not recognised as such.

As mentioned in the previous section, there seems to be a need to transform the desire for revenge into something righteous. Our literature and films are full of stories of the underdog or the victim avenging and we rejoice as the baddies are brought to apparent justice. This idea of goodies and baddies is a huge over-simplification, which we will return to later. It certainly is not there in those who have chosen to forgive who see the complexity in what has happened and can appreciate many perspectives. This lessens their desire for punishment and the demands of society for so-called justice.

Of course, there is a legitimate need for public acknowledgement of the crime and some sense of accountability for it. If a perpetrator were publicly to take full responsibility for their actions, that would change the dynamic. But that rarely happens and so the courts provide a place where 'what happened' can be judged. The problem is that punishment as a concept doesn't work and keeps the cycle going.

Others carrying our shadow

The denial that we are all capable of committing atrocities means that we are very likely to judge those who have done so very severely, forgetting their humanity. They carry our inhumanity so we can seem fully justified in projecting our self-hatred on to them, and punishing them. In the film *Fambul Tok* (2011), we saw that those who had killed neighbours or relatives were forced to do so by the rebels or be killed themselves. The context defined their actions. Rarely were they simply bad people.

Solzhenitsyn expresses this very well:

> If only there were evil people somewhere insidiously committing evil deeds and it were necessary only to separate them from the rest of us and destroy them. But the line dividing good and evil cuts through the heart of every human being. And who is willing to destroy a piece of his own heart. (p.75)

The wish to avenge is perfectly understandable, but if we inquire within we realise how much of ourselves the other is carrying. There is a tribe in Africa (quoted in Ben-Shahar 2010) where when there has been an individual offense, the whole community takes responsibility for it. They all get together and see the individual as their responsibility and rather than blaming and punishing they see that they have collectively failed this person in some way. Imagine a society where the crime rate went up and politicians asked themselves what they had done wrong and asked to meet with the offenders! And not just the party in power, but all of us, as we acknowledge and take responsibility for our interconnectedness.

Locking the situation and the other and therefore ourselves in place

As the sixth-century Greek philosopher Heraclitus said, 'No man can step into the same river twice, for it is not the same river and he is not the same man.'

Revenge keeps us locked into the past, and seeing the other through the lens of the past. But it is possible they may have moved on – and whether they have or not, we are locking ourselves into the past. My stepson realised this. He came back home to find his room trashed by a so-called friend who was looking for money for drugs. He was consumed with rage until he had a flash of insight that liberated him from holding on. He realised that the other person would have no awareness of this and that the only person he was harming was himself. He understood the idea that revenge was like taking poison and expecting the other person to die.

But the other party could have moved on. And I am very interested in social structures that offer the opportunity for both parties to move on or to see the bigger contexts, like the organisation Fambul Tok. Here perhaps our nearest equivalent is the restorative justice system where perpetrator and offender meet, often with transformations for both parties. This structure allows the humanity of the perpetrator to come through whereas previously they were seen as inhuman. This requires great courage from both parties, as in all likelihood both will feel very vulnerable, and I believe revenge is an avoidance of this vulnerability. I will explore this further in the next section. As a rule in the West, we do not have systems that support vulnerability. It is usually seen as a weakness to be vulnerable. 'Never admit you are wrong or that you have made a mistake' is quite a strong cultural injunction.

There is a small example of the power of my colleague's vulnerability, which helped to define my life's work. As I mentioned at the beginning, the work I have done on forgiveness stemmed from not writing a book on revenge. The full story is that my friend suggested a book on revenge to which I readily agreed, but I found he was not writing anything. I got very angry and would not speak to him. He tried to speak to me on several occasions, but I held on to my self-righteous position. Finally, on about the third or fourth time, I relented and went round to his house. He said, 'I am not the person who messed you around. I have changed.' I saw that was true and realised in an instant that to have held on to my anger would be to be angry with someone who did not exist.

In other words, are we willing to see the other as changed as I did with my co-writer? And as a society do we set up structures like Fambul Tok that enable us to see the bigger picture? Restorative justice, which brings victim and offender together, enables both to be changed, but despite its success, there is far less energy put into this than into the penal system. The clamour for revenge is too strong.

Inability to feel vulnerable: shame and loss of identity

Connected to the question of identity is shame. If you step on my toe, it might hurt but it is not such a big issue unless I feel my manhood threatened and then it becomes a very big deal. In gang culture, a gang member who might have knifed another will give as his reason that the other showed him no respect. And characteristically, in shame we feel we have lost our identity – we wish the earth would swallow us. It is one of the most unpleasant emotions to experience and most of us would do anything to avoid it. Justified rage is a good cover, a desperate way to get respect, which can be normalised when families, tribes or nations feel their collective identity has been destroyed and the shame is too much to bear. The Treaty of Versailles after the First World War, where Germany was forced to pay huge reparations, is perhaps the most striking example of a shamed nation extracting its revenge. This demonstrates that in any negotiations it is important that neither party feels shamed.

In the course of my studies on revenge, I came across a book called *Bloody Revenge* (Scheff 1994). It summarises hours and hours of videotape of couples in therapy. The authors trace all the arguments the couple have in the sessions to a shaming episode that happened just before the row broke out that neither party was conscious of. So the often-vicious rows were triggered by a shaming episode – a look of disgust or contempt that may have only lasted a split second. The book links the same emotional process of shaming in families to nations feeling shamed and feeling justified in going to war.

On this theme of shame and loss of identity, two examples from Shakespeare have meant a lot to me: Shylock from the Merchant of Venice, and King Lear. Shylock's famous speech in which he justifies his subsequent actions to take Antiono's pound of flesh comes straight after his daughter has eloped with a non-Jew taking all his jewels and he is feeling humiliated because everyone knows. King Lear promises revenge on his daughters after they reject him and he has lost everything. His whole identity has been stripped. Both have cause to grieve at the loss of their daughters and their social status and feel humiliated and therefore resort to fantasies of revenge.

Marina Cantacuzino (2015, p.7) quotes the father of a girl who was killed by a suicide bomber: "'The suicide bomber was a victim, just like my daughter, grown crazy out of anger and shame." He did not go for revenge because he faced his pain and this led to compassion.'

Revenge to avoid feeling self-hatred

Some time ago I went to a therapist to complain about what I saw as my wife's attacks on me. I knew intellectually that in my mind I was attacking her for what I saw as her attacks, but still felt wounded. The therapist listened patiently as I built my case and just calmly said, 'It has nothing to do with her, it is your own self-hatred.' I knew she was right. How we judge and talk about others is often a reflection of how we treat ourselves. When the internal critic is too painful to bear, we project it's wrath outward and find scapegoats who provide targets for our intolerance.

I do not know why humans have such self-hatred. It is often disguised, but if you ask people to share their inner voices, they are full of judgement towards the self. You fool, you're not good enough, you're lazy, careless. The list could go on and on. It is a relief to make another bad or wrong. We get respite from that self-attack, but in fact we increase it because as a rule we do not like ourselves when we are attacking another.

Revenge to avoid vulnerability: avoiding feelings of loss and grief

The speech by King Lear mentioned above ends with 'You think I'll weep. I'll not weep. This heart shall break into a hundred thousand flaws or ere I'll weep. Oh fool, I shall go mad.' He is using revenge fantasies to protect himself from feeling his grief and indeed to keep madness at bay. Inability to acknowledge and feel grief is a very important reason for holding on to revenge. In our society we do not have rituals around grief, with the result that we have unresolved grief in our individual and collective psyches: 'Resistance towards mourning can be masked in several ways. People often try to conceal their resistance by turning it into acts of revenge. (Bohm and Kaplan 2011, p.30)

Our society has fallen in love with change and newness, with the denial of the loss of the old. In one organisation where I was a consultant, there had been a merger and both sides felt enormous loss. There was no obvious revenge, but people withdrew their goodwill. As soon as loss was acknowledged, there were tears, deep sharing, and decisions to move on and recommit. It was similar in the week-long conference on forgiveness I organised in 2013. In the middle of the week, we had a long grief ritual on the basis that forgiveness cannot happen easily when there is unresolved grief. For many this was the highlight of the week and enabled them to let go.

Connected to grief is regret, which I see as a sort of revenge on oneself. In regret, we are mourning what could have been but doing it in a way that endlessly recycles the pain. We are attacking ourselves for what we could have done, or didn't do, as opposed to attacking others for what they did or did not do. Just as revenge is a pre-occupation with the past that reflects an inability to move on, so is regret.

A response to shock and trauma

I think many of the conflicts that get re-enacted in families and the world stage are motivated by trauma that has not been worked through. The connection between post-traumatic stress disorder and revenge is one that merits further research.

Betrayal and self-betrayal

In a classic paper on betrayal, James Hillman (1975) looks at revenge as a way of dealing with a feeling of having been betrayed. In fact, without betrayal there would be no revenge. What makes the paper a classic is that he asks us to acknowledge that we are betrayers as well as ones who have been betrayed, and that betrayal is part of the human condition. How we respond to it determines whether we move on or stay stuck. In the paper he is inviting us to look at betrayal in order not to stay stuck in it, and this is what I am intending to do with revenge.

In this section, I have mentioned self-betrayal and I think this happens more frequently than we care to acknowledge. So often we have the information but have chosen to ignore it, so when this charming man turns out to be a confidence trickster we feel betrayed, and justified in our wish to avenge. Our capacity for denial or self-deception is huge, as outlined in the book *Wilful*

Blindness (Heffernan 2011). This self-deception can apply to groups as well as to individuals, as we see in cults. From the outside, the evidence that the leader was a fraud was obvious. How much in our individual and collective feelings of betrayal and subsequent wish to avenge could be avoided if we are willing not to betray ourselves and see the situation for what it is? This means seeing ourselves for what *we* are. But which of us has not deceived ourselves and then wanted to blame the other? The blame culture, which we find ourselves in, starts with us.

Projective identification: I'll show you how it feels – shifted revenge

Projective identification in its simplest form is to make others feel what we cannot feel ourselves. So the bully maybe wants another to feel their fear. If we have been hurt, it is a natural response to want to do to others what has been done to oneself to show them how it feels. Revenge would be doing it to the one who did it to us. In shifted revenge, we are not doing it to them, but to anyone, not necessarily the person who hurt us. Often this is unconscious. I have seen this working with couples as, for example, the woman who has been abandoned by her father seducing and leaving men, or the man who has been overwhelmed by his mother refusing to commit to the woman who loves him and invoking powerlessness in her.

Part of revenge is to see the other suffering the way we did. A friend who works with abusers says that they want the moment of satisfaction when they see the terror on the other's face – a replication of what was done to them. In that way, abuse can be passed on for generations and has nothing to do with the person or people who committed the original abuse.

Context: the media and a society of litigation and punishment – a blame culture

Throughout we have emphasised the cultural reinforcements for revenge and touched briefly on punishment and the legal system as forms of revenge. A few years ago there was a Channel 4 programme called 'Why Doctors Make Mistakes'. The programme showed that people almost always sued because they did not feel heard or recognised. And it is difficult to admit mistakes when we live in a blame culture, but the denial keeps us in a vicious circle as the other is more likely to attack us when we do not come clean. I think vulnerability is not easy in our culture, and we have seen how inability to feel vulnerable contributes to revenge cycles.

In *The Forgiveness Project*, Marina Cantacuzino describes a father who had lost his daughter because she had been given the wrong drug at around the time of the Iraq war. A journalist thrust a microphone in front of the father asking him how he felt about the doctor who had given the wrong drug, expecting no doubt to hear a wish for the offending doctor to be punished. She describes how the father's merciful and compassionate tone felt out of sync with the bellicose rhetoric of revenge and payback that had been grabbing all the headlines.

The blame and punishment culture can also be seen in the under-using of restorative justice. When the meeting between offender and victim happens, re-offending is so much less likely as the offender is more inclined to face up to what he or she has done. The offender is given a chance to move on. It also brings closure to the victim to see that the other is human, and this lessens their desire for revenge. Why, if it is so successful, is it not done more often? Could it be that society's wish to avenge is too strong? I have sometimes wondered whether revenge could be a socially reinforced addiction.

Conclusion: letting ourselves out of prison

I see revenge as keeping us locked in a prison of our own making; forgiveness as releasing us from the prison; and writing about revenge as helping to understand more about the prison itself and the attraction of staying there with a view to encouraging us to get out, dismantling the justifications for staying there.

Often, we do not recognise that we are capable of atrocious acts and it may be circumstances rather than the goodness of our natures that have stopped us. In wanting revenge, we become the same as the perpetrators – an eye for an eye makes the whole world blind – and we distance ourselves from embracing the humanity in everyone. In doing so, we become a little more inhuman ourselves in the process.

My aim in this article is to help us understand the pull of revenge, particularly the social reinforcements, and perhaps lessen the attachments, the justifications and the inability to feel vulnerable which keep it locked in place.

Acknowledgments

Ben Fuchs who suggested we write about revenge and co-ran a forgiveness conference with me, and my wife Joan Wilmot who has supported me on many levels to explore this topic.

References

Ben-Shahar, A. (2010) *Self and Society*. AHP(B) Association of Humanistic Psychology in Britain.

Bohm, T. and Kaplan, S. (2011) *Revenge*. London: Karnac.

Cantacuzino, M. (2015) *The Forgiveness Project*. London: Jessica Kingsley Publishers.

Fambul Tok. (2011) DVD. Available from Amazon.

Hall, J. (1993) *The Reluctant Adult*. Dorset: Prism Press.

Heffernan, M. (2011) *Wilful Blindness*. London: Simon and Schuster.

Hillman, J. (1975) *Betrayal in Loose Ends*. New York, NY: Spring Publications.

Scheff, T. (1994) *Bloody Revenge*. Oxford: Westview Press.

Solzhenityn, A. (2003) *The Gulag Archipelago 1918–1965*. London: Harvill.

Chapter 10

A PASTOR LOOKS AT FORGIVENESS

Stephen Hance

Forgive us our sins,
as we forgive those who have sinned against us.

Jesus of Nazareth

To forgive is to set a prisoner free and discover that the
prisoner was you.

Lewis Smedes, Forgiveness – The Power to Change
the Past, Christianity Today, 7 January 1983

I am a pastor. I have been an ordained Anglican priest for 22 years
at time of writing, but you could say I have been a pastor for ten
years longer than that, since I was about 17 years old when I began
to lead a youth group in the parish church that I belonged to. Youth
groups throw up every pastoral issue under the sun. People fall in
love and out of love. They find faith, lose their faith, and find it
again. They want to leave home because no one understands them
and then decide they have the best parents in the whole world.
They fail exams, apply for university, and change their minds about
what they want to spend their lives doing. They read their religious
texts for the first time and ask all the questions older people want
to ask but don't dare because they're supposed to know the answer
by now. Occasionally, something really serious happens.

I led that group for a couple of years and then another when
I went to university; I then went to theological college and later

I was ordained. I served as a curate, then as vicar of two London parishes. I thought I would be in parish ministry all my life, but after 20 years or thereabouts I took on a new role as a canon of Southwark Cathedral and Director of Mission and Evangelism for the Diocese of Southwark. It's a different role, but still concerned with helping people to develop and grow, as people and in their faith. Part of me is still a pastor.

As a parish priest, I spent a good amount of time engaged in what might be called 'pastoral counselling'. This was by no means counselling in a professional or technical sense. I do not have the experience or training for that. When on occasion it seemed to me that someone I was meeting with needed professional counselling I would raise that as a possibility and help the person concerned access whatever services they seemed to require.

By 'pastoral counselling' I mean something much more informal and low key, something that might be a precursor or a lead in to formal counselling or therapy for some, but for many more was sufficient to enable them to take the step they wanted to take in their life or faith. Most clergy of whatever denomination will know what I mean. Pastoral counselling usually flowed out of a conversation perhaps after a service. 'Vicar, I wonder if you have time for me to come and chat to you about something?' Or, 'Vicar, could you pray with me about something I am wrestling with at the moment?' An appointment would be made, usually at the vicarage, often just with the two of us present, but sometimes with a third party present as well, especially where the person seemed especially vulnerable or upset. I always preferred to book these appointments for times when I knew I wouldn't be in the house on my own.

The theme of forgiveness was perhaps the most common which emerged during these conversations and moments of pastoral prayer. I came to believe that difficulties in forgiving others and in feeling that one had been forgiven were close to the root of many of the inner struggles that members of my flock were facing. The stories that follow are summaries or simplifications, and to some extent amalgamations, of more than one situation. But they act as quite concrete examples of the role that forgiveness played in many of these conversations and in the personal growth and progress that often followed.

The first set of challenges I observed around forgiveness were to do with coming to a place of feeling that one had been forgiven oneself. The stories that I am drawing on here take place within the context of a faith community, an Anglican church to be specific. They involve people who, with varying degrees of confidence and conviction, would describe themselves as Christians. As a person of Christian faith myself, who has lived all his life within that faith tradition, my understanding of forgiveness has been shaped by that tradition. Forgiveness is a theme that is close to the heart of Christianity. Christians typically have a strong sense of the imperfection and sinfulness of humanity, noting our ability to hurt and wound each other, to neglect and damage the planet, and to pay little attention to God. Christians see this sinfulness as both corporate and individual, and in need of forgiveness by God. The core of the Christian Gospel – a word that literally means 'good news' – is the declaration that God himself has taken the decisive action in making such forgiveness possible in the death and resurrection of Jesus, in whom Christians believe God is revealed as fully present. How precisely this happens is contested among Christians, but for our purposes that is unimportant. The point is that most Christians have a strong belief that God's attitude towards them is one of gracious forgiveness, in which deliberate sins as well as accidental ones can be forgiven completely, with no record kept.

Yet despite this intellectual conviction, I observed that many of the struggles of those who sought pastoral counselling were around feeling unforgiven by God. A young man would sit in my study and confess that he had found himself looking at pornography or thinking lustful thoughts about members of the opposite sex (or his own sex). He had prayed and asked God to forgive him, but somehow in his heart he didn't feel forgiven. Perhaps this was because his feelings and desires hadn't really changed despite that prayer. Perhaps he had found himself wrestling with, or giving into, the same temptation again. As a result, he felt that he was now beyond the reach of God's forgiveness. His prayer life had dried up. He no longer wanted to come to church or receive Holy Communion, as he felt so unworthy to be in God's presence. Sometimes these conversations would end with a tearful wail: 'I know God is forgiving, but how can he forgive *this*?'

The conversation that followed would usually begin by trying to set the sins or perceived sins that had been confessed into some kind of context. It was striking to me how many people felt that the most common or trivial of sins were somehow unique, as if they were theirs alone, as if neither God nor I had ever come across such a thing before. This was especially true where matters of sex and sexual desire were concerned. Those struggles were often confessed in whispers, with a great deal of shame. And it seemed to me that shame was a big part of the issue. It is one thing to believe that one has been forgiven for what one has done. But there are some (perceived) sins that seem to touch rather on who one is, and experiencing forgiveness and acceptance there is a much more complex issue. I decided that most things we might count as sin are really very small and trivial, and that part of the role of pastoral counselling was to help the other person see that too.

But then there were other confessions where the sin confessed was definitely not small or trivial at all. Most often when such sins from the past were confessed to me they had already been detected and responded to appropriately, for example by legal process, some time in the past. I am not talking here about the altogether more complex issue of a confession to a priest of abuse or other criminal action which has not been detected and punished and which in some traditions the priest may feel obligated to keep to him or herself, the 'seal of the confessional'. I discovered that it is one thing for society to say that a person has paid the debt for their offence, but it can be another thing altogether for that person to feel forgiven and free to begin a new life. Ironically, this can be true in a particular way when a person has experienced a religious conversion subsequent to the offence being committed. For some, their new faith does a better job of underlining how wrong their past behaviour was than of offering them a new start, which is of course the most fundamental message of Christianity.

In this situation, I came to understand the power of the Christian sacrament of absolution. In Christian thought, absolution is not a prayer or wish for forgiveness. It is a declaration by the priest that God has indeed forgiven and that the power of the sin and the guilt and shame that may accompany it is no more. Of course, to be experienced as effective, this sacrament must be believed and received. But I have seen the power it has when this does happen. At a deep level, there are few things more personally freeing and uplifting than the removal of a sense of personal guilt to be replaced by a sense that one has genuinely been forgiven and can walk into the future unshackled from the burdens of the past.

In the quote at the beginning of this chapter, Jesus makes a connection between two aspects of forgiveness, what we have termed the vertical and the horizontal. The implication, with which many Christians would concur, is that knowing oneself to be forgiven by God is intrinsically linked with the ability to offer forgiveness to others. It is the experience of having received grace – another key theological term for Christians – which makes it possible to offer grace to others. This grace is offered regardless of whether the other is in some sense a 'worthy' recipient of it, just as God offers grace to us who are unworthy. But the inverse connection is made here too. Withholding the grace of forgiveness from others makes it ultimately impossible for us to receive that same grace of forgiveness, from God and perhaps from other people too. This is the point that Jesus makes powerfully in the parable of the unmerciful servant in Matthew's Gospel, chapter 18, verse 23 to the end.

The story Jesus tells is a striking one. It begins with a king, a wealthy man, who decides it is time to call in various sums of money he is owed. One debtor, who owes a huge, unimaginable debt, is brought in. Realising that this man cannot begin to pay, the king orders that he and his family be sold into slavery in order to go some way towards paying back what they owe. The debtor breaks down at this verdict, pleading for patience. Moved with pity, the king goes further, granting not just more time to pay, but cancelling the debt altogether. Now this man is free, his debt forgiven.

But that's not the end of the tale. The newly forgiven one does not go back out into the world full of joy and generosity. Quite the reverse, in fact. Almost immediately after receiving his freedom he encounters another man who owes him a fairly small sum. Again, the debtor pleads for mercy, this time on a much smaller scale, but this time it is denied. The one who has been forgiven a great amount refuses to cancel a much smaller debt, or even to allow time for repayment, but has the one who is indebted to him thrown into debtors' prison until he can repay – presumably never, since this man is now unable to work or make money.

At this point in the narrative the king reappears, fully appraised of what has happened since his generous gesture of a short time before. This time he is angry, not inclined to show any more mercy than the one to whom he offered mercy has shown to another. Now this first debtor will share the fate of the second – debtors' prison until, somehow, the debt can be repaid. And Jesus says in conclusion that this is how God will treat those of us who receive divine forgiveness but refuse to show that same forgiveness to others.

We can read this parable as making a weak or a strong connection between our experience of offering and receiving forgivenesss. In the strong version, God intentionally refuses to forgive those who will not forgive their neighbours. In the weak version, God's forgiveness, while it may be offered, cannot be received or experienced by the one who will not also offer it. It is as if unforgiveness is a dam that prevents the whole stream from flowing until it is cleared.

In either of these forms, this belief gives a pretty strong impetus to the Christian practice of forgiveness, and may lead some people to declare that they have forgiven when in reality they have not and are not yet in a position to. Some of us will recall news interviews with people who have recently experienced a terrible loss almost immediately insisting that they have forgiven the perpetrators, and we have been unsure whether to admire them or yearn for them to have the space to acknowledge anger and hurt, albeit as part of the journey to true forgiveness.

As a pastor, though, my experience has been that forgiveness does not come easily to many of those who long to receive and offer it, despite their desire that it should. A woman sat in my study and spoke of some inner turmoil she was experiencing. With gentle probing, it became clear that this turmoil was connected to her complex feelings about her father. She had admired and loved her father very much, but he had been a remote and absent figure through her childhood, one whose approval she craved but whose love she was never sure she had. Many of those feelings had transferred themselves into her faith and attached themselves to her conception of God, a particular problem for a faith in which the idea of God as Father is so much a part of the tradition. She came to see this, and desired to forgive her father as a means to reshaping her conception of God. But as we got closer to the nub of the conversation it became harder and harder for her to speak in terms of forgiveness. She began to talk in her father's defence, reminding herself of challenges and pressures he had faced that made his behaviour understandable and, perhaps, therefore excusable.

After the conversation, we agreed that she might say a prayer in which she chose to forgive and release him. Again, as she got towards the word, she couldn't bring herself to utter it. She prayed for him, understood him, expressed gratitude for him – everything except the thing which she wanted and needed to say, that he had let her down, but that she was now choosing to forgive him. It took her a long time to find her way there – but when she did, the impact was immediate. A new lightness came upon her, and over the next weeks and months it stayed with her. Her faith came alive in a fresh way and she was able to see God from a new and much more positive perspective, as her image of him was decoupled from her image of the man who had failed her.

It's worth noting that the father was not in the room while this was going on. As far as I know he had not asked for forgiveness or acknowledged the hurt he had caused. This woman's forgiveness of him was not conditional on his repentance. Nor did it change the reality of what had transpired or the impact it had had. She did not say that his past behaviour did not matter. It would not have been true forgiveness if she had. Rather, she acknowledged that he had behaved in a way that he should not have done – at least as she had seen and recalled it – and that this had hurt her. Acknowledging the real harm done was a necessary step on the way to forgiving it and moving on.

One of the aspects of this approach to forgiveness, therefore, is that it is not conditional. It is not primarily about the restoration of the relationship, although it can be a mile marker on that journey. This is an important point given that restoration of a relationship may not be a possible or even desirable outcome. We may not know where the person who has hurt us is, or it may not be wise or safe for us to make contact with them. We may not know how they would respond to our initiating a conversation about what has happened. They may be dead. None of that is a bar to the kind of forgiveness we are talking about here. This kind of forgiveness is essentially about an inner peace-making. It involves acknowledging the hurt that has been caused and facing up to the impact it has had, being honest about the internal legacy it has left and not minimising it. Then it entails a conscious act of forgiving, releasing the right to vengeance and any sense of moral superiority or indebtedness. For a religious believer, it may include asking the help of God, and remembering the forgiveness of God which one has experienced oneself. And all this can happen without the person who is being forgiven ever knowing anything about it. As the quote at the beginning of this chapter says, to forgive is to release someone from prison and then discover that the prisoner was yourself.

But if our approach to forgiveness is not conditional, if forgiveness may be offered regardless of whether it is sought, regardless of whether there is remorse or repentance, don't we in fact end up colluding with and minimising the impact of behaviour which ought to be challenged and recognised as evil? While it may be laudable for someone to offer forgiveness to someone who has wronged them when there is sorrow at the hurt caused, does not unconditional forgiveness operate in a profoundly amoral way, offering 'cheap grace' and a bland assurance that past actions do not matter, when in fact they matter very much indeed?

Again, I think Matthew 18 helps us here. With those stark closing words – 'This is how my heavenly Father will treat each of you unless you forgive from the heart' – Jesus reminds us that in the Christian or indeed theistic world view the person harmed and the person who has done the harming are not the only two characters in the story. There is also the person of God in every story of forgiveness and judgement, and God reserves the right to judge. Ultimately, from the Christian perspective, God is the only one who *can* judge.

Seen from this angle, when a person forgives they are not saying, 'This harmful act that was perpetrated against me did not in fact matter very much and so I choose to forgive it.' That would be to excuse rather than to forgive. Instead, the one who forgives from a Christian perspective is saying something like, 'This act caused me harm and hurt me. However, I know that do not have the full perspective that would allow me to judge what has been done. Only God has all the information to reach a right judgement. Furthermore, I know that in carrying resentment and anger against the perpetrator, I end up struggling with things that are too big for me to handle without losing my peace of mind. And so my act of forgiving is in reality an act of handing over responsibility for judgement to the one who is able to carry that responsibility and to exercise it wisely, so that my own sense of peace and well-being might be restored.'

As a pastor, I have seen people experience this many times. It isn't always a quick or dramatic experience and it can't happen under pressure. It doesn't happen because someone else says it must, nor with the simple passage of time. It is a path that must be freely and intentionally chosen, and chosen regardless of whether there was any response or engagement from the person being forgiven. But when it is chosen, it can indeed lead to an experience of inner freedom.

A woman felt a deep despondency and heaviness. As she reflected on the cause of this feeling she recognised that she needed to forgive someone who had hurt her very badly years before. She spent some time coming to a place where she felt that she was now ready to forgive and did so as best as she knew how. To her disappointment, the sense of heaviness remained. Something in her said that the forgiveness was not yet complete. So she wrote a letter to the person who had hurt her, a letter written not to make her feel superior or to make the other person feel bad, but to reach out in love and to say that whatever bad feeling there might have been in the past was now gone. She took the letter to the post box and as she posted it she felt the despondency lift. She walked home a changed person.

So it turns out that forgiveness is not a chore or a duty, but a key – a key that can unlock a door for those who have been hurt and those who have hurt them alike. That's why after 32 years as a pastor I still hope and pray for those with whom I work to know the transforming power of giving and receiving forgiveness.

Chapter 11

THE ROLE OF FORGIVENESS AFTER INTERPERSONAL ABUSE
Danger or Road to Recovery and Healing?

Christiane Sanderson

Forgiveness is not just an event but a process and, like child sexual abuse and domestic violence in the family, it consists of complex dynamics which need to be understood and worked through before it can be considered. In addition, to avoid replicating the abuse of power and control, forgiveness must not be enforced no matter how well meaning. An essential aspect of healing from interpersonal abuse is to restore control and self-agency to survivors so that they can make meaningful, autonomous choices. To impose forgiveness as the road to recovery is not only potentially dangerous, but can lead to re-shaming and re-traumatisation. Survivors of interpersonal trauma need time to legitimise their abuse experiences, and validate the full range of concomitant emotions before considering the process of forgiveness and assess to what extent it will aid their recovery and healing. It is critical that families, partners, friends and clinicians support survivors in processing their experiences and do not contaminate this by imposing their own beliefs or expectations to forgive.

This chapter will explore how the complex dynamics inherent in interpersonal trauma can make premature forgiveness dangerous, not only for survivors, but also for others in their social world or community. It will also examine who forgiveness is for, the danger of reinforcing the ubiquitous self-blame that survivors feel, especially when abusers do not accept responsibility for the abuse, and the role of self-forgiveness. To ensure ethical practice, clinicians need to respect survivors whether they choose to forgive or not, and be careful not to coerce survivors to forgive and impede the healing process. The therapeutic focus needs to be on working through the abuse experiences, validating the full range of emotions, and supporting survivors to make autonomous choices.

Who is forgiveness for?

Forgiveness is imbued with myriad socio-cultural and religious meaning and is considered by many to be not only a moral virtue but also a moral obligation (Sanderson 2012; Tener and Eisikovits 2015). Advocates of forgiveness argue that forgiveness will release survivors from negative emotions such as anger, rage, resentment and the desire for revenge, which in turn frees them to lead to more satisfactory lives and improved relationships (Enright and Fitzgibbons 2000). What is often not acknowledged is that feelings of anger, rage and the sense of betrayal need to be legitimised, validated, felt and processed for healing to occur. This challenges the notion that to forgive facilitates healing, and argues that healing must come first before forgiveness can take place.

All too often, forgiveness is driven by social expectations to preserve the sanctity of the family, or to repair family disunity, and maintain social order (Lamb 2002a; Lamb and Murphy 2002; Murphy 2002). Often families or partners persuade or coerce survivors to forgive in order to avoid negative feelings or conflict so that the family can be restored. However, forcing forgiveness diverts empathy and compassion away from the survivor and onto the abuser. In addition, forgiving the abuser and not holding them accountable can lead to endangering others and colluding with continued abuse. Many survivors forgive their abuser on a daily basis in order to avoid destroying the family, only to discover that the abuse has continued and put others at risk.

Difficulties can also arise when some family members forgive the abuser while others do not, leading to a fracture in the family. It is not unusual for those who have not been directly abused to expect the survivor to forgive without fully understanding the pain and harm done. This is compounded in sibling abuse whereby parents may minimise the abuse by perceiving it as banter, horseplay or consensual sexual experimentation. As a result, some parents may hold both children equally responsible for the abuse, or if they favour the abuser over the survivor, will insist on forgiveness so as to restore the illusion of a normal, happy family. This is of huge advantage to the abuser, as splitting family loyalties increases divisiveness, which fuels their sense of power and potency (Sanderson 2013).

A common assumption is that forgiveness will release survivors from a myriad of negative emotions such as anger, resentment and the desire for revenge, which allows them to lead more satisfactory lives and form improved relationships (Wilson 1994; Freedman and Enright 1996). Implicit in this is that forgiveness is the right, or virtuous, thing to do, irrespective of the harm done or whether the abuser is remorseful or repentant (Enright and Fitzgibbons 2000). Moreover, any reluctance to forgive is typically seen as a fundamental flaw and a source of shame, which reinforces an already omnipresent sense of guilt and inadequacy, raising the question of who forgiveness is actually for.

If forgiveness is truly for the good of the survivor and yet they are shamed for not forgiving, this can lead to re-traumatisation. Making survivors feel ashamed for not being able to forgive or guilty for not making amends or repairing the family (Herman 2001; Lamb 2002b; Sanderson 2012, 2013) imposes a huge responsibility of restoring family unity on the survivor. This not only adds to the elevated sense of guilt and responsibility that many survivors feel, but also metastasises their already crippling sense of shame making the survivor feel even more flawed and inadequate (Sanderson 2015). Survivors are invariably saturated and encumbered with not only their own shame but also the shame that the abuser has disavowed (Sanderson 2015). To drench them in more shame for not forgiving is tantamount to abuse and merely allows the abuser to continue to behave in a shameless way and abuse with impunity (Herman 2001; Sanderson 2015).

The danger of forgiveness in interpersonal abuse

The nature of interpersonal abuse that thrives on deception and manipulation of others gives rise to a number of dynamics that can make forgiveness dangerous. This is particularly so in the case of domestic violence, where pleading for forgiveness is an integral part of the cycle of abuse (Walker 1984; Sanderson 2008) and remorse and assurances of change are used to prevent the partner from leaving so that the cycle of abuse can continue (Walker 1984). Similarly in child physical and sexual abuse, abusers consistently show remorse and ask for forgiveness and yet continue to abuse (Sanderson 2008). There is robust evidence that perpetrators of child sexual abuse and domestic violence find it difficult to change their abusive behaviour without specialist treatment, and forgiveness merely serves to support the abuser's cognitive distortions in minimising harm done (Herman 2001; Sanderson 2004, 2008). More importantly, they are more likely to perceive forgiveness as a weakness which fuels their sense of omnipotence while putting those who forgive at increased risk of harm (Herman 2002; Murphy 2002). Finally, forgiveness can be dangerous in exacerbating the 'duping delight' many abusers feel when they get away with manipulating others (Ekman 1992). Given these complex dynamics, it is imperative to exercise caution when promoting forgiveness in cases of interpersonal abuse in order to minimise the risk of collusion in further abuse.

The assumption that a lack of forgiveness gives rise to resentment and desire for revenge must also be deconstructed. The majority of survivors merely want the abuse to stop as they yearn for a healthy relationship with the person they love yet who abuses them, and desire an acknowledgement of harm done (Sanderson 2013). It is when abusers do not take responsibility, or are not held accountable, or continue to abuse with impunity, that feelings of anger and resentment arise. This not only fuels survivors sense of betrayal in being coerced to forgive but also replicates abuse dynamics. This is compounded when family members, siblings, partners or children exert pressure on the survivor in order to preserve the family, no matter how dysfunctional or abusive. Many survivors find it hard to withstand such expectations as they already feel guilty for causing upset in the family, making it hard to resist the sense of responsibility to restore family unity.

Traumatic bonding

This pressure from other family members reinforces the elevated sense of responsibility they already feel. Survivors typically feel responsible for their abuse and tend to protect and forgive the abuser by blaming themselves. This is a core feature of traumatic bonding (Sanderson 2008, 2014) in which the child or domestically abused partner blames themselves for the abuse in order to preserve a positive image of the abuser. As they are dependent on the abuser, they cannot afford to hold the abuser responsible for the abuse, or express anger or rage, as this could escalate the risk of further harm. To manage this, survivors have to suppress any negative feelings and, rather than hold the abuser responsible, they blame themselves. This is further compounded when the abuser blames the survivor, or portrays him or herself as the victim as a way to elicit empathy and compassion (Sanderson 2008, 2013). Given the degree of forgiveness for the abuser inherent in traumatic bonding, it is much more pertinent to explore the value of self-forgiveness.

Self-forgiveness or self-acceptance

While self-forgiveness is an important aspect of healing it can only be done with an acknowledgement that the survivor is not to blame for the abuse (Sanderson 2010). To avoid colluding with the elevated sense of responsibility it is critical that survivors establish what they are forgiving themselves for. They need to be mindful that the responsibility for the abuse lies solely with the abuser. They also need to know that their reactions to the abuse such as freezing or sexual arousal are outside voluntary control and represent normal, physiological responses to danger that aid survival (Sanderson 2010, 2013). Furthermore, they cannot be held responsible for not being able to foresee, prevent or stop the abuse, for submitting to it, or having an inability to disclose, as to fight back or break the silence and secrecy increases the risk of further harm. It is essential that survivors identify the thoughts, feelings and behaviours that were under their conscious control and forgive themselves for these rather than trauma-related reactions that are not under voluntary control.

Survivors must have permission to feel the more negative emotions that they have without feeling guilty so that they can accept what happened to them and begin to feel compassion for themselves. Most importantly, survivors who feel that their abuse is so pernicious to be beyond forgiveness must be respected, irrespective of social expectations or personal beliefs (Holmgren 2002; Lamb 2002b). In working through their abuse experiences and feelings, survivors can shed their self-blame and move towards self-acceptance, which is a more potent aid to healing than forgiveness or self-forgiveness. It only through self-acceptance that the survivor can genuinely release the power the abuser had, or still has, over them and begin to heal. As the process of healing unfolds, some survivors may come to forgive the abuser, while others may feel compassion for the abuser and yet choose not to forgive (Sanderson 2012). Forgiveness does not have to be binary but needs to be seen on a spectrum to include empathy and compassion for self and others.

Alternative ways of healing

Forgiveness is not the only way of healing. Indeed, it is more likely that healing will lead to forgiveness rather than forgiveness predicting healing. The danger of premature forgiveness is that the avoidance of anger and aggression may masquerade as empathy and compassion while paving over justifiable anger, rage or aggression. Forgiveness is a process not an event and cannot be bypassed by premature forgiveness as this leads to pseudo-forgiveness (Lew 1990; Hunter 1995) in which feelings are suppressed and buried, while the risk of compromised mental health is increased (Holmgren 2002; Lamb 2002b; Murphy 2002). Thus, premature forgiveness, with its outward focus on social expectation and pleasing others, may prevent the necessary internal changes that lead to genuine empathy and compassion.

Authentic forgiveness must be seen as a process, not an event, which will affect survivors in different ways. Survivors vary enormously in terms of their abuse experiences, how this impacts on them, and the process of recovery. There is no simple, one-cap-fits-all (Sanderson 2013) solution to trauma or the adoption of forgiveness. An alternative approach to healing is to integrate the trauma. This is best achieved through the use of a trauma-informed practice model which advocates a phased treatment approach comprising three stages: stabilisation, processing the trauma, and integration (Herman 2001; Sanderson 2013). In this model, survivors need to work through the first two stages before they can begin to forgive those who have harmed them. It is only when the survivor has worked through the hurt and losses associated with the abuse and has permission to experience and validate the full range of feelings, including sadness, hurt, anger and rage, that the survivor can begin to feel empathy and compassion for self and others, including those who have harmed them. This allows them to integrate the abuse, begin to live in the present and hope for a better a future.

Forgiveness as therapeutic process

Forgiveness must never be imposed but worked through as part of processing the abuse, and clinicians need to support the survivor whatever their decision. They must be mindful of their own attitudes and beliefs with regard to forgiveness so that they do not impose their own expectations or contaminate the survivor's process of healing and forgiveness. Therapists working with survivors of interpersonal abuse must ensure that they maintain an ethical framework with regard to forgiveness which does not collude with social expectations to forgive. They must avoid imposing their own view of forgiveness onto their clients and adopt a supportive stance, whether the client chooses to forgive or not. A survivor who does not wish to forgive must know that they will not be judged or shamed, in the same way that the survivor who does wish to forgive must not be shamed for wishing to do so. Therapists must also guard against encouraging premature forgiveness in survivors who, in their yearning for belonging and acceptance, are afraid to explore the full range of their feelings and fully acknowledge harm done.

In helping survivors to process their abuse experiences, practitioners must be aware of the survivor's motivation to forgive and to what extent this is due to religious and socio-cultural expectations, or social pressure for family unity, or to have the family they never had. In contrast, they also need to explore any social pressure to not forgive because such abuse is considered to be unforgivable by others. Practitioners also need to address the concept of forgiveness which underpins their theoretical model to minimise the risk of survivors wishing to forgive to please the practitioner rather than because of internal motivation. The therapeutic process must provide a range of options around forgiving or not forgiving without judgement or prejudice and explore advantages and disadvantages for each individual survivor's circumstances so that they can make informed decisions that balance their own needs and their right to make autonomous choices. Clinicians must also acknowledge that to not forgive can represent a legitimate response to an offender's continuing actions and place in society and that to not forgive can come from a place of strength and self-respect (Lamb 2002b).

In conclusion, forgiveness, whether self-forgiveness, or forgiving others, is a very complex and demanding process and must always be a personal choice. There is no conclusive evidence that forgiveness is necessary for healing. Some survivors find it extremely helpful, while others do not. The process of forgiveness is not just confined to the survivor but radiates out to others such as family members and the wider community. Each of these will need to exercise personal choices around forgiveness rather than have it imposed. While empathy for the abuser is important, especially if they too were victims, this also should not be demanded of survivors but balanced with clear acknowledgement that harm has been done. Forgiveness is a process in which the full range of feelings needs to be experienced without judgement so that the survivor can integrate the abuse experience and can discover empathy and compassion for self and others, including the abuser, and in which he or she can make autonomous choices around forgiveness.

References

Ekman, P (1992) *Telling Lies: Clues to Deceit in the Market Place, Marriage, and Politics.* New York, NY: W.W. Norton.

Enright, R.D. and Fitzgibbons, R.P. (2000) *Helping Clients Forgive: An Empirical Practical Guide for Resolving Anger and Resolving Hope.* Washington, DC: APA Press.

Freedman, S. and Enright, R. (1996) 'Forgiveness as an intervention goal with incest survivors.' *Journal of Consultation and Clinical Psychology,* 64 (5), 983–992.

Herman, J.L. (2001) *Trauma and Recovery.* Second Edition. New York, NY: Basic Books.

Holmgren, M.R (2002) 'Forgiveness and Self-Forgiveness in Psychotherapy.' In S. Lamb and J.G. Murphy (eds) *Before Forgiving: Cautionary Views of Forgiveness in Psychotherapy.* New York, NY: Oxford University Press.

Hunter, M (1995) *Adult Survivors of Sexual Abuse: Treatment Innovations.* Thousand Oaks, CA: Sage Publications.

Lamb, S. (2002a) 'When Forgiving Doesn't Make Sense.' In S. Lamb and J.G. Murphy (eds) *Before Forgiving: Cautionary Views of Forgiveness in Psychotherapy.* New York, NY: Oxford University Press.

Lamb, S. (2002b) 'Women, Abuse, and Forgiveness: A Special Case.' In S. Lamb and J.G. Murphy (eds) *Before Forgiving: Cautionary Views of Forgiveness in Psychotherapy.* New York, NY: Oxford University Press.

Lamb, S. and Murphy, J.G. (eds) (2002) *Before Forgiving: Cautionary Views of Forgiveness in Psychotherapy.* New York, NY: Oxford University Press.

Lew, M. (1990) *Victims No Longer: Men Recovering from Incest and Other Sexual Child Abuse.* New York, NY: HarperCollins.

Murphy, J.G. (2002) 'Forgiveness in Counselling: A Philosophical Perspective.' In S. Lamb and J.G. Murphy (eds) *Before Forgiving: Cautionary Views of Forgiveness in Psychotherapy.* New York, NY: Oxford University Press.

Sanderson, C. (2004) *The Seduction of Children: Empowering Parents and Teachers to Protect Children from Child Sexual Abuse.* London: Jessica Kingsley Publishers.

Sanderson, C. (2008) *Counselling Survivors of Domestic Abuse.* London: Jessica Kingsley Publishers.

Sanderson, C. (2010) *The Warrior Within: A One in Four Handbook to Aid Recovery from Childhood Sexual Abuse and Violence.* London: One in Four.

Sanderson, C. (2012) *The Spirit Within: A One in Four Handbook to Aid Recovery from Religious Sexual Abuse Across All Faiths.* London: One in Four.

Sanderson, C. (2013) *Counselling Skills for Working with Trauma: Healing from Child Sexual Abuse, Sexual Violence and Domestic Abuse.* London: Jessica Kingsley Publishers.

Sanderson, C. (2014) 'The role of shame in child sexual abuse.' Optimus Education Safeguarding Hub, 20 March 2014.

Sanderson, C. (2015) *Counselling Skills for Working with Shame.* London: Jessica Kingsley Publishers.

Sanderson, C. (2016) *The Warrior Within: A One in Four Handbook to Aid Recovery from Childhood Sexual Abuse and Violence.* Third Edition. London: One in Four.

Tener, D. and Eisikovits, Z. (2015) 'Torn: social expectations concerning forgiveness among women who have experienced intrafamilial sexual abuse.' *Journal of Interpersonal Violence,* DOI: 10.1177/0886260515593296.

Walker, L. (1984) *The Battered Woman Syndrome.* New York, NY: Springer.

Wilson, H. (1994) Forgiveness and survivors of sexual abuse: Relationships among forgiveness of the perpetrator, spiritual well-being, depression and anxiety. Unpublished doctoral dissertation, Boston University, 1994.

Chapter 12

FAMILIES, FORGIVING AND WITHHOLDING FORGIVENESS
Meaning and Family Process

Honor Rhodes

For many people, those with faith and those, like myself, with none, their first encounter with the idea of forgiveness comes from religious observances. For devout Christians, there is a simple and relentless injunction contained in the Lord's Prayer, 'Forgive us our trespasses as we forgive those who trespass against us.'

The supplicant asks that they themselves be forgiven and, without a missing beat, adds that the act of forgiving is one that they have already undertaken, and will do so in future seemingly unconditionally. The prayer itself acts as a moral imperative, to pray is to be required to forgive. We shall explore 'pseudo' and partial forgiveness later but the possibility of these states is raised here, surreptitiously, at the heart of Christian teaching.

There is a clear social function to acts of forgiveness, apart from any moral construct, in that it can act as punctuation. Instead of retaliating for a wrong, some people seem to have the capacity to put that hurt to one side and offer an asymmetrical and often unexpected response. Perhaps they do this because they can imagine the mind of the wrongdoer and can find some understanding. Despite being hurt they can see that a genuine mistake was made, for example. Some people appear to forgive because it is required of them, by their religion or their family, by coercion or inducement. This is a state of pseudo-forgiveness and it can be deeply problematic for those of us who meet it in our work with families and their complex family systems. As workers we can be drawn into enabling 'transactions' between parties, settling for words of apology and potentially resentful acceptances; with thought and toleration of discomfort we can help families achieve more.

Our training for work with families, whether we are social workers, teachers, health visitors, housing or police officers, has probably not invited us to think about family troubles and distresses using a forgiveness lens. More actively we may consciously avoid language in our pluralistic practice that may seem to derive from a Judeo-Christian tradition; but it is far more likely that it is simply not a feature of thinking about families.

We will have read and been taught something about communication patterns, parenting and relationships and what research tells us about the family life cycle and its challenges. Unless we are thinking about it particularly we may not recognise the troubles that stem from the need to negotiate forgiveness for what they really are. We might miss the chance to have a thought as to how we might work specifically with someone who is withholding such a resolution from another. Or, as painfully perhaps, seeking an absolution that never comes.

As a social worker in London's East End, I worked with many families where issues of guilt and a desire for forgiveness were at the heart of the troubles a family faced; rarely did I or they understand it as such. It is only now, working at Tavistock Relationships and after much reading and thinking, that I wonder if practice could be improved if we were able to talk about forgiveness as a part of our enquiry work with families. We have known for a very long time that families' secrets and lies can distort communications and emotional responses as Pincus and Dare (1980) described. In helping families describe themselves to us, as they draw a family tree that seems a puzzle, we might take a moment to wonder with them whether the emotional ties include unforgiveable and perhaps unspeakable things. This is particularly useful in those families whose genograms contain sudden disappearances and severed connections. We will all have met some families who can't mention names of relatives and where they have no intimate knowledge of new arrivals or deaths in a relatively close branch of their wider family tree.

For some practitioners, though, there is a real question as to whether thinking about forgiveness is useful at all. Some people consider that forgiveness is a semi-judicial construct, not an unmediated emotional response and therefore a matter of personal morality rather than an area of possible change and influence. This seems to be a missed opportunity to have a conversation of meaning with families with a chance for change that might otherwise prove elusive.

There is interesting research on the use of communications theory and its relationship to forgiveness, including restriction of choice and a sense of obligation (Carr and Wang 2012). Here the notions of power are explored; Carr and Wang suggest that we find it easier to forgive those more powerful than ourselves, as a sort of 'tribute' gift. However, we more readily withhold forgiveness from those family members, work colleagues or friends and acquaintances who are felt by us to be less powerful than ourselves. Here the denial works in the non-forgiver's favour to prompt further displays of contrition, further offerings of goods we value or an increase in indebtedness 'cashable' later when the need arises. While this sounds mercenary or sadistic, it reflects the truly human desire to render our social, emotional and material environment more favourable to our personal experience. It may be that this potential abuse of power is one of the reasons why forgiveness is problematic in family work. We ourselves, or colleagues, will have worked with vulnerable people who assert their right to forgive abusers, not once but time and time again.

The entrancing Channel 4 documentary programmes in the series 'The Secret Life of Four Year Olds' and the companion episodes on five- and six-year-olds are illuminating generally, but particularly fascinating when viewed with an eye to wrongs and slights, forgiveness and social capital. They are not only fascinating but painful to watch as we see the casual and intended hurts that register as pain on children's faces, with fierce verbal or physical retaliations from some or angry tears and protests to powerful adults. What we see too is the adult's, or supervening authority's, intervention that is usually one of requiring the 'wrongdoer' to apologise and for the 'victim' to accept that apology, with the usual injunctions to now play together 'nicely'. This appears an even-handed response, and certainly requires the least emotional engagement from the person appealed to as judge. There is often a problem here, visible to us as viewers, who have seen calibrated intention to hurt, perhaps as a retaliation for an earlier injury that might have been worse but was not visible to the arbiter. We might also see the equivalent of the 'dive' in football, a child showing distress in order to attract adult attention and punishment for another. The rough and ready reckoner used by most adults of 'six of one and half a dozen of the other' works by distributing activity to both parties, often to neither's satisfaction. A wrongdoer who had an explanation for their actions goes unheard and the victim may well receive less than they consider their due in the satisfaction of watching the other's punishment.

This also takes us into the interesting and problematic territory of the requirement to apologise. It can seem the most natural and sensible thing in the world to suggest that a child apologises for an apparently hurtful action and the other accepts this apology without further exploration or negotiation. This may seem sensible but for many children, and the adults we grow into, the requirement from an authority to offer apologies and in return to offer forgiveness can be painful and, in some cases, impossible. We have all received a cursory, 'sorry', in our lives, and we know that this is no authentic apology; we may offer an equally inauthentic, 'that's fine, don't worry', back. Some part of this is merely pathic, social speech occurring when we are bumped in a crowd, but we can find ourselves apologising or being expected to forgive a hurt that is more serious and preoccupying than an accidental push in a queue.

Ritualising the seeking and granting of forgiveness is a valuable social act. It allows us to leave hurts behind and accept that the past that surrounds them is closed and needs no further negotiation. The performance of this act works poorly in practice where the hurts are significant and aggravated, perhaps repeated over time, deliberately and sadistically wounding or attacking something we hold very dear. In these cases, forgiveness, to be truthfully, as opposed to inauthentically, offered requires some authentic contrition on the part of the wrongdoer.

These thoughts about real and false acts take us to the heart of the problem in that it is human nature to view forgiveness as binary – one either forgives or one does not, one seeks forgiveness or one does not. The idea that our capacity to relent and forgive fluctuates, that we can wish we had not expressed our forgiveness so unequivocally, that we 'gave it away too easily' is an unspoken but deeply felt experience, and may relate to the enforcement of the requirement to say 'sorry' in childhood, or the power exerted over us by the wrongdoer.

In thinking about our work with families, this is the emotional terrain in which domestic abuse and violence exists; where a penitent abuser is forgiven only to be violent or controlling again. Perhaps the seeking of forgiveness is real, if temporary, and perhaps the granting of absolution is the same; there is something very hopeful for both parties in the resetting of the emotional clock, the wiping of the slate that records the wrongs. The temporary nature of this fragile peace is clear, and without intervention the pattern of often escalating violence and the seeking of forgiveness continues.

Many of the families we have worked with have members who have either struggled to forgive or to be forgiven. Sometimes the wrongs are historic and the wrongdoer may be old, ill or dead, but this in itself does not prevent a lasting sense of injustice for some. For example, the parent who still finds themselves furious with their own mother or father, for being not enough loved, for being abused, for not being a favourite. For some families, the wrong and the pain are very fresh – perhaps there had been infidelity, a secret gambling or other addiction; the act may be of smaller magnitude but still a strain to be negotiated – the damage to household goods or the child who loses an expensive coat.

The question in our minds is how we might help these particular people in this particular family best? For this we need to have some form of 'working model' in our minds of how we all, as humans, develop the capacity to forgive, both as a general psychological process and what the specific act of forgiving in a particular family might be either confounded or supported by. This is not to suggest that forgiveness is the 'coin' at the heart of the work but that we can help both sides use imaginative sympathy, compassion or 'mentalisation' (Bateman and Fonagy 2011) depending on our own understanding of change making.

There has been some considerable research on forgiveness, but only a few researchers have looked at the psychological processes required to move from a state of vengeful hurt to one of more positive thoughts and feelings as outlined by Fincham, Paleari and Regalia (2002). In this last positive state it is plainly more possible to accept an apology if one is offered and is experienced as sufficiently authentic or sincere. This is also especially true where the hurt is less significant.

Only a few professionals seek out a chance to think with families about this, largely because it is an area in which we have plenty of highly personal experience and very little by way of formalised intervention tools. On occasions, we can be faced with the need to equip ourselves better when we find our planned family work is obstructed by a singular event that has created such a hurt that it now requires both apologies and restitution.

Equally, our work may bring to the surface a long-standing resentment of such magnitude that we need to ask where it came from, what it means to all members of the family, why it has been sustained and why it has come to the foreground now.

For some families and individuals, true authentic forgiveness is a bridge too far, an unachievable state, and we are left to consider with them what can be achieved in its absence. A good enough position in one family I met was the acknowledgement that a wrong had been done to them; they had been badly swindled by a trusted friend. They would never be reconciled to the betrayal and were never going to be compensated but they wanted to be able to talk about the episode without the level of rage and turmoil that had surrounded it and that had affected the children badly. We used the thinking about rituals to help manage their distress; with some help and practice the parents found a 'script' or a story that they could use to explain to themselves and others what had happened. The act of telling their betrayal and recovery story helped reduce the pain it caused them and gave them a sense of choice and agency, this was itself important in helping them to imagine that in future they could trust others without being betrayed.

The painful nature of betrayals and insults is seemingly obvious, but, as with physical pain, our experience of slight or light insults and hurts is a subjective one. For some people, angry words can be damaging and deeply problematic, for others these would ignored, returned in kind or not seen as any form of behaviour that could require a forgiveness if the other person asked for it. This raises the question of measurement and the use of a standardised, well-tested, reliable clinical tool that could be used to assess the subjective hurt and any corresponding capacity to forgive.

This subjective nature makes the work by Fincham *et al.* (2002) on a forgiveness scale interesting and useful. They built the scale using the idea of a 'forgiveness pathway' after extensive research. The scale measures a five-stage process from the realisation of the hurt to a final setting aside of any grievance through resolution. Whether one might use the tool or not, the five Rs acronym developed by the research team helps us to frame questions as to where someone identifies themselves to be on a forgiveness pathway – or not as the case may be. The steps identified are: realisation, recognition, reparation, restitution and resolution; the process through hurt to seeking resolution seems both logical and consistent with our sense of natural justice.

Paleari, Regalia and Fincham (2009) have gone on to create a specific measure for marital forgiveness, again assessing the amount of subjective hurt but this time building on three specific lines of research enquiry that form subscales measuring benevolence (capacity to forgive), avoidance (shunning) and retaliation (inducing regret in the wrongdoer). This breach of trust is one of the most common reasons for relationship breakdown, whether partners are married or not. It is very preoccupying for the adults, but children are also deeply affected by the emotional turmoil that surrounds it and we need to have a practice vocabulary that enables us as workers to engage with pain of this magnitude, whether it arises from infidelity or some other action.

Other researchers (Cowan *et al.* 2009) have used similar ideas to create family interventions. One such is a co-parenting relationship group work programme where the attending co-parents are helped to understand the consequences of conflict and other damaging communications and behaviours between them. An attack turns one's partner into an enemy; evading their concerns and needs turns them into a stranger; and choosing to confide enables our partners to act as our allies. Much of the work focuses parents' minds on what their children need from them; ironically our children need to see the ordinary conflict we so often hide from them – and more than that they need to see the working out of apologies, forgiveness and resolution. This equips them with the internal mental model of low-level conflict as healthy and resolvable, that authentic apologies can bring reconciliation, that forgiveness can be sought and offered (Tavistock Relationships 2016).

As workers with families we need to ask the 'actors' within the family to look at the possible path from hurt to forgiveness and if they can believe it is worth their time and emotional investment. What we need to resist doing is becoming the equivalent of the busy teacher who might ask both sides to make up through 'sorries' and forgiveness. We need also to hold in mind the complexity of the task, the emotional snakes and ladders that confront families when they are working on something very hard and painful.

The way we, as workers, ask questions and offer our thoughts about what is going on matters, in that we have some capacity for helping make complexity a little simpler or pain a little less sharp. It is the 'relational' aspect of our work that helps most effectively here, the bringing in of the other's standpoint and helping all to try and imagine what was going on in another's mind that allows for some of the relief that comes with understanding. A parental couple, raging with each other about one's lateness home from work and the other's lack of tolerance found some sympathy and generosity for each other when they really tried to imagine the pressures their partner felt. This did not in and of itself resolve their difficulties but it gave them a technique to reach for when they found communication hard going.

Throughout our lives we exchange apologies and forgiveness, sometimes in unthinking and socially defined ways, sometimes in great anguish and pain. It is always worth reflecting what we ourselves have learned and continue to learn from the experience of needing forgiveness and giving it ourselves. Around us are images of forgiveness, religious iconography and occasional news stories of astonishing people who forgive those who have killed their children. These families are those we carry round as a yardstick and measure ourselves against, knowing or worrying that if we stood in their shoes we would not be forgiving but baying for blood or capable of carrying out mad and bloody vendettas.

We rarely think of those who are implacably unforgiving and we see even fewer images of the unforgiven. They are represented by either the medieval dead being tormented in hell's fires or news clips and documentaries on war criminals or modern street gangs notorious for their unrelenting violence and utter contempt for the laws of nation or society. These are outcasts who have placed themselves far from any relationship with forgiveness; they stand beyond the pale, beyond the lands of civilisation and humanity, proud of their isolation. It is hard to imagine their minds, and most are so damaged by their experiences that any conversation on atonement, contrition and forgiveness would be incomprehensible. Perhaps it is not for them that forgiveness could be sought and found.

Some of the greatest writers of the 20th century were preoccupied by forgiveness, unsurprising after two world wars of hideous brutality. For the families we try to help, these great conversations are usually less of a preoccupation. In our work, we need to help those who feel that they have no choice but to endure a state of anger, a sense of injustice and a persistent desire for reparation. This state of heightened arousal can affect ordinary everyday activities, sleep and digestion. For some hurt and angry people, our most important job of work is to persuade them to release the rope that ties them to the injury. They may never experience the contrition of the person who hurt them but they may, using a ritual perhaps, use forgiveness to improve the quality of their life. For some it will be plain that they cannot forgive, particularly those who need some act of reparation. For these family members we can help by working to create a different story where they are able to exercise more power and agency, where they describe themselves as less broken and more hopeful, where a degree of understanding and acceptance stands in for forgiveness. This, for most people, will be good enough.

References

Bateman, A. and Fonagy, P. (2011) *Handbook of Mentalizing in Mental Health Practice.* Washington, DC: American Psychiatric Publishing Inc.

Carr, K. and Wang, T. (2012) 'Negotiating forgiveness in nonvoluntary family relationships.' *Communication Studies Theses, Dissertations, and Student Research.* Paper 18.

Cowan, P.A., Cowan, C.P., Pruett, M., Pruett, K. and Wong, J.J. (2009) 'Promoting fathers' engagement with children: preventive interventions for low-income families.' *Journal of Marriage and Family,* 71(3), 663–679.

Fincham, F., Paleari, G. and Regalia, C. (2002) 'Forgiveness in marriage: the role of relationship quality, attributions and empathy.' *Personal Relationships,* 9, 27–37.

Paleari, F.G., Regalia, C. and Fincham, F.D. (2009) 'Measuring offence-specific forgiveness in marriage: The Marital Offence-Specific Forgiveness Scale (MOFS).' *Psychological Assessment,* 21, 194–209.

Pincus, L. and Dare, C. (1980) *Secrets in the Family.* London: Faber and Faber.

Tavistock Relationships (2016) *Parents as Partners: a summary of findings.* Available at: http://tavistockrelationships.ac.uk/policy-research/policy-briefings/910-parents-as-partners-a-summary-of-findings-2016.

Chapter 13

BIRTH PARENTS, ADOPTION, IDENTITY AND FORGIVENESS

Amanda Boorman

Adoption has a life-changing impact on those involved. It is one of the most powerful interventions it is possible to make on behalf of a child. Being permanently severed from one's birth family as well as one's cultural and historical roots is, for adoptees, a situation within which they have little or no choice. It is life changing.

Current adoption systems differ from previous practices which, in general, would have been based on social morality around unmarried mothers. Now they will almost always have involved an assessment and judgement which deems a birth family unfit to parent safely. Within this process, neglect, abuse, addiction, mental illness, emotional harm and future risk of harm may have been cited as the cause of family breakdown and child protection interventions.

The psychology within this situation is complex and may involve anger from all parties. Anger from professionals who witness neglect and abuse or feel powerless to support properly without resources. Anger from adopters at the abuse or neglect perpetrated on their potential child. Anger from the adopted who lose so much. Anger from original families who lose loved ones, often after scant resources or lack of empathy for their personal or family situation.

Some of this anger may also stem from fear and shock at the enormity of the sad situations that become so life changing.

If this complex anger remains unresolved among those supporting a child it can unwittingly write an adoption script that becomes hard to challenge and create emotions that can ultimately colour an adoptee's sense of identity and self-worth. Similarly, if an adoptee is viewed as being angry rather than being grateful to be 'saved' from their first family, this shuts down communication and understanding.

To call for forgiveness in adoption could be seen as asking parties to forgive the unforgivable. The anger felt by all can seem justified and immovable. For adoptees, the dual emotions of anger and loss can cause a potent and potentially fixed position from which it may be hard to recover without fair and truthful acknowledgment from the parties responsible.

As a family that has been involved in the current British adoption system we have attempted to put forgiveness at the heart of our emotional lives. It has not been an easy nor a straightforward approach but it is one that we believe has brought up many opportunities to work at having healthy family relationships. From our personal learning and experience we feel we can support practice that places truth and forgiveness as not only a humane approach, but also as one that can be transformative to both adoptive family life and to the wider culture and politics of adoption in itself.

Recent adoption reforms under the Conservative government were launched by Martin Narey, the newly appointed ministerial adviser on adoption, and following his 2011 report *Adoption: a Blueprint for a Lost Generation*. The report, commissioned by *The Times* newspaper, highlighted his belief that adoptions needed to increase in numbers and that the adoption process should itself be without barriers that may cause delay.

Within the proceeding reforms, focus was placed on the marketing of children in the care system available for adoption, and the recruitment of adopters. Local authorities and adoption agencies received Department for Education funding as adoption reform grants to achieve these goals. Within this reform, £150 million was transferred from early intervention budgets. Early intervention policy and practice works towards preventing family breakdowns and avoiding care proceedings.

Criticism of the report and subsequent reform could include suggestions that it over-simplified several issues with its rhetoric. The use of language included concepts of children 'languishing' in care and social workers tolerating unacceptable levels of neglect and abuse due to them being inherently 'soft' on failing families and even anti-adoption. An overall feeling in the dialogue was that there are good parents waiting to take in the children of bad parents if only barriers could be removed. This failed to address the complexity of individual and cultural experiences, or question the effectiveness of adoption systems and practices as a whole.

Within the ongoing reforms, participation from adopted people and birth families relating to their emotional experiences of the adoption system was missing in favour of tackling recruitment figures and post-adoption support for adopters. This process sets up systems of inequality, which in themselves may mean that any open dialogue and empathy leading to opportunities for forgiveness are scarce.

In the rhetoric of adoption, the 'adoption triad' is often mentioned (see Figure 13.1). This describes the position of adoptees, birth parents and adopters. The triad is represented by a triangle with adoptee, birth parents and adopter making up a point or side each.

Figure 13.1: The adoption triad

It is more accurate to think of adoption as involving more than three parties and as a moving chain of events which therefore involves both individuals and complex systems acting and reacting within differing power relations.

The triad or triangle does not illustrate the wider political and cultural context within which adoption takes place, nor the emotional cost to some involved compared with others who are less affected emotionally.

The system of adoption would be better illustrated either by a linear table or an upside-down triangle that features the most powerful at the top and the less powerful at the bottom of the hierarchy (see Figure 13.2 for example).

Figure 13.2: The adoption triad (2)

Without acknowledging the power imbalances in the culture, methods and systems of adoption, it would be difficult to support a course of action that seeks to have forgiveness as its aim. For example, it might appear to a lay person that the main act of any forgiveness may have to come from an adoptee towards their birth parents, particularly if severance was due to neglect or abuse. However, if a birth parent was neglectful due to managing a mental illness while being powerless and unsupported by health and social care services, the adoptee would have every right to feel angry towards the systems of health and social care as well as the parent.

In order to further illustrate the complexity of a modern adoption system alongside the emotional complexity of adoption itself, we are, with consent, sharing our family history below as a case study. The areas where forgiveness were considered, needed or actively sought as a positive intervention are clear within the narrative.

Birth family

Diane has a learning difficulty and attended a special school as a child. When she was a few months old her father James was killed at sea. He was a fisherman and was the ship's mate. While fishing, his crew dragged up an old mine which exploded killing several of the men on board the ship. The story was covered by the press, and public memorials to the men took place.

Diane was the youngest child of James's four girls and her mother Margaret became widowed in her twenties.

It can be presumed that loss and grief may have affected her mother's parenting capacity and that becoming a single parent to four young children must have been a great struggle both financially and emotionally.

Diane reports being abused as a child by a male relative of her father's. As a young girl, she became difficult to manage for her family as her behaviour was viewed by them to be aggressive and challenging. At the age of 12, Diane was abused by a predatory male who also abused other young girls in her home town area. The police became involved in safeguarding the children. During the subsequent arrest of the perpetrator and the investigations, Diane told her mother about the abuse she had suffered at the hands of her relative, but her story was not believed.

Diane was placed into care at the age of 12 as her family felt unable to cope any longer with her anger. During her time in care she reported that she and other children were being abused by the children's home manager. Although nothing was done at the time, many years later an investigation was instigated by the police after other adult women came forward. As part of this investigation, Diane was asked to visit the now closed down children's home site and walk the investigators around the areas in which the abuse would have happened. No prosecution was achieved, as key witnesses dropped out from appearing in court. Diane has never had any abuse officially acknowledged nor has she had any counselling or apology as a result of being abused in care as a child.

As a vulnerable adult, Diane had relationships with violent men and also had a problem with alcohol to which she was extremely sensitive. Drinking caused her anger to become uncontrollable.

Diane lost her first child who was stillborn. She was estranged from her family, who found her offending behaviour within their communities difficult to manage. By this time, her oldest sister was in the local police force.

In her thirties, Diane met Frank, an older man, who rescued her from a violent partner. Despite a large age difference, they became a couple and had three children together – two boys and one girl.

Frank was a gentle man who had become a widower when his wife died suddenly of a heart attack. They had five grown-up children and had not been involved with the police or social care.

Frank was a very proud man. He was suspicious of social workers and non-compliant to any offers of intervention. He was very fearful that his children would be removed and face the same type of experiences that Diane had while in care. In some senses, he could be considered to be over-protective. In reality, he was angry and scared.

Frank taught Diane to read and write and, despite her difficult behaviours, he was a loyal and committed partner and father. Frank kept much of her abusive behaviour towards him secret as he was ashamed, and this resulted in him being alienated from his wider family. Diane reports that he never retaliated when she bullied him.

The three children were born close together. Diane struggled with parenting and the home atmosphere was both chaotic and frightening for the children. Diane frequently argued with neighbours in the street and was aggressive towards Frank in front of the children. The police were often called to the house and on many occasions the calls to police were made by Diane herself, pretending to be a complaining neighbour. Diane admits neglecting the children, often leaving them alone while she went out as a coping strategy. Records show very regular attendance at hospital with the children for minor ailments. This was clearly a cry for help.

Diane loved the children and Frank very much but was inconsistent in being able to express her affection in healthy ways. Her learning disability remained undiagnosed before removal of her children and she had no support from any learning disability services.

Before the permanent removal of all three children they were often removed by police into temporary foster care and rarely as a group of siblings. They had many moves in and out of emergency foster care. Sometimes the moves happened at the end of a school day without the children going home.

Extended family members attempted to support Diane with the children but as single mothers with small children of their own and little help available from the authorities, this was an impossible task.

Diane and Frank's middle child Jane, along with her brothers, was permanently removed into foster care at the age of four. She was separated from her siblings and her care plan was to be adopted.

The plan for her siblings was that her younger brother, then three years old, would be adopted and her older brother, then six years old, would go into local authority care.

Adopter

I was approved to adopt a child as a single mother following a year of assessments. As a qualified social worker, I was aware of some of the issues faced by women living in poverty as well as those with addiction and special needs. Adoption was a first choice for me and as far as I was aware I could become pregnant if I chose to. My choice to adopt did not result in me having to address the loss of any pregnancies or birth children. It was important to me that any birth family losing their child to me had been supported in every way possible and that adoption was the only viable option in the best interest of the child. I was assured by the adoption team involved that the parents were beyond help, non-cooperative and potentially dangerous were they to see me or Jane in public. At the point of placement, I had scant information about any extended family and no photographs of them or of Jane as a baby and toddler at home.

Jane was placed with me at the age of five with no plans for any birth family contact at all. After several weeks of placement, I came to the realisation that I could not effectively parent somebody else's child without having a clear understanding about the family history that came before. The reports on the birth family were fairly damning and little family history was included other than the addresses they had lived and the incidents leading to child protection interventions.

We were encouraged to keep our home location private and to avoid certain areas. There was an overriding opinion that Jane's parents may be a danger to us were they to see us in the street or find out our address.

The life-story book about Jane came from the foster carers caring for her directly before her placement for adoption. It was as if she was born when she arrived at their home. It contained pictures of occasions and outings that had taken place in the year she had been within the foster family. There was nothing from her birth parents and no photographs of relatives.

When asked to take Jane to do a 'goodbye' forever contact with her two brothers I questioned the lack of a plan for sibling contact. I found it extreme for three children, then aged four, five and seven, to be totally separated and have no connection with each other. They were isolated from one another, scattered geographically, and would each end up with a different surname, legally no longer related to one another.

Adoptee

On placement, Jane was a very anxious and angry child. Initially my thoughts and emotions were focused on blaming her difficulties on her mother. I felt very angry towards a parent who had caused so much distress and damage to such a young person. I could not imagine how anybody could be so 'evil'. Forgiveness was far from my mind.

Jane was a very open and friendly child and sought closeness and relationships despite her obvious difficulty in trusting those around her.

She expressed her distress in very challenging ways, including hurting herself and others. She was cruel to animals and was unable to be left alone with other young children.

Within the first six months of placement she had been permanently excluded from her first school for presenting with challenging behaviour and was struggling at a second.

Jane was very sensitive to any change in routine, could not comfortably be cared for by anybody except me and could not allow me to pay attention to anybody else. The worst upset for her would be caused by social work visits when she always believed the professionals were there to remove her.

In the first year of being placed with me most of my strategy and focus as a parent was attempting to manage her behaviour and seek support for her from adoption professionals. The spotlight was firmly on her as the problem rather than looking at the systems within which we were required to exist.

This approach was one that resulted in the pathologising of her difficulties and led her into complex areas of assessment of need and a complexity of possible diagnoses that ultimately failed to address the core emotions of grief, loss, anger and fear.

If these emotions could be recognised, validated and understood I felt it more likely that a path towards the consideration of forgiveness and healing could be forged.

Although I believed Jane's behaviour to be in line with her experience, it was hard to get professionals to address the matter of life history and identity as a potential solution.

I was able to overturn the decision to end contact with her brothers and we had begun to see them regularly. The relationships between them showed love but also insight into the lack of boundaries they had been given while they were living with their parents.

After the adoption order

Once the adoption order had gone through I decided to search for Jane's parents. My feeling was that her difficulties were in part due to the severance from her family and a total confusion about her identity and future safety. I could see some positives from her family within her and felt her capacity to love and be loved showed me something that could not have been instilled within a year of foster care.

I contacted post-adoption services and after some initial dismay and criticisms over my request for contact with the family, alongside months of unpleasant wrangling, it was agreed that I would be assisted to meet them. I did not discuss this with Jane at this stage as I felt I needed to assess them myself and without triggering her. I arranged to meet them at local authority offices with social workers present.

The meeting was nerve wracking but wholly positive and extremely emotional. I had expected to receive hostility at best, but received genuine warmth and openness. Within that moment, the seeds of forgiveness were planted on both sides.

Following on from my initial meeting with them we met on several occasions and independently of any professional services. This was partly due to the disapproval of support services around my decisions. During the visits I filmed messages from the parents for their children. Diane and Frank were able to give me the stories and histories of their families and also those of them as a couple with three children. The information was invaluable for me to better understand their circumstances and to understand Jane's needs.

Another effect of the openness was that I was given information that enabled me to feel empathy for their circumstances. As well as expressing shame at failing their children, they also expressed anger at the systems they had been involved with. In Diane's case this included care systems from her childhood.

With this information, I was able to prepare Jane to manage the emotions around talking about them as I knew I had informed answers to any questions she may ask.

These discussions led on to preparations towards seeing some photographs of them and then on to watching the films of them. Although Jane was only seven years old at this point she was able to understand the concept that her parents were unable to keep her safe but that they loved her. The films brought about an immediate change in her feelings of identity and her self esteem improved. I attempted to get therapeutic support for her during these periods of discussion but was unable to access any suitable services.

When Jane was eight years old I arranged for her to meet her parents again for the first time in four years. As she ran down a hotel corridor, arms outstretched towards them, the noise that came out of her as she screamed 'Mummy' was visceral and unedited.

On reflection

Jane and I continued to have regular meetings with both her siblings and her parents over the following years. I also reintroduced her oldest brother to his parents and arranged and supported letter-box contact with her youngest brother and his adoptive family.

We spent many significant occasions such as birthdays and Christmas as a group, and many positive family experiences were gained.

Although I had to closely supervise time we spent together to support Jane, I did not witness any inappropriate behaviour from either of her parents over many years. With my support, Diane was able to take advice on how to communicate effectively with her children and to apologise to them directly for her failings.

As Jane became older I was able to discuss more complex themes of forgiveness with her. There was always a clear and strong message from me that what had happened to her was unacceptable and she was happy to consider and discuss what it meant to forgive but not forget. She would articulate that although she wanted to see her parents and actively enjoyed being close to them, particularly her mum, her body would react with adrenaline in their presence. She expressed that the most difficult part for her of maintaining a relationship with her family was at the point of goodbyes. She was unable to trust that it was not the last time she would see them again.

We spoke openly as a group about how things led to crisis and Diane was honest about her experience as a child in a way that was age appropriate for Jane. As in any family, the family history was told in different ways and unfolded slowly as the children grew to adulthood.

It could be said that we represented the notion of the adoption triad, working through the relationships on all sides. There were, however, obvious limitations within this set up. It became very clear that within our individual histories were the impacts of the systems we had experienced both before and after coming together as a result of adoption.

We found that gaining professional support either emotionally or practically for the health of our ongoing relationships was very difficult and largely impossible. Without that, working towards forgiveness was harder and less clear.

The practice we experienced reflected the wider cultural and political messages about parents who are involved in the child protection system: that the permanent removal of a family's children signified such a level of 'badness' that it must be considered an ongoing risk to maintain any relationship with them.

While Jane had many assessments for her behavioural difficulties via educational psychologists, specialist therapeutic support for loss, anger and grief or proactive life-story and identity work was unavailable. We were also attempting to get Diane an assessment for her learning difficulty and some therapeutic support for her childhood experiences of abuse. (Diane finally got an assessment, diagnosis and support for having a learning difficulty when all her children had gone past the age of 18.)

In requesting this style of intervention, I was heavily criticised as an adoptive parent and Jane's needs often became lost in a constant dialogue of misunderstanding and frustration with professionals.

The result of not being able to get support was that, individually and as a group, we became angry and had unforgiving feelings towards services. We were dismayed with the systemic failure of adoption support systems to encourage forgiveness and reparation in the interests of children's rights to access their personal history as a means of forging healthy identities.

It is at this point that we became acutely aware of the irony that we could not easily forgive the systems that had neglected Diane and failed to support her in maintaining a relationship with her children. The same local authority that failed to care for her safely as a vulnerable child with a learning difficulty then removed her children with the decision that she was so bad that she must never see them again.

As an adopter, I found it hard to forgive a system that had encouraged me to accept there was good reason to severe Jane from her family and for me to put forward her life story that suggested her parents were beyond forgiveness.

Supporting forgiveness

For practitioners working with adopted children and their families it can be a daunting task to facilitate contact and, in particular, ongoing relationships between birth and adoptive families. Current adoption policy does not encourage openness in adoption and therefore resources are scarce around support for contact and complex relationships.

It can be difficult for adopters to cope emotionally with the thought of managing long-term connections to birth families, especially if they only have negative family history from the perspective of child protection documents.

Clearly there are cases where parents have been so dangerous and abusive that they are an ongoing risk to their children and severance is required for child protection. In these cases, forgiveness would be a very hard place to expect a person to reach. However, the question of exactly what circumstances should lead to the punishment of losing your children to another family forever should be asked by those with the power within the triad of the state, practitioners and adopters. This should be done in all individual cases and before the adoption order is made.

It is crucial that recordings not only reflect the difficulties and negative aspects of a family and its parents but also find some things to record that were positive.

Independent therapeutic social worker and practice educator Wendy Showell talks about practice which supports forgiveness:

> Don't display a negative, judgemental approach to parents when we're in case conferences – model for children that we may not like what somebody is doing but we understand the situation that has made them not resourceful enough to parent…even if it's just that the parents absolutely loved their child but were not able to do this, I think that's really important. (Showell 2017)

Based on our experience as a blended birth/adoptive family that has managed to find forgiveness of the systems and each other, we feel that we would have benefited from ongoing early years support to maintain relationships with each other in the best interest of the children. As an adopter, I would have appreciated a more rounded and thorough family history about Jane from the start, as well as a suggestion during the adoption process that I should meet her parents in order to make my own assessment on behalf of my family. I spent a long time feeling that Jane's mother in particular was beyond forgiveness. I would imagine Jane at the age of five would have sensed this from both social workers and myself.

Diane would have liked easier access to her local authority files and more detailed and accurate information about events leading up to her children's removal. She spent many years feeling angry at the lack of understanding and support towards her as an abused child and woman. Had she been able to go through a therapeutic process of being acknowledged and apologised to, as well as received empathic support as a learning disabled woman, she may have been able to parent more positively.

Alongside better access to information we would have liked therapeutic support, both individually and as a group, which encouraged truth, empathy and forgiveness where appropriate.

Although we actively requested this style of support we didn't receive it and the process of reparation was slower and less steady as a consequence. We feel practice using principles of restorative justice and family group conferencing alongside family and individual therapy with attachment and relationship at its core would have been in the best interests of the children.

Forgiveness has to be a process and it is different for every individual person and of course feelings may also change over time. It would never work to attempt to force a person to forgive to make others happy or because it's a 'good' thing to do. It can never be fake or forced as this could feel very uncomfortable at best and abusive at worst.

With the right support, however, services that can listen with empathy, validate angry and difficult feelings, record events with sensitivity, and practice in a non-defensive or judgemental manner are more likely to provide the circumstances where the seeds of forgiveness can be planted. Positive social care can be practised where a different view of circumstances can be considered and perhaps, if positive for the individuals involved, feelings of forgiveness can be acted on to improve the emotional lives and mental health of those involved.

As Dr Jenny Molloy, care leaver, author and patron of the British Association of Social Workers, says, 'We have to understand that to forgive is not to say that it was ok, but to free ourselves from the pain. We are reclaiming that power and saying to the world, we have a choice' (Guardian 2017).

References

Mattison, K. (2017) '"Now I feel free": why social workers must be ready to help care leavers forgive.' *The Guardian*. Available at https://www.theguardian.com/social-care-network/2017/jul/03/feel-free-social-workers-ready-help-care-leavers-forgive, last accessed 15 August 2018.

Chapter 14

FORGIVENESS AND END OF LIFE

Steve Nolan

Sara's father Bill had just died, and I was asked to go in to see her as she sat with him. Tearfully, she told me that her dad had been 'a difficult old bugger', who had left the family home when she and her brother were teenagers. After leaving, Bill had no contact with Sara or her brother for five years; as a consequence, Bill's relationship with his son had always been difficult, and they had not been in the same room with each other for over 20 years. In contrast, Sara had refused to give up contact with her father and, since his illness, she had persuaded first her brother then their mother to visit Bill in hospital. Initially, Sara's brother resisted the idea, but she told him, quite plainly, that he needed to see his father and sort things out, before it was too late: 'You can't put it right when he's six feet under!' So father and son met. The fact that, during their meeting, Bill didn't manage to say sorry to his son, was in keeping with the father he and his sister had known: 'He would never admit that he was wrong'. However, when Bill's ex-wife visited him, he managed to tell her that he had lots of regrets about his life. Sara reported that her mother was normally a very calm woman, but in response she became forceful in telling Bill that she had had a good life, that she had no regrets and that he should put the past behind him and regret nothing. In Sara's words, 'They had the conversation they should have had 25 years ago. But they had it there – in a hospital bed, on a medical ward.'

Sitting with Sara and her dead father, I was impressed by her honesty about their relationship and how, in the full knowledge of what her father had been, she had forgiven him, not finally on his deathbed, but *in vivo*. There was nothing conditional about Sara's forgiveness; it was not the one-off 'Now-you've-said-sorry-let's-put-it-all-behind-us-and-hope-you-will-be-different-from-now-on' kind of forgiveness, the kind that wipes the slate clean and starts afresh. Sara's forgiveness accepted that her father would never mend his ways, that he would never become the man she had wanted him to be, and that she remained open to being hurt by him in the future. Sara's forgiveness was unconditional, but it came from her realistic appreciation that this was how he was and this was how it would be, and that she could either live her life uneasily resenting this reality or she could acknowledge it and make the best of it. The authenticity of Sara's hospice vigil and her quiet tears testified that she had chosen the latter.

To the extent that she managed to forgive her father, Sara's forgiveness was an act of grace, to Bill certainly, but also, and perhaps equally importantly, to herself. And it was of a different kind to the forgiveness that was exchanged between her parents. Bill's inability to admit that he was wrong meant his admission to his ex-wife that he had lots of regrets was as close as he was likely to get to admitting guilt (in religious terminology, a confession of sin) and asking for forgiveness; in which case, his wife's response, that her life had been good and that he should put the past behind him, implied the forgiveness he needed. The difference between mother and daughter was that one had found some compensation for the way Bill had treated her, while the other forgave without expectation of anything in return. In each case, they cancelled his debt to them. Despite Bill's inability to apologise and ask forgiveness, Sara's act of grace addressed his unfinished business, and to that extent he achieved what some would consider a 'good death'.

The idea of a 'good death' has re-emerged after generations lost in the cultural unconscious. Promoted by the philosophy of hospice care and what has been termed the 'revival of death' (Walter 1994), in its modern form, a 'good death' seems to mean dying without pain and with other symptoms well controlled, in familiar surroundings and in the company of those we want close, and, most characteristically, 'being treated as an individual, with dignity and respect' (Department of Health 2008). The contemporary cultural emphasis on individualism means there are now 'no scripts when it comes to dying' (Beckerman 2006, p.54). This may be a great positive of modern dying: genuine, person-centred freedom that benefits each of us with personalised choices about how we want to be cared for in our dying and the way we want to be memorialised in our funeral. Yet, while personalised choice liberates some to die their own way, for those who are unprepared for their dying, it can overwhelm, bewilder or even paralyse their decision making. The question Tony Walter poses is urgent: 'With religion, community and family providing little instruction [about how to die and how to grieve], will people know how to determine their own exit from this world?' (Walter 1994, p.3). Yet it was not always this way.

In 14th-century Europe, the 'Black Death' pandemic (1346–1353) heightened medieval consciousness of death, claiming up to one in three of the population and focusing an awareness that divine judgement would fall on the individual sinner, rather than on the collective sin of humankind (Duclow 2015). To educate priests and laity, the Church began to sanction catechisms that included instruction on ministering to the sick and dying. By the mid-15th century, manuals on 'the art of dying' (Latin: *ars moriendi*) had been written and were in wide demand, the coincidental invention of printing presses making them easily available. An anonymously authored text, *Ars Moriendi*, was one such manual that was especially popular in its adapted shortened form as a collection of paired woodcuts, each pair illustrating the five temptations that a dying person must overcome as they face death. Of particular interest here is the depiction of the 'Temptation to Despair' and its partner the 'Triumph over Despair (hope for forgiveness)' (see Figures 14.1 and 14.2). In the first illustration of this pair, six horrific demons gather around the deathbed and taunt the dying soul with sins he has committed in his life. These include perjury, murder, fornication and avarice. Burdened by despair that his sin will finally carry him to hell, the dying soul looks gaunt and furrowed. However, in the second woodcut, he is calmed by visions of St Peter, St Paul and St Mary Magdalene, as he realises that, if the perjurer who betrayed Christ, the murderous persecutor of Christians and the one caught and publicly charged with fornication have been forgiven, then his sin is not beyond redemption. Turning to Christ crucified, the dying man finds forgiveness and his demons are vanquished.

Figure 14.1: Temptation to Despair   *Figure 14.2: Triumph over Despair (hope for forgiveness)*

Over generations, the *ars moriendi* literature evolved in step with developments in theology, but each iteration implicitly assumed that the dying person should be made aware that their end was close so that they could prepare themselves to make a good death. This is striking to contemporary readers, but medieval and pre-modern anxiety about one's fate in the afterlife was real, and advice always included an encouragement to 'humble ourselves before God, [and] be instant in prayer for the pardon of our sins past and present' (William Perkins 1595, cited in Autton 1966, p.14). For this reason, priests, ministers and close associates of the dying person were frequently provided with prayers appropriate to the deathbed.

Concern with the afterlife may no longer be the widely held priority it was in medieval dying, but the urgency around making choices at the end of life and the need for 'a common framework for [healthcare] communication' (Leget 2007, p.318) has prompted some to revisit the *ars moriendi* tradition (Leget 2007; Verhey 2011). Dutch ethicist Carlo Leget has attempted to update the tradition, on the premise that the ancient themes 'still play a pivotal role in the dying process' (Leget 2007, p.315). Leget finds the 'Temptation to Despair' and the 'Triumph over Despair (hope for forgiveness)' have continuing relevance in contemporary concern with 'forgiving and reconciling'. The intimidating threats of mocking demons may no longer trouble contemporary souls, but Leget argues, 'It is an important and good goal to strive at peace and harmony both with respect to the patient's inner life and the relation with his relatives' (Leget 2007, p.317).

The psychospiritual value of 'forgiving and reconciling' is attested by Peter Houghton. As a counsellor working with dying people, Houghton recalls that he had frequently counselled people to do 'last things': 'That is, wind up their lives, finish unfinished business, *make amends or apologise where necessary*, and say thank you. So when I realized I was going to die I decided to take my own advice' (Houghton 2001, p.19, emphasis added). Faced with his own imminent dying due to end-stage cardiomyopathy, Houghton took his own counsel and describes the impact apologising had on him:

> Apologizing…was a surprise, some felt things were in the past and had passed by. They were no longer alive to them as they were to me. Others thanked me and pointed out it was myself I harmed more than them. Still others felt there was nothing to forgive and never had been. It was confusing. Had I lived too long with the pain of bad things when they had really passed away? It gave me a new perspective. These things were over, were part of my life, made me more human, and they had not led to hatred as I thought but to renewal, even if I was the salutary lesson for that renewal. For the first time I felt able to accept myself, my life and not to worry about the darkness in it. (Houghton 2001, pp.20–21)

Houghton's words are striking. His apology, his asking for and receiving forgiveness from people he considered he had offended, liberated him from his anxiety about the darkness in his life. But perhaps what is most significant about Houghton's experience is the realisation that the forgiveness of others allowed him to forgive himself. It is telling that the impact of certain things he had done was felt more by him than those he thought he had offended, with the result that he lived for so long 'with the pain of bad things when they had really passed away'.

In reality, it is often it is easier to forgive others than it is to forgive ourselves; often the person I most need to forgive is *me*.

Perhaps the key to forgiving ourselves is, as Houghton found, in being forgiven by another. And this may be where medieval dying was at an advantage over contemporary dying. For although the medieval soul lived under the shadow of divine judgement, with its ever-present possibility of eternal hellish torment, the *ars moriendi* brought reassurance that, through the Church and its sacraments, God had mercifully provided a sure and certain means of salvation: forgiveness in Christ through priestly ministrations. Faithful medieval souls could ultimately be assured that, rightly appropriated, they would be forgiven by the divine Other.

Yet the psychospiritual dynamic of forgiveness at the end of life is not limited to medieval souls. The Christian narrative of forgiveness through Christ's atoning death still retains its power to liberate those it has shaped.

I sat with Janie in the hospice garden one hot summer's afternoon as she chain-smoked her way through her life story. Brought up in the Roman Catholicism she had inherited from her Irish father, Janie had recently discovered an unpretentious and welcoming Methodist church community that had taken an interest in her and her life. She liked the minister and had asked her to take her funeral service. To say that Janie's life had been difficult would be to gloss over the harshness of her hardship. Her mother, who had wanted to abort her, left Janie in no doubt that she preferred the children of her first marriage. The married man with whom Janie had a relationship physically abused her. Their toddler died in a freak accident, falling out of a moving car when an unsecured door suddenly swung open; unable to save the child, Janie understandably, but wrongly, blamed herself for the fatality. Separated from her child's father, she found love with a man who treated her kindly. They enjoyed several years together, but when he died suddenly from an aneurism, Janie again (wrongly) blamed herself, convinced herself that if he had been with someone else he would have lived. On top of all this emotional pain, Janie alluded to her multiple illnesses: cancer, diabetes and recent significant surgeries. Once more, she blamed herself, but Janie was also struggling to make sense of why God was allowing her to suffer so much: 'I know I was brought up Catholic, and I know all about "Catholic guilt". But why do I feel I need to make sense of it?' I heard Janie's question as expressing her sense that all that had happened had happened *to her* (rather than to her child or her partner) because she was a bad person! In Janie's mind, God was punishing her.

Rather than try to convince her that she was wrong to think in the way she did, I suggested to Janie that her 'Catholic guilt' might be eased if she made a confession. I explained that I could get a priest to come to see her or we could do it together. As I am a Baptist minister and, therefore, not a priest, this was an unorthodox suggestion, not strictly within the terms of the *ars moriendi*, but I was concerned that in waiting for him to arrive Janie would 'miss the moment'. As it was, Janie preferred to make her confession with me, so I suggested we start with a prayer together, then she could tell me her story and I would end with a prayer of forgiveness. As she began to speak, Janie interrupted herself and told me there was something that had troubled her for many years, something she had not told anyone before, something of which she felt ashamed and that she felt she needed to confess. I reassured Janie that she need only tell me what she felt she really wanted to. With that, Janie made her confession, and when she finished, I extemporised a prayer.

> Let's pray: In the name of the Father, and of the Son, and of the Holy Spirit. Let's be aware that here we are, sitting together outside on this lovely day, with the birds singing, and the flowers around, and we are in the presence of God. And he made us, and he understands us. He knows that we want to be loved, and that sometimes we meet people and things arise within us that seem beyond our control. But God loves you, Janie, and he doesn't judge you. He accepts you, and he forgives you, and so, in the name of Jesus, you are forgiven. A lot has happened in your life, Janie, a lot of very difficult, traumatic things; things that you are not responsible for. You *weren't* responsible for your husband's aneurism. And you *weren't* responsible for your child's accident. And you *weren't* responsible for your parents' separation. These things happened, and God knows that they happened, and his heart is broken for you. And so we pray now: Dear God, please be close to Janie. Let her know that you are close to her, that you

accept her and love her and forgive her. Let her feel your love, holding her and filling her, and let her know that she is free. In the name of the Father, and of the Son, and of the Holy Spirit. Amen.

Janie ended our prayer with, 'Thank you. That feels good.'

Janie's confession may have been unorthodox, but it was certainly in the spirit of the *ars moriendi* tradition as it intended to convey the psychospiritual benefit of forgiveness and reconciliation with the divine Other and facilitate her own inner peace and harmony. Although Janie was no longer a church-goer, she nonetheless had been shaped by the Christian narrative of forgiveness through the atoning death of Christ; in other words, it was her belief that God would forgive her sin and that she would be accepted by the divine Other. To that extent, her confession effected her experience of forgiveness – she felt herself forgiven and had a sense of inner peace. Had she been on her deathbed, she may very well have made a 'good death'.

For those not shaped by the Christian narrative of forgiveness, the non-religious analogue of acceptance by the divine Other is non-judgemental acceptance (what psychotherapists term unconditional positive regard) by a significant other or others. This was Houghton's experience; it was also Bill's experience. In their different ways both men received the grace of forgiveness from those they had, or believed they had, offended. It is only possible to guess at the psychospiritual effect this had on Bill, but Houghton is explicit: for the first time he felt able to accept himself and not worry about the darkness in his life (Houghton 2001). Similarly, giving her father the gift of unconditional forgiveness – a realistic forgiveness that did not pretend to forget – allowed Sara to accept her relationship with her father for what it was and let go of the darkness in his life.

References

Autton, N. (1966) *The Pastoral Care of the Dying* (The Library of Pastoral Care). London: SPCK.

Beckerman, D. (ed.) (2006) *How to Have a Good Death*. London: Dorling Kindersley.

Department of Health (2008) *End of Life Care Strategy – promoting high quality care for all adults at the end of life*. London: Department of Health.

Duclow, D. (2015) 'Ars moriendi.' *Online Encyclopedia of Death and Dying.* Available at: www.deathreference.com/A-Bi/Ars-Moriendi.html, accessed on 14/11/2015.

Houghton, P. (2001) *On Death, Dying and Not Dying.* London: Jessica Kingsley Pubishers.

Leget, C. (2007) 'Retrieving the *ars moriendi* tradition.' *Medicine, Health Care and Philosophy* 10(3), 313–319. See also, Leget, C. (2017) *Art of Living, Art of Dying: Spiritual Care for a Good Death.* London: Jessica Kingsley Publishers.

Verhey, A. (2011) *The Christian Art of Dying: Learning from Jesus.* Grand Rapids, MI: Eerdmans Publishing.

Walter, T. (1994) *The Revival of Death.* London and New York, NY: Routledge.

Chapter 15

FACE TO FACE WITH ENDLESS MERCY
How a Christian Community Forgives

Richard Carter

The Good News is that there is no relationship beyond mending in God's providence and good time, that the most final of separations, and that the most bitter of betrayals, will not stifle the possibility of resurrection.

Rowan Williams

There are defining moments in all our lives, moments which change things so that after the experience we know things will never be the same: moments which we return to in our memories and rewind, memories that can hurt like unhealed wounds, but which can also become the source of who we are and who we want to become.

In my own memory I return to Easter day 2003 and the three months which followed on the Island of Guadalcanal. It was the day we learned that one of the Brothers from our community, The Melanesian Brotherhood, which I served as chaplain, had been tortured and murdered by one of the militant militia. For the preceding years, our community had been working for peace. On this island of Guadalcanal, torn apart by fighting between two island groups, it was our Christian community that had for many become a symbol of hope. They alone had been able to cross the roadblocks and barricades. They had brought medical supplies, searched for the missing, protected those fleeing from the fighting, ferried the wounded to hospital, and carried back the dead for grieving relatives. They had even camped between enemy lines, visiting the camps of the militants, trying to awaken a consciousness that a better way was possible. It had seemed they had lived charmed lives. They had weaved their way through bullets unscathed. They had seemed to embody the faith of so many that God and goodness would prevail and that prayer was answered in a real and palpable way.

On the day we heard of Brother Nathaniel's murder everything changed. These Melanesian Brothers were as mortal as everyone else. There was no divine protection, just the reality of a young man bleeding to death in the misery and rain of the Weather Coast and no one there to help him. There was no miraculous intervention of the God of love. Six of the Melanesian Brothers went to search for him and they too were taken hostage and did not return. Our community, who previously the nation had looked to as the Christian peacemakers, were now being directly targeted, accused of being spies and collaborators themselves. The peace advocates had no one to advocate on their behalf.

What happens when actions have been committed that cannot be repaired or undone? What happens when we cannot see any way out or any way through? I suppose it is then that real faith begins. We begin to enter the really unknown, and it often doesn't feel heroic or holy at all. It's about trying to get through the flood of chaos and trying to keep those you care about from drowning, while trying to keep your own head above water. And part of that knowledge comes from the fear deep in the pit of your stomach; it is the realisation that actually you can never ever change what has happened, never turn back the clock. And in that sense there is no forgiveness. And yet there is knowledge too, deeper than I have ever known, that the love and the care we hold for one another is the only thing which can possibly redeem the future. And that knowledge night and day becomes our prayer.

After three months of waiting and praying we heard the news we had most feared: that the six brothers who had gone to look for Brother Nathaniel had also been killed on arrival. The day I heard,

I wrote a letter telling a little of the story of each one of those seven peacemakers and at the end of that letter I wrote these words:

> Of one thing I am certain. These seven peacemakers will live on in the hearts and minds of the community. Their sacrifice seems too great and hard to believe. Our community has been awake all night telling the stories of these Brothers and trying to come to terms with the enormity of their loss. And yet beneath the trauma there is a peace too – the knowledge that each of these young men believed in peace and in goodness. They knew there was a better way. They were prepared to oppose violence and prejudice and to risk much. At the end of the day they stand against all acts of brutality which are at present disfiguring our world and bravely and boldly and with love, lived what many proclaim only in words from the safety of a church. Oh how much the Anglican Church at this moment in time could learn from their witness. And when there are real issues of life and death at stake in our world, is not this what the Gospel should be?

I wrote those words trying to summon up hope and courage. My words were, at that moment, an act of defiance, claiming that those whose lives had been irreversibly lost were the victors. Perhaps I was whistling in the wind to escape the real force of the anguish. But somehow I knew I had to give voice to those who could no longer speak for themselves. The email I sent this message in from a small internet shop in Honiara got sent on by others around the world. It resulted in a wave of support and prayer which seemed to uphold us through the deluge. All I can say is that, 12 years on, the words I wrote are in fact more true than I could ever realise. These seven Brothers are constantly present in my soul. It is with them, if only I have the courage, that I want to stand too. There is a Cherokee story of a young man who comes to his elder and says, 'There are two wolves within me. One of them is wild and full of violence and hatred, the other is full of gentleness, compassion and love. I am fearful. Tell me, which of these wolves will win?' And the elder answers, 'Which one will you feed?'

The death of those seven Brothers was a horrific act of violence. Nothing will ever take that away or lessen that. The six Brothers who came to search for Brother Nathaniel were surrounded by a group of the militant leader Harold Keke's men where they came ashore on a beach on the Weather Coast of Guadalcanal. The militants' group was led by Ronnie Cawa, Keke's henchman. They shot Brother Robin Lindsay and Brother Francis Tofi dead. They shot Brother Alfred Hill in the arm and then beat him to death. They took the other three Brothers back to their camp where during the night they forced them to make confessions on a tape recorder saying that they were enemies of Keke. You can hear Ronnie Cawa shouting at them what to say. Then they lined them up in front of a single grave and shot them in the chest and buried them. One of their killers was only 15 years old. I can still feel the thick blackness and horror of that evil committed against these Brothers. But I can also remember Brother Francis Tofi's words to me the last time we met before he died, when I warned him his life was in danger. He said to me, 'I would be frightened to die if I was doing something which is evil but I am not frightened of dying doing something which is good.' I realised, then and now, that he had a greater courage than I, but somehow my calling was to live out of that goodness and bear witness to his life. The last word he wrote for me was the word 'courage'. Perhaps the stories we tell are not ever completely as they are, but as *we* are.

You see, this act of evil was carried out against a group of Brothers who had committed themselves to God. Their Christian story somehow had the means to transform this. I do not mean to make sense of the senselessness of brutality, but to reveal that that brutality does not have the last word. In our promises as Brothers we promise 'I want to live the Gospel, O Lord give me grace.' After their death it was as though the Gospel story continued. It was the Gospel itself which provided our community with the context to find a way forwards and provided a narrative shape that does not end with crucifixion. Was this just wishful thinking, trying to provide a story of redemption despite an unredeemable tragedy? Was this an attempt to close down the story rather than to be honest to its horror? I do not believe so. Strangely the word *forgiveness* did not greatly enter the narrative. But it was unquestionably forgiveness which was the journey we were on.

First, one's own forgiveness. Because the first thing that overwhelms you is your own sense of powerlessness; the haunting fear that you should have done more to stop the events that took place. As Chaplain of the community, I agonised that I had failed to protect the community I served. The pain of those who have died can enter into the marrow of your own life. I remember meeting Brother Caulton, who was one of the Brotherhood leaders I had always respected, in the vestry after I had celebrated Holy Communion. I told him that I felt broken after what had happened and that I felt like giving up for I had failed as a Brother. He replied that he had noticed I had lost my 'Spirit' but that this 'Spirit' was needed more than ever at this time. He told me to let go of my feelings of guilt. I realised that guilt was the right word. If forgiveness is to begin it must begin in us; in the place of my own weakness.

I remember feeling stripped down, as though this tragedy had torn away all pride, all pretence, and all illusion. Surprisingly in this poverty there was an invitation into relationship. God is there at the bottom of the fall. The grace that is forgiveness often begins at the point of nakedness and emptiness. But Brother Caulton's words were also correct in another important way because he said to me 'your Spirit is needed'. It was the realisation that I was not alone but part of a community, and just as the wound of this violence had been inflicted on all of us, so would the healing and the forgiveness need to be for all of us; this realisation gave me strength. We were the body of Christ. In the journey of forgiveness, each part of the body had a part to play. Our grief and loss were not individual, they were shared. And just as this community had been the source of strength through conflict, so we needed each other during the healing.

There was need to understand the meaning of God's mercy within our community itself as it found a way of coming to terms with this trauma. This was, for many, a profound transformation in their understanding of the Christian faith: Christ not as triumphant king, but the one who empties himself and is mocked and stripped and wounded by sin. The one who is with us, intimately with us, even in those experiences of complete abandonment. For the months we had believed that the Brothers were being held hostage, we had kept a vigil of prayer, night and day. It was those prayers which held us now, joined by the prayers of those from around the world. They grounded us and kept us close to the cross. Death was not a stranger to us as a community – rather something we had contemplated and knew intimately. We dug the graves of the Brothers with our own hands and waited for their bodies to return. The government declared a national day of mourning and as the police trucks carried their bodies the 16 miles from the cathedral, people came out to the side of the road to watch them pass. At the community motherhouse we assembled – hundreds of us – to welcome these martyred Brothers home. Brothers came forward and carried each coffin followed by grieving relatives. In our community chapel of St Mark's we told and sang the story of their lives and deaths. 'Blessed are the peacemakers for they shall be called the sons of God.'

Our faith had prepared us for such a time, with the daily offices of prayer, the simplicity, the Eucharist, the devotion and attentiveness to the things of Christ. At this funeral the huge crowds surged forward in a wave of grief and yet the Brotherhood, like bulwarks against this ocean of loss, contained this and gave it a form and a structure and a dignity. This was living Christianity – a faith that daily entered into our community through the pores of the skin; this was not an alien ritual, it was in our very bones. This was the Gospel, it continues beyond death. That night they lit candles around the fresh graves. Hundreds gathered and the community of our Brothers and then the Sisters sang deep into the night. This was not forgiveness, but the beginning of it, like land prepared. The word for 'buried' in Papua New Guinea Pidgin is 'planted'. We did not bury our Brothers, we planted them. We were saying with our words, with our rituals, with our songs, with our very love, that death has no dominion. And we were saying in the language of our faith that the brutality of those who had taken the lives of these brothers had not taken them or us from the God we serve; rather it had united us even more inseparably.

A funeral does not end the grief, it is a rite of passage along the way. I noticed the way some of our Brothers who had witnessed the brutality were distant and detached or unable to settle, and their pain belonged to all of us. Somehow their story needed to be expressed and heard. I arranged for a Jesuit priest and clinical psychologist Fr Peter Hosking, who had worked with victims of trauma in Vietnam, Cambodia and East Timor, and Felicity Rousseaux, who had worked in trauma counselling with Survivors of Torture to come from Melbourne. With them, we put together a programme to address the experiences we had been through. Peter and Felicity were quick to realise how different this situation was from working in a secular context. The Brotherhood had provided the tools and the structures of community for healing. We had to build on this, addressing the pain they had been through, able to use the Christian narrative and values of the Christian community which formed them. Praying, loving, healing, all go hand in hand.

We should not speak too quickly of forgiveness. Forgiveness may be the final destination but talking about forgiveness at an early stage may sound like an insult to the depth of the loss, trying to shortcut the pain. Forgiveness cannot be talked about by one who has not experienced the jagged, unreconciled loss. Beware ever telling someone that they must forgive. For it is like saying to the person that the pain within them is of their own making and the grief they feel in the pit of their stomach is their fault, something they must get over. It is like saying that the loss, the most unique, irreplaceable life, can be dismissed in a word. That is not forgiveness, that is continuing the torture. Forgiveness is not acceptance of evil; it is discovering a grace from beyond us to transcend even the worst evil. The journey is the journey to the place where you can see that the crucified is the risen one and that the crucifier is in fact the crucified. And where you can begin to say, 'Though as perpetrator you may have shown no mercy, I long for you to know what that mercy means.' But before you have arrived at that mercy you have to know that mercy of God yourself.

I had no desire to forgive those who showed no remorse. I was satisfied that Keke and Ronnie Cawa and those who had killed our Brothers had handed themselves over and were in prison for life. But I did not want revenge. What I wanted, more than anything, was to believe that the lives lost had not been in vain. I felt a deep aversion to violence and that to actually mirror the perpetrator in the longing to cause hurt to another was to let the perpetrator win. I recognised that there was a choice in all of this. Some of those who became Keke's henchmen were not innately evil, they could have become members of my own community schooled in the Gospel. Instead, they followed a different branch in the road; an almost negligible choice at first. Young men, with little opportunity, who were led to embrace a cause that gave them purpose and meaning. But rather than being schooled in prayer and compassion, they were being initiated into the paths of hatred. In this process of radicalisation, violence simultaneously made them prisoners of fear, but also offered the opportunity of power. A gun in their hands gave them perhaps the first power they had ever had: the power to terrorise, to change things, to kill. How could they do these things? They did them because they were conforming to the delusional narrative of those of whom they had become part. They did them because they feared humiliation themselves, and, having seen what was done to the enemy, were silenced by fear. They did it because they themselves had blood on their hands and once you yourself have become the murderer the only way forward is to believe the psychosis of the group that justifies your brutality and claims your horror as righteousness. In a conflict like this you witness the compulsive power in violence, a lustful brutality – an adrenalin and a hype that compels people into the savagery of a battlefield to do actions from which they will never escape or recover. They were, you could argue, simply following orders of their leaders, swept up into something they had not understood.

But we are changed by our actions. We can come to mirror the hatred of those who claim these murders as victory. No, I did not forgive these actions. How could I? But I pitied those who had carried them out. I could understand in my own soul, God forbid, how we enter the lie. And I could taste in my own stomach the fear that could prevent me from standing up to the mob and becoming the scapegoat myself. Was I not, too, the child in the playground who had feared being singled out or made the victim? Was I not, too, the one who had longed to conform, to make myself acceptable to those in power? Would I have had the courage to risk all, even the brutality of a lynch mob, to stand up to my accusers, ready to become the scapegoat rather than compliant in their narrative of hate? Both the crucified and the crucifier are not strangers. Etty Hillesum, who was imprisoned in Westerbork Nazi concentration camp, and died in Auschwitz, wrote, 'The rottenness of others is in us too... I really see no other solution than to turn inward and to root out the rottenness there. I can no longer believe we can change anything in the world unless we have first changed ourselves.'

We organised a retreat in our community for those who had witnessed the violence. We were a community, we had the strength of not being alone, we could bring healing to each other. We began to realise that the fears and traumas that isolated people could be shared and that there was a commonality. Our bodies and our minds were responding to events deeper than our conscious rationalisations. What were these common fears and traumas? The sense of an all-invasive fear, the belief that we were somehow to blame for what had happened; that in some there was an anger that was within that could not be controlled or explained; that they believed no one would ever understand; that the violence within us continued; that all that had happened was like a DVD forever repeating and replaying the brutality; that the nightmare did not end when we woke up. There was a sense of being withdrawn and that the life that continued around us was not something we were part of. There were those who felt the pain of being deeply wounded and believed these wounds would never heal; the projection of others' delusions onto them disturbed their sleeping and their thinking so that they were still prisoners. And to those of us who were numbed by all we had been through, life seemed far away; we felt like men underwater, unable to regain the surface; the sense that we would never be free; that forgiveness was impossible.

But alongside these symptoms of grief there were paths to healing: the need for and discovery of a safe space, the place of safety where life was no longer threatened; the constant reminder that it was over and that somehow we had got to the other side; the goodness and compassion of those around us; the realisation that there was a great strength in gentleness. Good food and drink could become a taste of restored communion, sharing with those who had been through similar situations and understood in their own bodies what we were experiencing. There was a sense that we could minister and heal one another, a sense that the simple things of life continued and we were part of them. The daily rhythm of prayer in the morning, evening and night was something to which we could constantly return – a continual reminder of God and the community's presence and participation in the healing work of God. Human love, laughter, tenderness and touch could be like a balm and antidote to the horror of violence. Our wounds were not simply signs of violence, they were also the signs of resurrection and we who had witnessed the pain were the ones who now had somehow been called as a community to live out the fullness of life of those whose lives had been taken from us, to live out of their life. Forgiveness is not a word, it is this journey to Emmaus. We have been given a narrative: the story of Christ. It is a story that we will go on telling and acting out, because it is the story of our own lives through death to the place of belonging. We have abandoned the God of miraculous power for the God of love and, astonishingly, in this exposed place, this place of seeming weakness, we have discovered his true power. Nothing is so powerful as mercy. Nothing is so merciful as true power.

I have never been back to visit Ronnie Cawa or Harold Keke in prison, although some of our Brothers have. Perhaps one day I will. I wish them no evil. I bear them no hate. I long for them to know the mercy and forgiveness of God as we have known it: undeserved, freely given, born in the darkest place, the place where we thought that nothing would ever grow again, but the place where resurrection begins. No, forgiveness is not a word which can shortcut the pain or cover up the loss. Forgiveness is the broken hands of Christ stretched out to the world. It cost him his life. It is our own hands, like those of the father of the lost son held out against the odds. Forgiveness is not formulaic. Neither is it earnt. It is not transactional... I will forgive you if you... Rather, it is undeserved; it is the astonishing movement of God, the one who runs towards us, the father of the lost son – the one who says to each one of us 'You are still my son. For a moment you turned away but I will raise you up and embrace you forever.'

Many years have passed since the death of my Brothers. But their death is also a resurrection to which I return daily. How can you forget that story of their courage and love across division, when all around us today there are still so many stories of violence, prejudice and hatred. In St Martin-in-the-Fields in London's Trafalgar Square where I have been a priest for the last ten years, I have had the privilege of helping to provide sanctuary and welcome for refugees and many people seeking God's healing and peace. I have come to realise the vital ministry of communicating in word, in music, through sacrament, in listening, in action and generous welcome, the mercy of God. We have so often taken for granted the very nature of what it means to be Church. Here, in our midst, we have the place and the means to provide the meeting place between the lost and the God who waits with outstretched hands.

Yesterday I met with a group of people at the Connection at St Martin's, which provides support for homeless and vulnerable people in London. This group is a weekly time we call 'Spiritual Space'. I asked them to imagine being a disciple coming early in the morning to the tomb of Jesus after they had just witnessed the agony of his death. And there coming towards them out of the light is Jesus Christ himself. 'What would you ask him?' I asked them, 'And what will he reply?' I was not sure if this contemplation would work. Perhaps it would seem like make-believe, a fantasy far removed from the tough reality of their lives, facing destitution where nothing was changed by magic. But quite the contrary. They had many questions to ask. What would their future be like? Why does bad stuff happen even when you are good? What was God's will for them? One person in the group's answers I cannot forget. He is quiet in the group. So quiet, in fact, that I wondered if he had registered my question or even knew what I was asking him to imagine. But he said this:

> 'Jesus held out his hands to me and I could see they were still bleeding. They were wounded hands.'

> 'What did you ask him?' I asked

> 'I asked him if I could bandage his hands. I wanted to bind up his hands to stop the blood.'

> 'What did Jesus reply?'

> 'He thanked me but said he needed to hold up his hands in order to bless me. Bless me like this with open wounded hands. He said that the blood was a sign of his love for me. He was showing me now. With these wounded hands he was blessing me.'

There is a choir of those who have sought asylum in the UK called Woven Gold. Many of them have been victims of torture and violence. One of the songs they sing has these words: 'All that has beaten has not beaten me. I am more than a survivor.' I have witnessed this truth so many times. I remember holding a small memorial service at St Martin-in-the-Fields for a Congolese mother and her family, who had just learned that the daughter had been murdered in the Congo while she had been trying to gain asylum so that her family could be united. And the mother asked me the same question we have often heard, 'What is the point of praying and of God if our prayers are not heard?' Yet here in this mother was both the question and the answer – a mother who was filled with the love of the God she questioned. And the prayer within me was that she, and indeed we who joined with her, would not give up that struggle to reveal God's mercy, for if we did, that would indeed be the victory of hatred.

At the memorial service for Beni Diza from the Congo, the victim of human brutality and war, we gather around the altar at St Martin-in-the-Fields, the young son and brother of Beni leaning on this holy table, looking up to watch a piece of bread broken – a sign of human brokenness and death which will be a sign, a sacrament of life and hope – and a cup of wine, Christ's blood – the sign of our forgiveness. And this Congolese family, led by their eight-year-old son, holding a flickering candle, lead us out of the Church into the light and we feel our hearts burning within us. This family, like lambs among wolves. Outside in St. James' Park the sun is shining, the Horse Guards march past, a band is playing, flags fly, and the balloons we have given the children rise up into a clear blue sky. This is the good news, the beginning of healing. God's mercy. The first shall be last and the last first. This mother, the very poorest, the most broken or the smallest child can become the bearer of Christ's love to the world.

In Rome, I meet a very old and dear friend of mine. Her husband, who was the same age as me, has recently died, and my friend's grief and love for him is palpable. On the one hand, she tells me she finds the organised church hard to stomach. It seems aloof, alien, cold, unable to respond to her suffering, and yet the churches around Rome are, she says, also the places she seeks sanctuary, to light a candle and open her soul to the enormity of life and death and the loss of the man she loves. She is seeking God's mercy. In the

Basilica of St Bartolomeo I too go in search of mercy. It is a place I feel I belong because one of the altars is dedicated to the Seven Melanesian Brotherhood Martyrs I knew and loved. On the altar, symbols of their lives have been placed: Robin's cross from around his neck on the chain I remember so well, Alfred's walking stick, Patteson's belt. I kneel and pray, feeling that here my prayers will be heard. These men who knew me so well, how could there be better intercessors? Karl Jung argued that conflict can never be resolved on the level at which it arises; at that level there is only a winner and a loser, not a reconciliation. The conflict, the grief, must be somehow got above, like seeing a storm from higher ground – a transfiguration. I pick up a postcard. It is a mosaic of the face of Christ. I search the church for the mosaic but cannot find it. 'Ci.Ci,' says the man selling the postcards when I point to the picture. He takes out a key and leads me up a stone staircase to an upper room and there hidden away is this big, beautiful, oval mosaic of Christ looking down, gentle and strong, the scriptures in his outstretched hands. The risen Christ, as though waiting for me, present in this upper room, above the pain and loss of the path through which we find him. It is the face of an endless mercy.

And what is the message when I go down those stairs that I must take back? Well, the scriptures are open in Jesus hand. In Latin they read 'I am the way, the truth and the life.' The temptation in our memories is to become locked in ourselves. But today Christ seems to speak beyond: 'Tell your friend, tell your congregation, tell your own heart,' this Christ seems to say, 'I have set you free, not to live in the labyrinths of regret for all that cannot be changed. No relationship is beyond my healing and mending. Your love has a present and a future tense, an eternity. I hold nothing against you. Since this is through my mercy, do not lose heart. Only my love can engender love, costly love, stronger than death. To know my resurrection is to recognise that nothing finally kills the possibility of forgiveness. So look up and around you and recognise my face in the faces of the community of your life. Then you will know the meaning of my forgiveness.'

I look up. I am face to face with endless mercy.

I am going to go back down the stairs and tell my friend who is grieving. I know there will be darkness again and there will be doubt. But it is good for a moment to be here in this place of transfiguration. And to know that seeking God means, first of all, letting yourself be found by God.

Chapter 16

FORGIVENESS, THE INDIVIDUAL AND THE CONFLICT SOCIETY

Graham Spencer and Lord John Alderdice

All through the night of 14 November 1940, the German Luftwaffe bombed Coventry and by the morning, despite the best efforts of its Provost, the Very Reverend Richard Howard, the 14th-century Cathedral of St Michael lay in ruins. Standing in the still-smoking ruins, he took a piece of chalk and wrote the words 'Father Forgive' on the smoke blackened wall of the sanctuary. Seeing the charred remains of two roof beams, which had fallen to the floor in a cruciform shape, Howard tied them together and had them raised above an altar of rubble for a later Sunday service. He took three bent and twisted nails that had come down with the medieval roof and made them into another cross, which has since become an iconic symbol of peace and reconciliation across the world. A few weeks later, on Christmas Day 1940, Provost Howard spoke on the radio of his commitment not to take revenge but, on the contrary, he promised forgiveness and reconciliation, declaring that he would work with those who had been enemies 'to build a kinder, more Christ-like world'. Coventry Cathedral has now one of the world's oldest religious-based centres for reconciliation.

It has lately become almost fashionable to make comments about forgiveness and reconciliation in the face of atrocities and attacks, and one could easily forget how startling his comments were at the time. He was, of course, speaking out of a faith in God guided by his followership of Jesus Christ, who from the cross two thousand years before, spoke those same words about his persecutors, 'Father, forgive them; they do not know what they are doing' (Luke 23:34, New English Bible (NEB)). Jesus had often spoken of forgiveness, and not just the forgiveness of man by God, but of the reciprocal forgiveness of man by man which was an essential element of his Gospel. Indeed, the model prayer that he gave to his disciples includes the passage 'Forgive us the wrong we have done, as we have forgiven those who have wronged us...' (Matthew 6:12, NEB).

Despite the passage of two millennia and the many generations of preachers of that Gospel, when Lord Longford turned his attention to writing the *Forgiveness of Man by Man* in 1989, he noted the paucity of systematic books on the subject. Much had been written about God's forgiveness of man, but, while it was much commented on, there was less serious examination of forgiveness as a characteristic of relationships between man and man. Even in the whole of the Standard Edition of the writings of Sigmund Freud (Stratchey and Freud 1974), who was one of history's most astute observers and analysts of human behaviour, there are only a handful of references to forgiveness. Freud was very sceptical that forgiveness, at least in the sense in which it was most commonly used, was either possible or healthy and, as Macaskill (2004) has noted, this was in spite of the fact that much psychotherapy and counselling involves dealing with the experiences of emotional pain as well other much more serious forms of interpersonal mistreatment. Until recently, most psychoanalysts seem to have followed suit and, deliberately or otherwise, overlooked serious examination of what forgiveness means in connection to resolving interpersonal difficulties, learning to move on, coming to terms with the past and letting go of hurt. And this is surprising given that all these point towards the problem of forgiveness. It may be that religious associations with forgiveness have left psychoanalysts uncomfortable about using the term or even referring to it, but in more recent times practitioners of other schools of psychodynamic psychotherapy have become more open to its exploration, especially when it is not defined through the lens of theological absolutism.

Psychotherapists of all schools have focused on the importance of ambivalence and how in interpersonal and intrapersonal relationships love and hate are always found in relation with each other, with a greater or lesser admixture, but nonetheless with neither of them observed in the context of what one might describe as 'pure culture'. This may be one of the misunderstandings that could deter the inclination to examine or interrogate forgiveness. Moreover, if forgiveness means to turn all negative thoughts and feelings into positive ones, it can quite reasonably be regarded as a reaction formation which is sustained by a refusal to engage with the angry side of one's personality – hate being replaced by love. In contrast, if the process of forgiveness is regarded as a gradual process of transformation, not from hate to love, but from a relationship that is poisoned by hate into one that is no longer characterised by such a negative preoccupation, then it becomes more understandable in psychological terms. This may be even more important when we consider associated large group phenomena, which are not merely the sum of the reactions of many individual people, but more often the functioning of people within a system that exerts its own dynamic and emotive determinants. In the same way that a person is made up of millions of individual cells and has capacities and functions that are beyond those of the cells as individual systems, so large groups have capacities and functions that go beyond the reactions and counter-reactions of individuals.

Yet most of the literature about forgiveness focuses on it as an expression of the individual response to suffering inflicted by another (Arendt 1958, p.241) and tends to highlight how for those who try to forgive, the struggle is invariably one of seeking to end a destructive tension between perpetrator and victim and reconfiguring that relationship away from pain and towards healing (North 1987). This is a transformation invariably inspired by efforts to prevent past pain from giving the victim–perpetrator relationship a destructive permanence, so ending any chance of the victim disassociating from its suffering hold.

Just how this happens remains a matter of considerable conjecture but speaking about the cognitive element of this process, Griswold contends that healing begins to take place when the 'why' of the victim shifts towards 'why' from the outlook of the perpetrator (Griswold 2009, p.105). In other words, where the pain of the victim begins to be seen in the light of the perceptions of the perpetrator – what did they think they were doing and why? Christ's words spoke of those who crucified Him not knowing what they were doing. While many of those who watched his final agonies taunted him, the response of the centurion who was watching was that Jesus was 'truly…a son of God' (Mark 15:39, NEB). In other words, by denying the humanity of the victim, the perpetrators lost some of their own humanity, whilst the centurion, by reflecting on the way that this crucified victim offered forgiveness and died in submission to God, was challenged and then transformed by the experience. Seen from this perspective, the act or gesture of forgiving from the victim may sometimes help (wittingly or unwittingly) to turn the perpetrator in on himself, to reflect on what he is doing or has done to another human being, and through that introspection enable him to see and reflect on the damage he has done to the 'other' *and* himself simultaneously. From this position, the victim–perpetrator relationship is recognised as an inextricable whole where, on reflection, the victim may come to acknowledge that the violation of his own humanity is evidence of an absence of humanity in the perpetrator and that his pain derives from that inhumanity, from a lack of being human.

The intensity of the victim–perpetrator relationship – cast as it is in the infliction of pain and defined by destructive power – is not just a matter of cognition, but of deep emotion. One would expect the perpetrator to find particular difficulty in accepting and confronting the humanity of his victim and similarly the victim would no doubt find it difficult to feel and think of their persecutor as human. Yet when the victim appears to be seeking and retaining a sense of hatred and a desire for vengeance (which is different from the wish for justice), the perpetrator may more easily avoid the need to confront his own inhumanity. Feeling the anger of the victim he may more easily rationalise his actions by way of the subsequent animosity he draws from the victim and which he uses as protection against the harsh reality of the horrible suffering he has brought to bear. Here, the possibility of the perpetrator facing up to the consequences of his actions is avoided precisely because he is able to use the victim's anger and wish for retribution to distance himself from the responsibility and consequences of hurting another. To put it another way, he is likely to use the animosity of the victim as a basis for avoiding apology, feeling shame and admitting guilt (it spares him pain). These comments should not be seen as a criticism of the victim who is unable or unwilling to forgive (which would surely add further pain and victimisation) but to note that there are consequences for not forgiving just as there are consequences for forgiving.

It is tempting to think that forgiving is in the interests of the healing of both parties and that it should always be portrayed as the implied natural end-stage of destructive relations, but is this the case? On this Marina Cantacuzino (2015), the founder of The Forgiveness Project, speaks about two views that appear self-evident but that she regards as mistaken and counter-productive. First, the notion that forgiveness is the natural and appropriate end-stage of the process of coming to terms with past hurts, and second, that the way to bring people to forgiveness is to talk about that pain. Her extensive experience, backed up by research evidence, suggests that while for some forgiveness is the route of healthy accommodation with a painful past, for others, to forgive is to abandon and betray friends and relatives who were injured or killed and to accept a moral relativism that they find repugnant. In addition, she has found that the more one talks about forgiveness to those struggling with their pain, the more difficult it becomes. This is a paradox overcome, in so far as it can be, by the telling of stories, especially by those who have themselves come through the suffering.

When a victim tries to embrace the process of forgiving in the context of, or in the wake of, intense suffering, there must be some engagement with the perception and memory of the pain, emotional and physical, and an attempt to think about that experience and memory in order to understand it in another light. From a cognitive perspective, such a transformation, if it were to happen, would require the reframing of pain within a new narrative or way of imagining that helps create distance from the suffering and despair. One way of doing this might involve the victim seeing the inextricability of the two opposing forces that lead to their pain – what we might call infliction and affliction – and see that release from the former is more likely to be achieved by re-imaging the latter. To forgive would therefore, if this action is pursued, appear to be about creating distance from pain by initiating and drawing from narratives that offer release from the recollections of action and control enforced by the perpetrator. In some cases, these may even be narratives or stories informed by others who have gone down the road of forgiveness. How this re-imagining might develop suggests not only a complex process of individual cognitive struggle, but also reckoning with a variety of conflicting emotional impulses that are neither straightforward nor predictable, and in some cases are likely to be affected by the perpetrator's reaction to their own abusive behaviour as much as the victim's inclination to forgive.

Here we come to the role of apologies and some aspects of restorative justice, which call less for the punishment of the offender and more for reparation, in so far as that is possible. Some of the damaging consequences of being a victim can result from a sense of powerlessness, of being 'at the mercy of' the powerful abuser, and where repeated thinking and ruminating reinforce that helplessness. There are other ways of transforming feeling helpless, such as when the victim identifies with the aggressor and becomes an abuser or perpetrator themselves – I am not powerless and in pain; I am the powerful one and I can inflict pain. The problem of helplessness may also be addressed and overcome in a more positive and nuanced way though when the offender (whether in the context of restorative justice or not) makes an apology in word and deed, and where reparative words and actions put the previously powerless victim in a position based no longer on feeling powerless, but with a new distinct sense of agency and empowerment.

Engel (2001) sets out three requirements for a meaningful process of apology:

- *Regret* for having caused the hurt or damage

- Acceptance of *responsibility* for the actions

- Willingness to *remedy* the situation.

She says that unless all three elements are present, the victim will sense that the apology is less than fulsome and honest, but that when all are present it becomes more possible for empathy to develop with the perpetrator, not least because he has shown recognition of the pain he has inflicted and has indicated a desire for change as a result. Nonetheless, even when accounting for the complexity of this relationship and the importance of the individuality of both the victim and the perpetrator, can we say convincingly that forgiveness is *only* a matter of individual decisions, beliefs, convictions, emotions and reactions?

As soon as we speak of restorative justice programmes we are implying the involvement of the wider community and its structures and formal relationships, and because of this perhaps we should ask whether forgiveness is an entirely internal matter or indeed whether powerful influences for good and bad forces lie outside the victim? To be more specific, what of the social conditions and circumstances in which hurt and potential forgiveness take place? Where is the space to forgive when society is divided in conflict and where the polarisations of loss and gain, along with the assertions of 'us and them', dominate understanding? We have already noted Marina Cantacuzino's observation that trying to press people towards forgiveness can be counter-productive and may even re-traumatise the victim, but if individuals, families and groups can obstruct forgiveness by being too eager to press for it, can they also stand more directly in the way of its emergence? In a society that is deeply divided by conflict and violence, the victim–perpetrator scenario often ends up with individual suffering being transformed or absorbed into communal suffering and used to demand punitive action against the opposing community from which the perpetrator comes and which should take responsibility for him. In social conflict, responsibility for individual actions quickly becomes a matter of organisational or communal motivation. Such motivations may be adopted not only by those who have been directly affected by pain but also by observers who, although not themselves suffering directly, still identify with the victim and may even on occasion exploit that identification to bolster moral certitude about the responsibility of 'the other' along with demands about what 'must be done'. In this instance, forgiveness is made more difficult because communal allegiances are heightened and incorporated into social discourses, which further entrench the intractability of division and conflict.

Where society is characterised by persistent and ominous strains of sectarianism, division and hatred expressed in words and actions become invariably read through the prism of conflicting terms of reference between the two sides, and elicit responses that tend to confirm rather than challenge the divergent tensions of communal and social identity. Individual action is primarily read as an extension of social and community loyalty, and forgiveness is perceived as a threat because it offers empathetic recognition of 'the other'. Such an inclination is usually felt to undermine the certainties that sustain group identity by keeping others outside the group and making imaginations of their dangerousness more convincing as a result. Because of this, the act (or perhaps more accurately, the process) of forgiveness can be seen as a danger to community cohesion, with the individual who forgives being regarded as worryingly uncritical towards those who inflicted the pain and who are invariably seen as the cause of conflict. By forgiving, the victim may be regarded as begging questions about identity and community commitment which can shake up the simple certainties of self-identification on which the unity of the community depends, and these certainties demand the exclusion of those not of the community who are easily scapegoated, discredited and even dehumanised.

This takes us to a further consideration – that of the identity of the large group or community. We have considered the individuals, whether victim or perpetrator, and how they may be affected and impacted by the larger group or society in which they live. But there are some emotive and behavioural tendencies that exist primarily as large-group phenomena. Fundamentalism, radicalisation and terrorism are all such examples. Even the so-called lone wolves believe themselves to be members of virtual groups. It is not just individuals or groups of individuals that can experience hurt, but whole groups of people may act in a particular way because of what has happened to their group, as distinct from them as individuals. At a relatively trivial level, millions of men around the world may be low in spirits on a Saturday evening because an internationally significant football team, such as Manchester United, loses an important game. Most of these men have never met each other, and many will never set foot in Manchester, but they function as a systemic entity and dealing with them requires recognition of and engagement with large-group emotive and behavioural processes. More significantly, large groups can have their own evolution or development, and when faced with a threat or crisis, may regress into primitive thinking and behaviour, exemplified by intolerance of the other and the collapsing of time so that past hurts are experienced as current injuries. Here, angry feelings that are unable to be expressed in words often, through symbols and rituals, lead to a breakdown into violence and, in the worst-case scenario, end with the chaos of war.

Provost Howard in Coventry was, of course, expressing forgiveness as a prophetic spokesman of his large group or community that had suffered assault and loss, and this is not quite the same thing as forgiveness in the individual context. He also took the road of forgiveness in time of war and was aware that the German attack was fully intended to wreak terrible havoc. Josef Goebbels, the Nazi Minister of Propaganda, had boasted, '...tomorrow morning Coventry will lie in smoke and ruins'. Yet it is precisely because of this potential to undermine the strict expectations and obligations of tribal and communal life that forgiveness can help challenge the intolerance that allows communities to disregard others and maintain a culture of fear and hate in the process. In a climate of communal division, such a move may be able to release the community from the trap of vengeance, but also poses a risk when it is taken to suggest a loss of commitment to love of one's own; where it threatens to discourage a loathing of the other and bring into question the polarisation that is essential to maintain community boundaries and so preserve emotive and physical distance from the enemy. On this point, one might even argue that pain and suffering are important to sustain collective suffering by keeping intact the justification for hostility and the integrity of the aggrieved community. As an example of this tension, Goebbels exemplifies the German reaction to the profound hurt and humiliation of defeat in the First World War and the continuing sore of the reparations and the Treaty of Versailles. In response, Provost Howard was attempting to break the cycle and find the space for a new way of thinking and relating, not between individuals, but between whole countries and even more widely.

Not being afforded the space to forgive can be a condemnation to continue existing in a past that makes pain inescapable and the infliction of more rather than less pain highly likely. As Arendt puts it 'Without being forgiven, released from the consequences of what we have done, our capacity to act would, as it were, be confined to one single deed from which we could never recover' (Arendt 1958, p.237). With this is mind, the desire to emphasise vengeance over forgiveness, as Arendt reminds us, encourages reciprocal actions that reinforce a culture of suffering. Those bound against forgiveness may be condemned to expected retribution and continuing pain. For Arendt, the value of forgiveness in this light arises because it 'is the only reaction which does not merely re-act but acts anew and unexpectedly, unconditioned by the act which provoked it and therefore freeing from its consequences both the one who forgives and the one who is forgiven' (Arendt 1958, p.241).

From this perspective, we might suggest that the propensity to forgive means being open to the prospect of renewal and disengagement (gradual or otherwise) from entrapment by the destructive consequences of pain. The presence of forgiveness, in a conflict, is therefore the presence of flexibility in a culture of rigidity, and points towards the possibility of change because of reflections and emotions which are now malleable rather than intransigent. This moment of culturally transmitted newness is also a means by which divisive communal order and sectarianism can start to become receptive to the politics of similarity and diversity and where social difference can be respected within a context of tolerance and expected mutual understanding, rather than split into dominating superior and inferior categorisations.

We cannot predict with any certainty that forgiveness will issue forth an early resolution of conflict, and let us not forget that Howard's remarks were made in 1940. The war had another five bloody years to run. Nevertheless, what is predictable is that in a culture of mistrust, loathing, hatred and dehumanisation, sectarian tendencies will flourish, because those tendencies contribute to the 'hardening of boundaries between groups' (Liechty and Clegg 2001, p.3), enabling distancing from others which may be reflected in a range of attitudes – from ignoring to humiliating – that emerge as the 'way of being in the world' of that community. The social discourse, the narratives that then dominate, will stress separation, threat and fear, and increasingly speak not only of an enemy outside, but a prospective and potentially dangerous enemy within, slipping from an embattled to a paranoid frame of reference. It is true that at an everyday level contrastive narratives have currency, but in a conflict they are largely framed within the kind of limits that reflect what Graham Sutherland (who designed the extraordinary tapestry in Coventry Cathedral) insightfully described as 'the precarious tensions of opposites' (Spencer 2014, p.411–419).

This discussion should not be taken to devalue or criticise a decision not to forgive, or indeed to suggest that 'unforgiveness' is not in itself worthy of deep consideration or examination (Brundholm 2008; Murphy 2005). We are simply making clear that the decision to forgive or not to forgive is one that may be made more or less likely depending on the social environment and dominant discourses that exist at any one time. We are also pointing out that the public articulation of forgiveness may cause significant problems when an individual's stance is interpreted as failing with regard to loyalty and keeping within the boundaries of the community. However, if the opportunity to forgive or even talk about the value of forgiveness is curtailed by a fear of considering the perspectives of the 'other' and a refusal to empathise, then this distance must invariably contribute to the persistence and pervasiveness of conflict psychology and so conflict society.

We have seen that any desire to transcend the limitations imposed by the conflict through statements or gestures which suggest a possible rejection of the stereotyping of differences and simplistic portrayals of the 'other side' brings risks. These may be less costly in societies that are not in conflict, though every society has those who show racist tendencies and loathing for those outside the boundaries of the dominant identity. But within a society embroiled in violent conflict, the repeated narratives and feelings of superiority (and inferiority) instil a way of thinking dependent on acute demarcations of good and bad, assert tight moral limits on what is acceptable and reinforce the view that others must be the primary cause of suffering. Within this landscape, the concept of 'victim' also serves as a useful device for mutual reinforcement of violent reaction and counter-reaction (Volkan 2013). In turn, the victim–perpetrator relationship is difficult to define when the perpetrator believes he has acted because of victimhood, so enabling retaliation to be displaced away from individual responsibility to the community and fused with the dynamics of the conflict itself. Indeed, in conflict societies, 'victim' and 'perpetrator' often function as interchangeable categorisations. Think of Jewish Israelis and Palestinians, where the responsibility for the infliction of pain is blurred into the wider social and political dimensions of dispute, violence and counter-reaction. In such circumstances, it is almost impossible to even talk about the value of forgiveness because the meaning of victim and perpetrator finds no common point of reference. It is used as part of the lexicon of conflict and as a driver for more conflict, not less (especially when both are interpreted through discourses about winning and losing). Moreover, each can be contested and used to reflect different understandings and expectations about experience and responsibility. Therefore, although those who wish to forgive are likely to carry the implications of this act personally (Spencer 2011), as a social discourse the concept of forgiveness becomes highly disputed and reliant on how each community sees its role (in comparison with the enemy) in the conflict.

But, if communities in conflict protect themselves by adopting moral certainties based on self-definitions of superiority that reflect moral expectations of community allegiance, then the logical extension of this is that they must see themselves as victims more than perpetrators, acting in self-defence against the immoral and destructive nature of others, who are necessarily and self-evidently perpetrators. And the deeper the fight, the more this same outlook will exist in the opposing community, adding to the struggle and to the complexity of claims about victimhood. Further, since neither community sees itself as the perpetrator of conflict, so each justifies violence as a legitimate reaction of self-defence against the violent and illegitimate 'other'. Because of this, in order facilitate any wider toleration for forgiveness as a means by which to help bring an end to conflict, the concept of victimhood must be challenged, since to persist with claims that the opposing community is the cause of the conflict and retaliating against others on that basis means that pain is merely transferred from one community to the other. In this environment, disputes about who the recipients of suffering and the owners of pain are inevitably mean further and sustained divisions about responsibility and expected reparations when violent conflict comes to an end. Then, without a wider social discourse on forgiveness, the past becomes the new battleground for conflict with all the potential demands for retribution, apology and shame that this entails.

Clearly, social discourse is influential in how individuals act and particularly in conflict societies when actions are interpreted much more as statements of communal identity. Perhaps, too, this question of identity must be approached more thoughtfully and sensitively in connection to wider debates and arguments about reconciliation in the post-conflict environment. But, ending the problems of division and difference which sustain conflict are, if anything, surely about the need to disengage from the conflictual way of 'being in the world' and this requires a re-imaging and reframing of suffering through new narratives that interpret relationships in new ways, moving from a struggle over victimhood towards a shared or common sense of suffering (Volf 2006). Finding ways out of conflict ultimately means a change in the culture, the identity, the very way of 'being in the world' of communities. It means re-examination of the 'victim' as a core part of communal identity, even when the external reality changes and the sense of 'who we are' is still informed by an old way of being. What may at one time have been an appropriate or at least understandable way of being becomes inappropriate, maladaptive and even self-destructive in the new context.

Change does not come easily or naturally just because the external political, legal and social reality has changed. Nor will it come about through external pressure or the mere passage of time. It will require new processes that allow for new stories, emerging opportunities, energising visions of what can be, all of which enable a profound and healthy change in the victim–perpetrator relationship so that it is no longer poisoned by the past. In some cases, and perhaps more than we expect, even forgiveness may be possible. For a community that has lived in conflict and sustained mutual hurting, this represents a path towards ending the humiliation, unfairness and entrapment of the past. In turn, the transition must be towards a shared future, a new collective moral sense and a route that leaves the destructiveness and pain of the past behind (Margalit 1996).

If some of the account we have given of forgiveness and the individual or the large group seems dry or complex and cerebral, perhaps a real-life example will be illuminating and enlivening. When one of us was Speaker of the Northern Ireland Assembly, he was approached with the request that he meet with chiefs and senior representatives of some North American first nation peoples. Uncertain about the reason for the request he nevertheless met with them at Parliament Buildings at Stormont in Belfast. The leaders described how they had come to the conclusion that one of the reasons why their people continued to suffer from problems with alcohol and drugs, with violence and abuse, and with a deep sense of alienation and unhappiness was because they had never found a way to forgive those of the ancestors of his people from the north of Ireland and south of Scotland who had come over to their country and treated them so badly. Accepting their concern, he asked why they were approaching him and they said that they wished to meet him as a representative of that historic community of people who had treated them badly and to have him witness them engage in a ritual of forgiveness in the Parliament Buildings. He responded positively and shortly afterwards a very moving ceremony was publicly celebrated with full regalia, singing and music in the Grand Hall of the Parliament Buildings. This led to further contacts and follow-up, and some ten years later there are significant signs of improvement for some of those peoples. Perhaps, in conclusion, we should remember that ultimately forgiveness is not a set of concepts but a change in the way of being of an individual or group that enables them to get beyond the pain of hurt, and that a meaningful ritual may make this more possible.

References

Arendt, H. (1958) *The Human Condition*. Chicago, IL: University of Chicago Press.

Brundholm, T. (2008) *Resentment's Virtue*. Philadelphia, PA: Temple University Press.

Cantacuzino, M. (2015) *The Forgiveness Project*. London: Jessica Kingsley Publishers.

Griswold, C.L. (2009) 'Forgiveness and Narrative.' In P. Godobo-Madikzela and C. Van Der Merwe (eds) *Memory, Narrative and Forgiveness*. Newcastle: Cambridge Scholars Publishing.

Engel, B. (2001) *The Power of Apology*. New York, NY: John Wiley & Sons Inc.

Liechty, J. and Clegg, C. (2001) *Moving Beyond Sectarianism*. Blackrock/Dublin: The Columba Press.

Longford, F.P., Earl of (1989) *Forgiveness of Man by Man*. Northhampton: Buchebroc Press.

Macaskill, A. (2004) 'The treatment of forgiveness in counselling and therapy.' *Counselling Psychology Review*, 20, 26–33.

Margalit, A. (1996) *The Decent Society*. Cambridge, MA: Harvard University Press.

Murphy, J. G. (2005) 'Forgiveness, Self-Respect and the Value of Resentment.' In E.L. Worthington Jr (ed.) *Handbook of Forgiveness*. London: Routledge.

North, J. (1987) 'Wrongdoing and forgiveness.' *Philosophy*, 62 (242), 409–508.

Spencer, G. (2011) *Forgiving and Remembering in Northern Ireland*. London: Continuum.

Spencer, G. (2014) 'Challenging Sectarianism.' In N. Hall, A. Corb, P. Giannasi and J.G.D. Grieve (eds) *The Routledge International Handbook of Hate Crime*. London: Routledge.

Stratchey, J. and Freud, A. (1974) *The Standard Edition of the Complete Psychological Works of Freud*. London: The Hogarth Press.

Volf, M. (2006) *The End of Memory*. Grand Rapids, MI: Eerdmans Publishing Company.

Volkan, V. (2013) *Enemies on the Couch*. Durham, NC: Pitchstone Publishing.

Quotations from the Bible are from the New English Bible (NEB).

Chapter 17

BEARING WITNESS
How the RESTORE Programme Helps Prisoners Change the Narrative of Their Lives

Marina Cantacuzino

One of the most surprising things I've learned during nearly a decade of delivering an offender rehabilitation programme in prisons in England and Wales is that in order to encourage prisoners to explore and embrace a more forgiving attitude towards themselves and others, it is often necessary to approach the subject from the opposite end of the spectrum – in other words, either by barely mentioning forgiveness at all or by first and foremost addressing the more urgent subjects of resentment, retaliation and revenge.

This is because when someone has been hurt or feels angry (and prisoners spend a lot of time feeling hurt, angry and victimised) it is important to provide a safe environment where people can express these often-inhibited negative emotions. Remorse or (self-) forgiveness is usually a secondary consideration. At the same time, it is also important not to push the need to forgive or over-emphasise the benefits of forgiveness. As the criminologist and Distinguished Professor at the Australian National University John Braithwaite eloquently wrote: 'Forgiveness is a gift victims can give. We destroy its power as a gift by making it a duty' (Braithwaite 2002, p.15). As founder of The Forgiveness Project, I have found myself having to tread carefully around this potentially explosive topic of forgiveness, because while I believe wholeheartedly in the healing power of forgiveness, I also know that if the topic is introduced prematurely or with too much force then it can easily become an obstacle or even an oppression.

That is why after three years of delivering a course for male prisoners, The Forgiveness Project decided to rebrand the programme as RESTORE, thus detaching it from the name of the charity. The name RESTORE felt much more appropriate, containing as it did the concept of recovery, restitution and repairing damaged relationships. Also, I had come to realise that even though the concept of 'forgiveness' in a prison context is extremely relevant, the word itself is so barnacled by notions of piety and self-abnegation that prisoners would often turn up on the course assuming we were a Christian organisation whose underlying purpose was to teach them how to forgive. Much time would then be spent explaining that the work had no faith bias and that while forgiveness was the lens through which we would explore true stories of personal transformation, there should never be an obligation to forgive or be forgiven.

Our aim is simply to create a safe space in which sharing life stories can help prisoners think about the impact of their actions on others, and thus rebuild their lives. RESTORE can be described as a three-day, intensive, story-sharing intervention that comes under the victim empathy umbrella. It uses restorative approaches to encourage offenders to explore concepts of forgiveness and reparation in a framework that fosters greater responsibility and accountability. We recognise that although convicted of offences, many offenders are themselves victims of abuse and violence and the course assists them in reconciling with their own pain as well as taking responsibility for the harm they have done to others. Using personal narratives as the stimulus for learning, the aim is to open offenders' minds to an alternative way of viewing themselves and the world around them, one that makes a crime-free life seem both attractive and attainable. Where appropriate and where possible, we also establish a pathway for offenders to go on to meet their victims in a face-to-face restorative justice meeting.

In our work with female prisoners, we have found the line between victim and offender is often blurred. For women, trust is therefore always a major issue. The way RESTORE facilitators have been able to win over that trust is by extending the course and introducing creative elements (art and poetry) in order to give expression to silence and peel away layers of resistance.

Inviting prisoners to listen to the stories of victims and survivors is the catalyst for change. But crucially these must be 'reconciling' or 'restorative' narratives – in other words, stories where the speaker has reconciled with the trauma of what happened, though not necessarily with the harmer(s). While pain is not ignored, the focus is on resilience and recovery. For example, Mary Foley tells of her devastation when her daughter Charlotte was killed aged 15 at a house party in 2005, but she also tells of how exchanging letters with the young woman serving a life sentence for the murder has helped her to heal. Foley says: 'I knew that if I didn't forgive, anger and bitterness would turn me into a person Charlotte would not have liked' (Foley 2010).

Often a prisoner's response to these healing narratives is voiced in words of astonishment, respect and inspiration. The inspiration comes from witnessing how reframing life experiences after a deep trauma not only requires considerable courage and imagination, but also opens up new possibilities. 'I have a stone heart and your story brought a tear to my eye,' was one prisoner's response to hearing Foley's story. Another wrote at the end of a course feedback form: 'I went in quite closed minded…as in "just another course" but the first morning kind of blew me away.'

The tone and content of the story told by RESTORE's storytellers are critical because a tale of hate will only engender more hate and close people's minds. I heard of an intervention some years back where relatives of drunk driving victims were invited by prison authorities to share their stories of pain and loss with offenders who had committed similar offences. The intention was to paint a picture of such devastation that the perpetrators would be shamed into never drinking and driving again. With the purpose being to prevent further harm, these victims did not hide their anger, despair, resentment or confusion. I am not suggesting that such emotions are unjustified or unreasonable, only that if you are trying to help offenders change their thought processes within a criminal justice setting then the 'scared straight' approach won't work. In this particular case it was no surprise to me that the prisoners were left with exactly the same emotions as the victims had arrived with – anger, despair, resentment and confusion.

A change in thinking only occurs with an open mind. Restorative narratives (real stories that emphasise forgiveness rather than revenge, or meaning-making rather than hopelessness) are much more likely to prize open a tightly shut mind, and are much more able to give people the inspiration to behave differently, than stories that emphasise hatred and vengeance. RESTORE also has an ex-offender sharing their own story of change, because giving prisoners a vision of what they might become is much more helpful than continually stressing what they have done wrong.

The key objective of RESTORE is to assist offenders in reconciling with the harm done to them (normally in childhood) and help them take responsibility for the harm they have done to others. Taking responsibility leads to self-empowerment and paves the way for taking constructive steps towards building better relationships. With women, the first step of self-empowerment is being able to break through the silence and start to speak their story. The concept of forgiveness is explored extensively during RESTORE through open, honest, heartfelt conversation as participants come to view forgiveness as redemption and as an opportunity to start afresh or reinvent themselves. Self-forgiveness means freeing yourself from old and destructive thinking patterns or opinions that no longer serve you. It opens up space for an alternative outlook, a new beginning. All indicators show that this in turn reduces re-offending behaviour as prisoners become more resourceful, adopting a vision for their future that does not involve crime.

It is probably apparent by now that The Forgiveness Project takes a nuanced approach to the concept of forgiveness. While our underlying aim is to use personal narratives to draw a line under the dogma of vengeance, our method is to explore rather than persuade, and we acknowledge there may be situations when it is neither possible nor desirable to forgive. The charity expresses no religious or moral agenda; it recognises there are no absolutes and no definitive answers, and the emphasis is always on inquiry rather than persuasion. The paradox of our offender work in both the male and female estate is that it is precisely in this open, non-prescriptive, unattached-to-outcome approach that hardened attitudes start to shift and people begin to gain real insight into themselves.

It is almost as if you have to give people the space to think and room to breathe before ideas around forgiveness can be confronted, articulated and embraced. Jane Sonntag, who at one time observed a RESTORE programme, wrote to me with these comments:

> The strength of the RESTORE workshop is that it does not deliberately lead either the victim storyteller or offender to a place of forgiveness, but allows each – in freedom – to meet and discuss issues related to crime, including responsibility, contrition and reconciliation. Alongside the facilitators' genuine commitment to the men, I was inspired and impressed by their constant and consistent demonstration of the absence of any emotional investment in the outcome. This gave the men a freedom to choose to be who they wanted to be or become.

Facilitation of RESTORE workshops adopts a 'leading by example' approach, neither didactic nor scripted but rather what learning theorists call 'modelling' (Bandura 1972), whereby behaviours, attitudes and identity-building factors are modelled by influential individuals – the pivotal role played in RESTORE by victims of crime and ex-offenders.

When cultural scientist Christina Straub examined and evaluated the effectiveness and impact of our work at Ashfield Young Offenders' Institute near Bristol (2013), she concluded:

> Acceptance and a non-judgemental attitude created an atmosphere of trust that encouraged prisoners to be honest and authentic. The group became a circle of confidants. Additionally, connections were forged between facilitators and participants during breaks between sessions. Providing hot drinks and biscuits created a frame for open encounters. (Straub 2013, p.13)

Straub also noted that since stepping out of the physical confines of prison was impossible, it was crucial to create a space that was as far removed from life in the cells as possible:

> This was something RESTORE continuously managed to achieve, as noted by a member of [the prison] staff stating, 'It was really good. It's been my eighth or ninth RESTORE and it never ceases to amaze me, when you get to the point when it does not feel as if you're in prison' (Fieldwork notes). (Straub 2013, p.14)

In a separate and independent evaluation conducted by Middlesex University's Forensic Psychological Services, researchers stated that participants would report how the safe environment created by RESTORE 'provided a rare opportunity for "pause", "calm" and "reflection"' (Adler and Mir 2012, p.25). Straub similarly notes:

> Perhaps the most important precondition that helped to set the scene for RESTORE as a place where you do not hurt each other by being disrespectful was the fact that at the start of the programme a complete stranger had stepped forward and exposed their rawest inner self. The person telling the first story (usually the victim) had already demonstrated what courage looks like. They would share highly sensitive and private experiences and emotions with the group – heartfelt empathy, connection and relationships could then be established on this basis. (Straub 2013, p.14)

One staff member at Ashfield noticed that the young men he worked with, who were normally tight-lipped and sullen, would engage with RESTORE in ways that astonished him. Referring to how the boys would listen and react to speakers' stories, he noted: 'You don't often get to see them responding and expressing empathy like that…there is not an opportunity to do it' (Staff interview Ashfield) (Straub 2013, p.12).

Since working in prisons I have come to recognise that prisoners' stories are mostly rooted in a ruined childhood and I have consistently and repeatedly witnessed how being exposed to victims' voices helps them identify and acknowledge their own pain as well empathise with the pain of others. Straub notes:

> Sometimes prisoners would note in their workbooks that they felt upset hearing the stories revolving around painful experiences and emotions like loss, fear, grief, or anger and rage. They often reminded them of their own stories [as victims] of hardship in life. One member of the group, for example, recalled how he felt 'really

upset because when [the victim] started telling her story about her son I was surprised that she didn't cry. I also felt heartbroken and didn't know what to say, I feel depressed remembering all of this.' On the other hand, they would also state how it made them feel calmer and happier to hear that even the most painful story could have a 'happy ending' with people finding peace and redemption through forgiveness ('I feel happy that I've done this project; I feel that before I judge someone for what they did to me or have done I can look on two different angles and see their point of view, so I can forgive them'). (Straub 2013, p.23)

During the workshop, as prisoners bear witness to these inspiring personal testimonies they are also asked to write reflections in their workbooks back in the privacy of their cells. This culminates in them sharing with the group some of the painful as well as redeeming events in their own lives, through creating their own lifeline on a single sheet of A3 paper. (A lifeline is a visual depiction of someone's life story using symbols, drawings, words and occasional phrases. It is a well-tested method to help offenders make sense of a life that may seem chaotic and unstructured.) For female prisoners, the use of creative arts became by far the most effective tool in supporting women to move away from crime and increase their desire to reform and make reparation.

The lifelines, workbooks and anonymous evaluation forms completed by all prisoners are both revealing and moving. Illiteracy is endemic in British prisons and yet at The Forgiveness Project offices in London we have shelf upon shelf of prisoners' writing – much of it articulate, beautifully written prose, but even those workbooks with broken sentences and sparse writing are no less powerful or meaningful. Themes which emerge again and again indicate that the cells and corridors of British prisons are overflowing with shame and remorse – offenders often long for an opportunity to make things right through apology or explanation. Many offenders fear that an apology would be inadequate and could never repair the harm. They seem to grasp the concept that forgiveness is particular and yet universal, that it brings relief and healing of painful feelings and broken relationships.

The RESTORE workshop is a model of learning, known as transformative learning, which encourages participants to observe and transform their perspective. Transformative learning acknowledges that true and sustainable behaviour change will only occur through the revision of 'world view'. Our world view represents a safety net; it helps us make sense of an unpredictable world and reinforces a feeling of certainty or control. In this way, world view transformation is never straightforward, and to a degree it always involves relinquishing the safety and security provided by an established former world view. The central method of RESTORE's transformative learning model is true stories, victims' stories and (ex)offenders' stories, all of them personal stories that are irrefutable and credible, and address deep emotional issues.

Perspective or 'world view' change usually happens slowly and incrementally as prisoners reflect, consider and verbalise new points of view, but it can occur more dramatically like a 'leap of faith'. For instance, it may stem from astonishment at hearing the story of a rape victim who has chosen to forgive her attacker because it is the only way she has found to free herself from the pain of the past. Some reflections from prisoners' workbooks spell this out. 'It made me emotional. It made me think of others in a way I have never done before.' 'Didn't really know what to expect but WOW what a mind-opening course, not just for me but for all in the group.' 'Before I wanted to really hurt the victim. Now I want to find out how the situation made him feel and say sorry.' 'The workshop has in a way softened me and the way I see things.' In short, by embracing a new world view, prisoners are able to break out of the cycle of retaliation, take responsibility for the harm they have done and learn to make amends.

Analysis of prisoners' workbooks and evaluation forms from RESTORE suggests that creating a safe space for open discussion and opportunities to consider concepts of forgiveness and reparation can change the way prisoners feel, speak and behave. It reveals that prisoners feel more emotionally open, shocked, moved, vulnerable, empathetic, supportive, supported, heard and understood by others. Participants in the programme say they feel less judgemental, more able to take a broader perspective and to challenge their negative thoughts. They express attitude change, for example revised views on the inevitability of their re-offending, and on the benefits of forgiveness over revenge; and many stress they wish to give back and restore, articulating a new desire to contribute to a wider community and even in some cases to mentor others.

In addition, staff and family members report that prisoners engage in different behaviours following participation in RESTORE; for example, they employ new levels of empathy, try to foster forgiveness of others and to forgive themselves. They begin to challenge their own anger, and no longer succumb to revenge desires, resisting or refusing to resort to violence.

Over the years of running RESTORE in British prisons we have found that prison staff who at the beginning of a course stand firmly on the side, often by the second or third day are drawn into the workshop and ask to get involved. At Ashfield Young Offenders' Institution (YOI) where we worked for three years (until it changed into an adult male sex offenders' prison) prison staff repeatedly expressed the desire and need to embed the ethos of the programme into the fabric of the prison. According to them, RESTORE's values of promoting forgiveness as a real alternative to retaliation and dealing with conflict in a restorative way would increase understanding and awareness between prisoners, as well as between prisoners and prison staff, and therefore increase safety on the wings. They felt there was a need to be 'empathetic and open' and recognised that RESTORE was doing exactly this.

However, staff at YOI Ashfield also recognised that the prison system was unforgiving and that their main strategy for maintaining security was to keep the emotions of the young offenders detached from their everyday contact with them. They also felt that an increased level of involvement with, and understanding of, prisoners was not included in their 'job description'. A clash of values was felt therefore between prison culture, which was about disconnection and being risk averse, and interventions like RESTORE, which promoted connection and mutual trust.

One staff member gave us an example of how she had to maintain boundaries within her work practice:

> You are not allowed to hug or anything like that; there is a general rule around hugging and you have to have personal safety. [But]

> I shake everybody's hands now, I know that seems a small thing but when lads come into our groups it's just 'Hi, alright, how are you?' And they sit down, but I noticed that you guys (RESTORE facilitators) shake everybody's hands as they walk in, as an introduction, and I feel it's a good way of showing them respect so they automatically know, ok this person is acknowledging me, they are respecting me, let's do this differently. So I take that on now because I definitely think that's a good way of starting a group. (Staff interview). (Straub 2013, p.18)

This gesture of shaking hands held symbolic value because it created physical connection and broke down barriers to make a different type of conversation possible.

Despite these fears and reservations, over and again I have seen prison officers moved and changed by their involvement with RESTORE. Starting out in purely a security role, some officers later ask to participate in the programme alongside the prisoners they serve. As a result, staff frequently tell us how they now have a better understanding of prisoners' backgrounds and needs. Staff also frequently report that RESTORE's values around looking at our mutual humanity, at what unites rather than separates us, could play an important role in building better staff–prisoner relationships that would ultimately promote enhanced levels of safety and order. Adler and Mir point out that:

> Staff and prisoners recognised that the workshops could change the dynamic between individual prisoners and officers and have a positive impact on the regime as a whole. Staff…clearly felt both that prisoners were changed and that this change could be carried forward into other domains within the regime, beyond RESTORE. (Adler and Mir 2012, p.37)

At HMP Parc in Wales we have even delivered RESTORE to 40 prison officers as part of a staff well-being initiative. Once again, just as with prisoners, the process succeeded in creating a safe space where people could reflect, connect, talk and heal. As one officer put it: 'Even though the guest speakers had such amazingly powerful stories, hearing my colleagues speak took the experience to the next level. I have felt happy, sad, joyous and relieved to find out the strength of the human spirit still alive and well in the British prison system.' A female officer commented: 'Every moment of every session has had a positive impact. Even the memories I blocked for 39 years.' And when asked how the process had changed him, another participant said: 'Loads of thoughts, such as changing my perception of others, more consideration to the people I work with, officers I mean as well as our clients!'

RESTORE's group process succeeds in breaking down differences and defences. Staff's professionalism is as much a steel fortress as is the expected macho culture of male prisoners or the voicelessness of female prisoners. You could define the RESTORE group as a sanctuary that protects and respects the individual's expressions of thoughts and emotions. A space is created where it is safe to share and show vulnerability, which can be daunting for prisoners since they do not want to lose face:

> Prisoners often highlighted the emotional impact of RESTORE, some of them noting that it was unusual for them to display strong emotion in prison as it didn't fit with the image that people typically maintain whilst in prison. ... Staff echoed and corroborated the idea that RESTORE can emotionally affect those prisoners who ordinarily present an image of strong, invulnerable masculinity. (Adler and Mir 2012, p.36)

My belief is that by looking at the world through a softer lens, a new frame of reference is created that is more reflective, perceptive and inclusive. In the case of prisoners, this shift is often expressed in terms of forgiveness. As one offender put it: 'Forgiveness is knowledge…because if you let go of the old stuff it leaves you free to receive the new.' And as another put it: 'Forgiveness is about opening the locked drawers of my life, examining and emptying the hurt of past wounds.' In time this may also mean that forgiveness rather than revenge becomes the predominant discourse and the more natural response to violence and conflict.

References

Adler, J.R. and Mir, M. (2012) *Evaluation of The Forgiveness Project Within Prisons.* Project Report. London: Forensic Psychological Services, Middlesex University.

Bandura, A. (1972) *Social Learning Theory.* New York, NY: General Learning Press.

Braithwaite, J. (2002) *Restorative Justice and Responsive Regulation.* Oxford: Oxford University Press.

Foley, M. (2010) 'Mary Foley (England)'. *The Forgiveness Project.* http://theforgivenessproject.com/stories/mary-foley-england, accessed 29/12/2017.

Straub, C. (2013) *Embedding RESTORE into the fabric of YOI Ashfield – Qualitative analysis of impact and effectiveness.* Evaluation report. Available at: http://theforgivenessproject.com/wp-content/uploads/2013/06/Evaluation-Report-YOI-Ashfield.pdf, accessed on 29/12/2017.

Chapter 18

ADDICTION AND FORGIVENESS

Christopher C.H. Cook and Wendy Dossett

The causes of addictive behaviour are complex and various, including genetic and biological factors as well as psychological and environmental causes. There are many pathways to addiction and it is not necessarily the case that anyone is to blame. However, problematic drinking and drug use, as well as other addictive behaviours, are not infrequently associated with the painful feelings that arise from unforgiveness, guilt and shame. The addicted person may be unable to forgive themselves, or others, or they may struggle with not being forgiven by others. Harm has been done which cannot be undone and, seemingly, the associated guilt and shame are indissoluble. Alcohol and other substances or behaviours seem to provide some kind of temporary relief and take away the pain. Of course, these are not effective ways of coping, particularly when viewed from the longer-term perspective. Even in the short term, the supposed grievances from which relief is sought may be excuses for, rather than real 'causes' of, addiction. Nonetheless, the association remains. Grievances of the past cannot be changed, forgiveness is hard to find, and patterns of addictive behaviour emerge as cause or consequence of a painful cycle of broken relationships, guilt and shame.

Whatever the causes of addiction, addictive behaviour also generates disharmony, moral irresponsibility and offences of diverse kinds which, as consequences rather than causes of the problem, make it difficult to find a way into recovery. Partners and spouses find it hard to forgive each other, children grow up unable to forgive parents or others who care for them, and the addicted person finds it above all hard to forgive themselves. All of this is perceived as a reason to drink more, or use more drugs, and the growing lack of trust feeds into a vicious circle in which the consequences of addiction fuel more addictive behaviour. The web of broken relationships, grievances and hurts can seem too tangled, too enmeshed, too tightly woven, for there ever to be any hope of a way out.

It is therefore not surprising that it has been suggested that forgiveness might play a valuable part in addiction treatment (Worthington, Mazzeo and Kliewer 2002; Lin *et al.* 2004; Scherer *et al.* 2012; Webb, Hirsch and Toussaint 2015). The evidence base for such interventions is still modest and forgiveness is often not seen as a central issue in addiction treatment. The literature of Alcoholics Anonymous (AA) certainly explores the need for forgiveness (Alcoholics Anonymous 2001, pp.78–79)[1] and the increase of the likelihood of forgiveness arising by working through the 12 Steps recovery programme. However, it is interesting to note that forgiveness is not explicitly named in the 12 Steps, whereas moral inventory, admitting wrongs, making amends and other practices are.

The question arises, then, as to whether or not forgiveness is truly important in understanding either causes or solutions to the problem of addictive disorders? It is not our intention to provide any definitive overall answer to this question. Rather, through the narratives and reflections of a number of self-identified alcoholics in recovery who have kindly shared their stories with us, we will seek to examine some of the facets of forgiveness and unforgiveness that emerge, at least in some individual stories, as important aspects of the experience of addiction and recovery.

The quotes used in this chapter to illustrate the problems of forgiveness associated with addiction are all drawn from the real-life experiences of members of AA who are now in recovery and who contributed their stories to the Higher Power Project (www.csargg.org.uk).[2] They are related in their own words, and

---

1   The *Big Book of Alcoholics Anonymous* was originally published in 1939. We have cited the fourth edition, published in 2001.

2   The HigherPower Project gratefully acknowledges the support of the Sir Halley Stewart Trust.

so the term 'alcoholic' is used as the form of self-identification customarily adopted within AA. It is recognised that this terminology is potentially stigmatising and prejudicial, and that 'person first' language is preferable when discussing those suffering with addiction issues. However, the recent shift away from such terminology fails to acknowledge the powerful act of *self-*identification undertaken by members of Alcoholic Anonymous. We consider it appropriate to allow our research participants to describe themselves. Differences of experience might also have emerged had we included the testimony of members of other groups – such as Narcotics Anonymous, or Gamblers Anonymous – although we note that the programme of recovery adopted by these groups is very similar to that of AA and that both substance and process or behavioural addictions are widely recognised to have many more similarities than differences. Confining ourselves to alcohol as a substance of addiction will simplify the discussion, while at the same time being illustrative of the wider problems of addiction to other drugs and behaviours.

Anonymity has been preserved, in accordance with both the traditions of AA, and the ethical demands of qualitative research. In order to further protect anonymity we have deliberately not identified which quotes were provided by which person, nor how many people in total have contributed these quotations. This has clearly disrupted the integrity of the stories that were related to us, but it is not our purpose to convey those stories in their entirety. Rather, we are focusing quite specifically on the theme of forgiveness, and closely related themes, as they emerge within those stories.

Where does it all start?

Leaving aside its precise aetiology, it seems obvious that difficult emotions both drive addictive behaviour, and addictive behaviour results in difficult emotions. Furthermore, the emotional life of a person suffering with addiction is both affected by and drives a complex personal life story in which damage to self and others becomes intertwined, situations become entrenched, cause and effect become densely entangled, and people are changed. A member of AA, a man in his fifties reflecting on his drinking after some years in recovery, wrote:

> Sadly, I had no idea why I was always in trouble. I had no sense of how separate I felt. I looked outwards, I pulled away more and more. At 16 I left home and took with me the knowledge that I was unforgivable. I proceeded to cross lines year by year. At the age of 48 my life was a sham. Deep down I felt wretched. The ability to mask it was all but gone. While I was alone, drinking in my flat, I would ruminate about my life. I could see clearly that I had lied and cheated every single person who had come into my life. I had used and abused friends and partners. It was unforgivable. Perhaps I was a sociopath or just simply bad.

By the time that the web has become this tangled it is no longer easily possible (if it is even possible at all) to establish clearly where the problem began. Even if its origins could be traced this would scarcely make it possible to disentangle the threads. We might say only that problematic drinking often seems to be associated with guilt and shame and unforgiveness at an early stage. Whether or not forgiveness or self-forgiveness could have halted the progression of the harmful behaviour years before can never be known.

Beginning recovery

Unlike some other approaches, AA considers abstinence as a prerequisite for recovery. Thus, in this context, the work of forgiveness can only begin when the drinking (or other addictive behaviour) has ended. A woman in her late forties told us:

> Pain and self-hatred (which is extreme lack of self-forgiveness) drove my drinking. Now I'm in recovery, no matter how extreme my emotions (and they still can be very difficult, especially around my childlessness), I would not use them to justify drinking. If I don't drink on them, I've got a chance of working on self-forgiveness, self-respect, balance, courage, on not being so driven by unconscious forces, and on being some use to others.

Those embarking on recovery having reached rock bottom often describe their lives as being 'unmanageable'. Relationships, jobs and careers, financial stability and legal standing have often been damaged or lost. In this complex situation of pain and addiction, no single act of forgiveness can offer healing. Indeed, it might not even be completely clear who needs to be forgiven, or for what. The phenomenon of blackout reported by many sufferers can mean they are genuinely unaware of acts of harm they may have perpetrated. They may also, for the same reason, be unaware of acts of harm perpetrated on them. The complexity of questions about who is responsible for harm done is confounded further by the presence of denial, minimisation and self-justification, which have become familiar and self-protecting patterns of thinking for the sufferer. Combine this with the overwhelming feelings of shame experienced at the very same time, and it becomes obvious that undoing this confusion will not be an easy task. Furthermore, we might legitimately ask more philosophical questions about freewill and agency in this context. The presence of addiction and associated harmful behaviours may not be best understood as being the consequences of personal choices, but as the result of powerful social, genetic and even political factors (Orford 2013). Another member of AA, reflecting back after some years, wrote about the early stages of her own recovery:

> My sponsor suggested that I took some time to write about times in my life when I had been hurt, as a starting point to begin to think about resentments. I found this difficult and confusing, because as a newly sober person, I had become completely unsure about how to understand the situations that had been so significant in my life. 'It's all my fault, I'm pathetic, let's have a drink' was a habitual line of thinking which was now no longer open to me.

It is easy to see how a natural response for sufferers to the presence of what AA calls 'resentments' is simply to drink. They report that drinking numbs the feelings of pain and hurt. People who drink irresponsibly are often, understandably, judged, criticised, controlled and even abandoned. Their behaviour invites this response, but the drinking person still has to somehow find ways to bear this hurtful treatment. Drinking is easy and effective (at least in the short term). For drinking to end, some other, equally powerful, strategy must be in place, or at least to emerge and strengthen over time. Forgiveness would appear to be the obvious solution. However, the accounts of those who spoke to us demonstrate that forgiveness is not simple, and in fact, there may be some cases where, for a range of reasons, it may not be appropriate or helpful. In other cases, honesty about the inability to find or offer forgiveness is the only way forward. As one person told us:

> It seems obvious, of course, that resentments are best addressed by forgiveness. Forgiveness certainly looked like something I ought to be working on. I listened to people in meetings who spoke about forgiveness, including one man who claimed to have forgiven his ex-wife for having an affair behind his back the previous year and then running away with her lover. I found this mystifying, but I didn't want to judge the man in question. People are mysteries to us after all, and who am I to say how he really felt? Yet I was deeply conflicted about my own experiences and for me to talk in such an easy or seemingly superficial way about forgiveness would have been inauthentic and insincere.

Certainly, such an honest admission seems better than any attempt to engage too quickly or too easily in something which may look like forgiveness, but which is actually far removed from it. Some writers on forgiveness (such as Bash 2007; Cherry 2012) have talked about the dangers of forgiveness that is too easy – 'forgiveness light' – and the stories that we received included examples of this kind.

> An early and immature attempt at forgiving and making amends (Steps 8 and 9)…involved wandering around saying 'sorry' to those that I had hurt and let down – based on the assumption that they would forgive me for everything immediately and gratefully accept me back into their lives.
>
> My thinking, behaviour (and ego!) hadn't really changed much – I'd worked on the first five steps in a treatment centre, but was still full of blame, resentment and fear. I had only paid cursory attention to personal change (Steps 6 and 7) because I didn't understand its importance, I didn't believe that I had much in the way of 'defects' anyway, nor that God would take them away, because I was agnostic and had no faith. I was in no fit state to really forgive.

However, to say that 'forgiveness light', or for that matter 'restitution light', are problematic, is not to say that forgiveness and genuine restitution will never be possible, nor that they may not play any part in recovery. For some, the process of undertaking Step 4 (a searching and fearless moral inventory of ourselves) leads to a realisation of personal responsibility for dysfunctional relationships in which the other party may previously have been entirely blamed. For the sufferer, realising and accepting that their own behaviour contributed in part to the harmful treatment they received can release the energy needed to understand, and to forgive.

> In Step 4, I had to look at my life from 'their' end of the telescope. Not mine. I never meant to hurt them, but I did. I had to imagine what it must have been like to live with me. They were hurt, frightened and let down. It was not surprising that they could be judgemental and heartless. Understanding my own part in the deterioration of these relationships enabled me to dial-down the blame and dial-up the forgiveness.

Continuing in recovery

If not drinking is a prerequisite for beginning work on forgiveness, then the subsequent work to be undertaken would appear to take many and varied forms.

Sometimes forgiveness is possible only with the help of others – something that is beyond our power to offer on our own, but which nonetheless becomes graciously possible through the support of others. One woman, writing of her experience of forgiving her father, whose drinking had caused great harm within her own life and family, found that forgiveness was an important part of her own recovery. She writes:

> For me, though, that 'ability' to forgive is not 'mine'. It's embedded in a community of forgiveness, made up primarily of my brother, sister and our partners, who have supported and helped each other shape our responses to difficult and sometimes dramatic situations. We all found the power to cope with Dad because we had each other.

Sometimes forgiveness is both possible and necessary, but requires a journey of thought that passes through treacherous and dangerous places before opening out again into a more pleasant landscape. Things get worse before they get better:

> Before I could sort out the wreckage of my life resulting from my addictive behaviour, I had to genuinely take stock of the nature and consequences of my behaviour towards others (Steps 4 and 5). This involved progressively becoming more honest about the part that I had played in the breakdown of relationships and where I had been dishonest, selfish, self-centred and inconsiderate. Eventually, I came to terms with the fact that I was largely the author of my own destruction, which led to profound feelings of guilt and shame (in addition to the intense feelings of fear and anger that I already felt). The support of my close friends in the Fellowship was invaluable at this time; they repeatedly told me that my behaviours were characteristic of the condition of alcoholism – that I was not an inherently bad person, just because I'd behaved badly. Before achieving anything further, I would need to accept and forgive myself.

Sometimes, and in happy contrast to this last example, forgiveness is easy:

> Forgiving my mother was easy because we loved each other deeply and I never really felt anything more than frustration towards her. She was a kind, caring and loving mother, who had exceptionally low confidence and self-esteem. She needed a lot of love, reassurance and support in order to struggle through life herself and I knew that she had been the very best mother that she could be.

On other occasions and in other settings, forgiveness is extremely difficult, and can only be accomplished through a willingness to change oneself, and to accept the complexity and ambiguity of life:

> Forgiving others and making amends was (and remains) sometimes difficult for me to handle, particularly when I'm convinced that I'm right and others are at fault. What has changed is that I've moved from a position of 'always being right' to one

of understanding that the polarised 'right' and 'wrong' approach seldom applies in real life – situations are usually complex and there are no absolutes, just different perspectives, values, standards and opinions in play.

A blanket assumption that forgiveness is an absolute goal, universally applicable in all circumstances, must be questioned. This woman's story below is one of healing that involves the considered and deliberate withholding of forgiveness. To forgive her abuser would, for her, imply a potential forgiveness of all other abusers, a move she cannot make. Aligning herself with other survivors seems central to her recovery from alcoholism. She indicates that self-blame had to end in order for her recovery to set in. Self-blame is a common avoidance coping strategy employed by victims of abuse, known to feed depression and addiction (Littleton and Breitkopf 2006). Perhaps forgiveness would feel too much like re-asserting the self-blame, which had taken so much work to undo. She says:

> I don't forgive my rapist. It would be wrong in my view to do so. I'm not just an individual. I'm a woman, and I stand in solidarity with others (regardless of gender) who have been abused. He abused his power, and caused damage to a young person, the reverberations of which are still felt 25 years later. Obviously, I don't think forgiveness means that 'what you did is ok with me,' and I understand the far more nuanced and psychologically healthy framings of forgiveness that might be practised in some circumstances, but even so, in this particular case, I steer clear of any thought of forgiveness. Like many other survivors of abuse, the most difficult thing for me to untangle was the truth that I was not at fault, and that the responsibility for what happened lay entirely with him.
>
> In my Step 4, my sponsor was very clear that I was not looking for 'my part' or 'my responsibility' for what happened to me that night, but I was looking for ways in which my coping mechanisms had distorted my personality, and contributed to my drinking. I knew that I drank partly because I was angry, but more because I was ashamed. I needed to face up to the fact that, yes, I had let other women down by not reporting it, and I needed to work on forgiving myself for that. For me, a big part of that work is my commitment to talking about it now, and including it in my

shares, in case it resonates for others. Most of all, I needed to stop using it as an excuse to drink, and the realisation that it *really* wasn't, in *any* way, 'my fault' was a big part of that. It has taken years of counselling, and of working the AA programme, to get to the point I am at with it. I now have a reasonable sense of security that this issue will not lead me back to a drink, though I am not complacent. But, in all honesty I am not sure what forgiveness would look like in this case. In other areas of my recovery I've been able to forgive, mostly because I have been able to see my part in the hurt I've experienced. This one really doesn't feel like mine to forgive. I've never wished my rapist any harm, though I do think he should have been made accountable for what he did, for the sake of all my fellow survivors everywhere and through history. He's dead now, so that can't happen. Interestingly though, I've had occasion to see how this aspect of my biography links me in a healing way to others. It would be wrong to say that I am grateful that I've been raped, that would be abominable in my view, but I'm profoundly grateful for the moments of connection with others, that wouldn't have happened had I not been raped. Our recoveries from alcoholism and sexual abuse spark off each other, and we can light the way for one another.

In other accounts, the experience of *being forgiven* is a mystery, a miracle and a joy, but by the same token also something that cannot be fully analysed, planned or understood:

By that time [my two children] finally came to accept that I wasn't drinking and that they could trust me to behave like a loving father and grandfather. The reparation of these relationships is one of the big joys of my recovery. We don't talk much about the past – although they are both able to laugh at my exploits when drinking. I'm not sure to what extent I've been forgiven. However, I do know that my new wife and I are an accepted and appreciated part of their lives and families, which feels like a minor miracle, and for which I'm immeasurably grateful.

People with addictions (whether in recovery or not) sometimes have amends made to them by others. When family members practice the AA programme they may consider it important to 'own' their part in difficulties and conflicts within the family. The practice of Step 9 ('We made direct amends to such people, except when to do so might injure them or others') may involve reparation being made to the person with the substance problem. This can be profoundly healing and can sometimes even catalyse recovery. Serious AA practitioners would say that while they might hope for such an outcome, it is not their motivation for undertaking it. Rather, their motivation is to do the right thing regardless of a self-interested outcome.

Here, a sponsor in AA explained to us how one of her sponsees made amends to her (story recorded with the agreement of both parties).

> My friend, who had been doing well for several months, had suddenly relapsed and gone AWOL [absent without leave]. Her mother rang me in despair. I was on holiday away from home and there was little I could do to help. I considered trying to come home because I was seriously worried. I did what I could by phone to try to help track her down, and to be as supportive as I could to her mother, but I feared the worst. My friend eventually turned up in hospital, thankfully not quite dead. She had been lucky.
>
> Over the subsequent weeks and months, as she got physically better, she picked up the programme again, and worked her way diligently through the steps with the seriousness of someone who knew her life depended on it. When she came to Step 9 she explained to me that I was on her list. This shocked me, as it would never have occurred to me that I should be. She explained that she had thought very deeply about what it must have been like for me, far away from home, meant to be getting some relaxation from my busy life, to be faced with the trauma of her relapse. She said she had thought about the awful anxiety and uncertainty about her whereabouts, the shock for me of visiting her in hospital when she was still so ill, and the frustration I must have felt after all the hours I had spent with her prior to the event. She said that she was deeply sorry and asked me to advise her what she might do to make amends. I was overwhelmed with feelings of love and respect for this woman, who had thought through my experience of her actions so deeply. I realised that I had probably never made

amends in quite this way, in a way that fully took into account the experience of the other person.

The experience marked a huge step forward in my own recovery (I was only about two years in at this point) and I realised the healing power of the programme at a deeper level. In relation to my friend, I had not realised there was anything to forgive. Addiction is an illness. I did not hold her (or anyone) responsible for her relapse. However, I could see how her articulation of amends was important to her, and forgiveness poured out of me. We agreed that her amends should be her daily commitment to practising the programme of recovery. She's still sober today and so am I. Her Step 9 has fed both our recoveries in profound ways.

Forgiveness in recovery is not only an individual matter. Institutions are affected by irresponsible drinking, and may also function as the locus of resentment or shame. The explanation of the Step 4 inventory in the main text of Alcoholics Anonymous (Alcoholics Anonymous 2001, p.65) asks practitioners to include institutions and organisations along with individuals, as they survey their lives for potential harm done. Here, someone describes their relationship with an employer, exploring the positive role of forgiveness received in the building of a new life in which greater integrity becomes possible.

> My performance at work had been seriously affected during the last few years of my drinking and I felt guilty about this. Once established in recovery, I was amazed to be approached by the organisation that I had worked for, asking me to do some work for them. This forgiving act was very important to me in building my new life and re-establishing my sense of self-worth. I was also able to repay the debt of time stolen from my employer by doing voluntary [work] in the same field – and I found that making amends in this indirect way dissipated my guilt around my past behaviour and promoted forgiveness all round.

In this example, we see the progressive nature of recovery. Only when recovery was established was the new offer made by the employer, and the guilt of the sufferer was transformed into positive and eudaimonic action. Making a distinction between what might become possible in later recovery that would have been unthinkable in early recovery seems important to some. In the next example, the development of honesty, self-knowledge and wisdom in a more mature recovery is evident.

> I sometimes think that it would be a good idea to put the record straight [with my ex-wife], but we've both moved on and it seems pointless and potentially dangerous to talk about the past now – we would almost certainly disagree on what happened and regress into resentments, self-justification and blame rather than forgive each other. I suspect that my true motive for wanting to 'put the record straight' is to bolster my stock with my children, who don't want to revisit the past anyway. So it's a bad idea! I guess that this has been a process of slowly forgetting and accepting rather than forgiving, but I no longer feel any negative emotions towards my ex-wife and wish her well, so it doesn't adversely affect my peace of mind or well-being.

The process of helping others in recovery therefore requires much wisdom concerning what is possible and what is desirable, but equally a willingness (at least sometimes) to confront failure to forgive. One AA sponsor, a member more experienced in recovery, seeking to help others in the early stages of their recovery, wrote:

> In my work as a sponsor in AA I have seen the consequences of the failure to forgive when forgiveness was appropriate, the power of resentments to destroy people's quality of life and ultimately their sobriety, and I've seen the negative consequences of premature forgiveness and people putting themselves under pressure to forgive the unforgiveable. I notice that women often suffer from the sense that they 'should' forgive, rather than looking at how the hurt they've suffered has driven them onwards into unhealthy behaviours over which they might have more power than they initially realise. Forgiveness and self-forgiveness certainly have an enormous part to play in turning the downward spiral of addiction into the upward spiral of recovery, but in my experience it's not straightforward, and it requires both continuous reflection and, importantly, occasional action.

Forgiveness is therefore a multifaceted and multifarious phenomenon in recovery and it is not possible to legislate regarding whether, when or how it should be invoked. Perhaps this is why the 12 Steps employ a different vocabulary and prefer to break the process down into its component parts. The steps also focus much more on responsibility for admitting one's own failings and finding willingness to change than on forgiving others, or focusing in any way on their behaviour. The literature says 'Putting out of our minds the wrongs others had done, we resolutely looked for our own mistakes. Where had we been selfish, dishonest, self-seeking and frightened?' (Alcoholics Anonymous 2001, p.67). A common informal injunction in AA is to 'avoid taking other people's inventories' and to focus on 'sweeping my side of the street'.

But acknowledging one's own failings and finding willingness to change and be changed (Steps 4 to 10) are not only a matter of forgiving others or being forgiven. Inevitably, they involve forgiving oneself as well. Forgiving oneself, forgiving others, and finding forgiveness from others, are all complexly interrelated:

> I would not have had the opportunity to learn to forgive without the experience of being 'unforgivable'. Perhaps by showing forgiveness we can spread forgiveness. But on a personal level, I would hope to be able to forgive both of my parents, purely because I want my son to have the ability to forgive me. I did my best for him – I really did and I still do.

> I live my life very differently today; I am able to forgive myself for my past. I did harm a lot of people. Sometimes that was deliberate. But, it's what I see today, 'Hurt people go on hurting people' and that was me.

Reflections and conclusions

The themes of the wider forgiveness literature would appear to be borne out by the accounts of forgiveness in recovery from addiction that we have considered here. Forgiveness can be easy – sometimes too easy. Forgiveness can be difficult to the point of impossibility. In some situations, forgiveness may not even be desirable, helpful or wise. Forgiveness may be mysterious and hard to fathom.

Forgiveness may be miraculous. But forgiveness often also seems to be bound up with processes of recovery, reconciliation and restitution. Ernie Kurtz and Bill White (2015), building on decades of research into a wide range of recovery modalities, named forgiveness as one of six dimensions of recovery spirituality (the others being 'release', 'gratitude', 'tolerance', 'humility' and 'being at home').

We cannot require people to forgive us, we cannot always forgive ourselves, and forgiving others might prove to be just too hard even to countenance. But willingness to be changed, to be made open to the possibility of forgiving and being forgiven, does seem, as Kurtz and White demonstrate, to be an important part of recovery from addiction.

References

Alcoholics Anonymous (2001) *The Big Book of Alcoholics Anonymous (4th edn)*. New York, NY: AA World Services Inc.

Bash, A. (2007) *Forgiveness and Christian Ethics*. Cambridge: Cambridge University Press.

Cherry, S. (2012) *Healing Agony: Re-Imagining Forgiveness*. London: Continuum.

Kurtz, E. and White, W. (2015) Recovery Spirituality. *Religions*, 6, 58–81.

Lin, W.F., Mack, D., Enright, R.D., Krahn, D. and Baskin, T.W. (2004) 'Effects of forgiveness therapy on anger, mood, and vulnerability to substance use among inpatient substance-dependent clients.' *Journal of Consulting and Clinical Psychology*, 72, 1114–1121.

Littleton, H. and Breitkof, C. (2006) 'Coping with the Experience of Rape.' *Psychology of Women Quarterly*, 30, 1, 106–116.

Orford, J. (2013) *Power, Powerlessness and Addiction*. Cambridge: Cambridge University Press.

Scherer, M., Worthington, E.L., Hook, J.N., Campana, K.L., West, S.L. and Gartner, A.L. (2012) 'Forgiveness and cohesion in familial perceptions of alcohol misuse.' *Journal of Counseling and Development*, 90, 160–168.

Webb, J.R., Hirsch, J.K. and Toussaint, L. (2015) 'Forgiveness as a positive psychotherapy for addiction and suicide: theory, research, and practice.' *Spirituality in Clinical Practice*, 2, 48–60.

Worthington, E.L., Mazzeo, S.E. and Kliewer, W.L. (2002) 'Addiction and eating disorders, unforgiveness and forgiveness.' *Journal of Psychology and Christianity*, 21, 257–261.

Chapter 19

CONCLUDING
REFLECTIONS

Liz Gulliford

This is a very rich volume which takes current thinking about forgiveness into increasingly complex terrain. While it would be impossible to address all of the many important topics raised by the contributors in this closing chapter, I have selected a number of key themes in order to create a synthesis of the best insights the book has to offer. In my opinion, one of the greatest assets this collection extends is a critical examination of self-forgiveness, a concept that has divided scholarly opinion. Another key theme is the failings of individuals and the failures and limitations of the systems in which their actions are embedded. A great many chapters in this volume reveal the critical interplay between these elements. A third theme recognises power imbalances between actors that impact on the human experience of giving and receiving forgiveness, while a fourth weighs the reasons for our ambivalence towards the concept of forgiveness. Possible alternatives to forgiveness are examined in many chapters across the collection, constituting the fifth theme on which I elaborate below. The practical question of how to promote forgiveness, which links to what we see as the final ground of forgiveness, is examined in closing.

Self-forgiveness

A major theme to emerge from the chapters of this collection is the difficult topic of self-forgiveness. Some people regard the idea of self-forgiveness as indulgent – they believe that only the offended party has the right to forgive. Other people see self-forgiveness as a logical impossibility; the structure of forgiveness requires that there be an offender and an offended party – the two cannot be one and the same person. In contrast to those who regard self-forgiveness as nonsensical or self-indulgent, a great many people see it as a necessary and intrinsic aspect of the hard-won course of forgiveness.

Cherry's thought provoking chapter offers an excellent synthesis of literature on self-forgiveness and tries to construct a useful concept of self-forgiveness. He hits the mark when he notes that there are 'species' of self-forgiveness, some of which might be 'cheap, hypocritical, unwise and unhelpful'. However, alongside this manifestation of self-forgiveness is a deeper, more reflective and self-aware approach toward forgiving oneself. Moreover, interpersonal forgiveness is often cheap and insincere; people *pretend* to have forgiven others for self-serving and self-deceiving reasons. As such, the accusation that self-forgiveness is any *worse* in this respect is misguided. Cherry seems to be right when he identifies the problem of self-forgiveness as when it is seen as an '*alternative* to other forms of forgiveness' rather than an 'a necessary *adjunct* in some cases, and in others a necessary *preliminary* to other forms of forgiveness'. It is not difficult to imagine a violation in which someone's whole sense of self-identity is called into question. In such cases, self-forgiveness would be an important means of becoming at one with oneself. Self-forgiveness can be virtuous and valuable because it 're-moralises' people, allowing them to admit and move on from their shortcomings. In some cases, this process may go a long way towards preventing similar mistakes in the future. In others, it offers a means of letting go of genuinely unavoidable failings.

Bowman's chapter demonstrates the necessity of self-forgiveness in a profession where mistakes are an inevitable part of diagnosis and treatment. Doctors and other health professionals do their best for patients, though errors of judgement and procedure unfortunately and inevitably occur. Diagnosis involves probabilistic reasoning – a rare brain tumour might well be misdiagnosed as something simply more *likely* to occur. Doctors work with a great number of unknowns. While victims and their relatives call for reassurances that such mistakes can never happen again, the unpalatable truth is that no promises can ever be made. In this context, self-forgiveness may offer a means through which medical professionals can – though not without difficulty – begin to let go of self-judgement and continue in their professional practice.

This 'letting go' of self-forgiveness is also a theme in the chapter by Liebmann, who recounts the story of Kevin, a lifer who spent 14 years in prison for murder. Kevin was overwhelmed that the victim's husband had no objections to his being released – a reaction Kevin said 'felt like seeing God'. Although Kevin worked on apologising to the victim's husband, in the end he felt this seemed insignificant; 'the only way forward was to forgive myself and try to live a better life'.

Cooper and Nolan both see forgiving others and forgiving oneself as intimately interconnected processes. For Cooper, the beginning of forgiving other people is learning to forgive oneself. However, Nolan conceives of self-forgiveness – a particularly important theme at the end of life – as being potentiated by having received forgiveness from others. Suffice it to say there is a connection between authentic self-forgiveness and other-forgiveness – a theme which is also picked up in the chapter contributed by Vajragupta who speaks of the importance of developing loving-kindness (*metta*) for oneself, in order to forgive oneself and others.

With respect to the theme of self-forgiveness therefore, a number of chapters in this collection acknowledge that the notion of 'self-forgiveness' can easily be abused – and often is. However, many of the chapters describe a welcome, constructive and valuable concept of self-forgiveness that is a far cry from simply 'letting ourselves off'.

Forgiveness: individual failings and systemic failures

A second major and hugely important theme this collection does a great deal to bring to light is the 'system' in which all interpersonal acts of forgiveness are embedded. Some chapters refer to tensions between individuals seeking to forgive and the effect this has on others around them, particularly where identity is at stake (see Spencer and Alderdice, Chapter 16). Other chapters speak of systemic failures, which unfortunately often go under the radar in the forgiveness process. For instance, Boorman references systemic problems within the adoption process. Often birth parents are cast as negligent and incapable when they themselves may be victims of a lack of support and adequate care. This goes unrecognised so long as the focus remains on the parent/s as the problem. Boorman notes that in such cases, 'the adoptee would have every right to feel angry towards the systems of health and social care as well as the parent'. Such systemic failures need to be brought to light in order for important change to be made, and to prevent simplistic accounts of the narrative of blame.

Bowman also recognises systemic elements of medical harm. She asks the important question whether our conception of forgiveness needs to extend beyond the individual to include systems, policies, organisational culture and procedures. The blame for medical errors is generally, uncritically and simplistically laid on doctors as *individuals*, but the failure to see recurring problems in the context in which health professionals work not only prevents change, but conveniently obscures the *need* for such changes in the first place.

The tension between the individual and the 'system' with regard to forgiveness also emerges in the chapter by Cantacuzino, where interventions like RESTORE, which promotes connection and mutual trust, are at odds with the prison system itself. In addition to being trained to maintain security by keeping the emotions of young offenders detached from their everyday contact with them, prison staff believed that the emotional labour of understanding prisoners was not included in their 'job description'. The result is a conflict between person and system. At the systemic or 'institutional' level prisons are about containment and risk avoidance, which fundamentally clashes with the attempt to break down defences and differences in RESTORE.

A clash of cultures is also a theme in the chapter by Adshead and Butler-Meadows. They note how forgiveness is undermined by the legal system. The process of constructing a legal defence makes it much harder for offenders to acknowledge guilt, impacting on their likelihood of seeking forgiveness later on. They also draw attention to how offenders in secure psychiatric settings experience tension and impenetrability around the issue of responsibility:

> It may not make sense for offenders to be told not to feel guilty (because their mental illness contributed to the offence); when they both feel guilty and are (in some physical sense, at least) guilty. Even more paradoxically, mental health professionals may take up incoherent positions regarding guilt and responsibility: they may tell offenders they were not really responsible because they were mentally ill; but if an offender then begins cheerfully to say that they are not to blame because they were ill, the offender may be accused of lacking remorse!

In addressing the 'system' in which forgiveness is embedded, Shohet invites readers to imagine a society in which there would be more acknowledgement of the impact policies and institutions have on individuals' lives. He references an African tribe where the whole community takes responsibility for an individual's offence to examine how they collectively failed this person. Clearly, a balance must be struck between individual agency and the influence of the collective to which they belong. However, in many cases the pendulum swings too far towards shaming and blaming individuals, rather than looking at the 'bigger picture'.

The chapters by Spencer and Alderdice and Shohet also call attention to the pressures exerted on the forgiveness process by large groups, particularly where identities are at stake. Forgiveness becomes embedded in a 'tribal' frame, where individuals, families and groups can hamper the process. To forgive can be construed as an act of betrayal: 'In a society that is deeply divided by conflict and violence, the victim–perpetrator scenario often ends up with individual suffering being transformed or absorbed into communal suffering and used to demand punitive action against the opposing community'. In the context of conflict, communal allegiances are heightened and individuals become enmeshed in a narrative that is not of their own making. The story may extend over generations, with the parts played within it following a predictable course of loyalty to one's forebears. Breaking out of one's appointed 'role' in the narrative by seeking forgiveness threatens the story and the identities of those involved. To call for forgiveness in these circumstances would be an extraordinarily courageous act.

Indeed, Shah-Kazemi speaks of the heroism of the former vice-President of Bosnia, Rusmir Mahmutćehajić, for his repudiation of vengeance against the Serbs in response to the atrocities perpetrated by Serbian militia against the Muslims of Bosnia in the genocide of the 1990s. In its place, Mahmutćehajić called upon his fellow Muslims to forgive their former enemies, highlighting the danger of victims becoming "so radicalised by suffering that they take on the nature of the perpetrators; (Mahmutćehajić, 2000, 144, cited in Shah-Kazemi, Chapter 3).

In their different ways, a number of chapters within this collection underscore the collective forces at stake in the forgiveness process. Some chapters bring neglected or under-recognised influences into the spotlight in order to expand the narrative of blame beyond the individual. This is important because individuals are frequently made scapegoats for systemic failures. Other chapters highlight tensions between the forgiveness of individuals and the 'system' in which moral actors find themselves. Often the forces exerted by such systems frustrate the process of forgiveness, either institutionally (as in the case of the criminal justice system) or because collective identities exert a powerful influence on individual behaviour.

Forgiveness, coercion and control

A third theme referenced across this collection acknowledges a darker side to forgiveness as a form of control in relationships where there are power imbalances between actors. Rhodes draws attention to how families often unwittingly collude in a shallow form of forgiveness in which parents encourage children to 'play nicely', forcing them to make amends for the sake of expediency. The adult's intervention usually requires the 'wrongdoer' to apologise to the 'victim', who is to accept that apology. This teaches children to paper over the cracks when things go wrong in their relationships. Over time and if children become parents themselves, the cycle could begin again with new actors playing their respective parts.

The potential exploitation of power within the family is also acknowledged in Sanderson's chapter examining forgiveness in the context of abuse; 'Often families or partners persuade or coerce survivors to forgive in order to avoid negative feelings or conflict so that the family can be restored. However, forcing forgiveness diverts empathy and compassion away from the survivor and onto the abuser.' In some situations, the roles of victim and perpetrator may not always be clear cut. However, special care needs to be taken in circumstances where there has been abuse because the balance of power in that situation has so severely run counter to the victim's wellbeing that many would question whether forgiveness is appropriate.

Going beyond the potential abuse of power in the family unit, Bowman identifies social structures that can work against the forgiveness process. For instance, in the medical settings Bowman describes, advocating forgiveness to victims of clinical failings can function as a form of social control, particularly when meetings are convened expressly for the purpose of promoting forgiveness of healthcare providers as a desired end. In many cases, forgiveness *is* – at least initially – more desirable for offenders than their victims. However, an honest examination of the impact of wrongdoing is an important prelude to adopting forgiveness as a goal – or perhaps for rejecting it as a response to wrongdoing. People can be coerced into a kind of forgiveness that rides roughshod over their experience of having been hurt. Great care should be taken to avoid the imposition of this kind of 'forgiveness' on others. Cook and Dossett's chapter offers an excellent illustration of the complexities around forgiveness as it is embedded in social structures and problematises any straightforward understanding of forgiveness as uncomplicatedly positive and helpful.

One final insight pertinent to the theme of power imbalances in forgiveness comes from Cooper's chapter and speaks to a point Rhodes makes about the benefits that can potentially be derived by denying forgiveness to offenders to increase their sense of indebtedness. Cooper highlights what he calls 'rabbinic realism' in the practice of absolving seekers of forgiveness from repeatedly having to petition for it after three sincere attempts, seeing in this tradition 'a way of balancing the ethical demands of a tradition with

ordinary human frailties and fallibilities'. While considerations
about the severity of the offence are crucial, the practice serves as
a 'break' in cases where forgiveness has been deliberately withheld
to indept others.

Ambivalence about forgiveness

Many chapters in this collection attest to the fact that forgiveness is
often touted as a panacea for troubled relationships, whose benefits
for mental health have been rather uncritically asserted. Although
these chapters constitute a collection about forgiveness, they do not
shy away from acknowledging a pervasive ambivalence towards it;
as Bowman puts it 'Forgiveness may be simultaneously comforting
and disturbing, constant and changing and desirable and repellent.'
In addition to examining uncertainties around the concept of
forgiveness, many contributors suggest alternatives to forgiveness
that might be more appropriate in some circumstances, while
others offer a bold and honest appraisal of the allure of revenge.

The attention placed on revenge is to be welcomed, for the
temptation to return an 'eye for an eye' runs deep in the human
psyche, and no book on forgiveness can be considered complete
without at least a sideways glance at the darker attractions of
vengeance and retribution. Thus, before examining the spectrum
of more temperate responses to wrongdoing on which forgiveness
falls, a brief glance at a more radical alternative is called for.

Shohet's contribution elaborates on the theme of revenge more
than any other chapter in this collection. This is not surprising since
this topic was the original focus of his research. He enumerates
reasons why we feel the pull to 'get even' in the wake of interpersonal
offence. In the short term, revenge is felt to restore victims' feelings
of power and self-worth; we didn't just lie down and 'take' whatever
was unfairly thrown at us. From a more objective point of view,
revenge affirms an interpretation of justice; if we are to do as we are
done by, revenge (in some cases) is thoroughly deserved.

Another attractive thing about revenge is that it cuts us off
from feeling pain, helplessness, shame and a whole range of very
uncomfortable feelings. Revenge allows our anger to burn white-
hot which distracts us so completely from the painful emotions

we *need* to experience to move on. As such – and as Shohet points out – this wish to avenge can become an addiction just as powerful as drugs and alcohol. In the same way, revenge becomes an all-consuming dead end that ultimately poisons those who are drawn to it.

Revenge can masquerade as a front for righteous indignation – a cause that is often taken up by those around the victim. To let go of the desire for retaliation can lead to reprisals from the community and accusations that justice is not being done. This links to the earlier remarks concerning systemic and collective aspects of forgiveness. Spencer and Alderdice recognise the need to disengage from what they call 'the conflictual way of "being in the world"'. The roles of victim and perpetrator, which result in an ever-increasing cycle of revenge, need to be transcended to halt the spiral of violence. The logic of revenge sees today's victim become tomorrow's aggressor. Unless a common sense of suffering can be shared in conflict situations, the escalation of hostilities will never cease. Revenge, as Shohet notes, 'keeps people tied to both the wound and the person who has done the wounding'.

The concept of 'unforgiveness' recognises that forgiveness may be an inappropriate or reckless path in some circumstances. Speaking specifically about child sexual abuse and domestic violence, Sanderson notes that in many cases forgiveness serves to support abusers' cognitive distortions. Abusers may feel that the forgiveness extended to them is on a par with their own sense of the gravity of the wrong, opening the door to minimisation and denial. Worse, however, is the sad reality that some abusive people take pleasure in feeling they have got away with manipulating others. In these circumstances, forgiveness would not be construed or accepted in the spirit it was offered, and this being the case, one could not expect the abuser to mend their ways as a result. Extending forgiveness to these individuals would be at best imprudent, and at worst could lead to them abusing and manipulating over and over again.

While the above example shows very clearly how wide the gulf can be between victims' and perpetrators' understanding of forgiveness – a gap that in some cases betokens wilful misunderstanding – there are far more innocuous differences of opinion regarding the meaning of forgiveness that nonetheless inhibit its realisation in human life. A good example of this is the adage 'forgive and forget', which has been very damaging in bidding people who have been hurt to erase all memory of their suffering. However, it is by no means the only misunderstanding associated with forgiveness.

Cantacuzino draws attention to difficulties associated with the word 'forgiveness' in the RESTORE programme, which she says is 'so barnacled by notions of piety and self-abnegation that prisoners would often turn up on the course assuming we were a Christian organisation whose underlying purpose was to teach them how to forgive'. While forgiveness is a *moral* – not a specifically religious or Christian concept – this is not an uncommon misperception about it. In fact, some years ago when I was co-editing a book on forgiveness (Watts and Gulliford 2004), I became aware of a number of individuals who were hostile to the newly emerging psychology of forgiveness as they were concerned that it obscured the Christian (and 'correct') understanding of forgiveness (Jones 1995; Augsberger 2000).

It is entirely appropriate for there to be different Christian, Jewish, Islamic and therapeutic understandings of forgiveness, provided these are seen as different expressions of a broader concept of forgiveness. No one tradition can lay claim to a monopoly on what 'true' forgiveness means – particularly if this serves to alienate people from the idea of forgiveness altogether. For many of the prisoners involved in RESTORE – and others – it is necessary to decouple forgiveness from the Christian connotations that would put them off even beginning to contemplate whether forgiveness might be an appropriate response in their situation. One aspect of ambivalence towards forgiveness lies in its associations and connotations, which could only benefit from closer scrutiny and discussion.

There are, however, other reasons why people experience forgiveness ambivalently. Rhodes reflects on the common human experience of wishing we had not forgiven someone so unequivocally – the feeling that we 'gave it away too easily'. This might occur when we have been socialised to forgive others to restore interpersonal harmony, or because our heartfelt desire to forgive sees us rushing into forgiveness too soon. Whatever the reason, the feeling of being pulled in different directions is commonplace.

Alternatives to forgiveness

Given how conflicted people often feel about forgiveness, the question arises as to whether there might be alternatives to it that allow people to move on with their lives in its absence. It is commendable that in exploring forgiveness, this volume examines other responses to pain. Cantacuzino emphasises that the focus in RESTORE is on exploring the contours of forgiveness rather than attempting to encourage, persuade or convince people to forgive. Talking about forgiveness is a crucial first step, for it seems there are a huge number of misconceptions about the concept that need to be critically examined – and perhaps even deconstructed – before people can decide on whether it is a conceivable option. For many prisoners involved in RESTORE, forgiveness will be neither possible nor desirable. Similarly, Rhodes acknowledges that in the therapeutic context; for some 'families and individuals true authentic forgiveness is a bridge too far, an unachievable state...' and asks what might be achieved in its absence. Victims could tell a narrative of 'betrayal and recovery' rather than a story of forgiveness. It is possible that over time these two narratives might ultimately weave together, though of course this should not be expected.

Bash makes the important point that it might be better not to think of forgiveness as just one type of response to wrongdoing, but rather a spectrum of responses whose parameters are set and circumscribed by the person bestowing forgiveness. Borrowing the notion of 'family resemblance', Bash asserts that 'forgiveness is forgiveness, if someone thinks it to be forgiveness, whatever the niceties of the details of a particular act of forgiveness. We thereby avoid an absurd – and judgmental – approach to another's actions, such as by saying, "What you have done is not to forgive, even though you think it is."'

Sanderson recognises that clinicians need to respect survivors whether they choose to forgive or not. Therapists need to take special care to bracket out their own preferences and ensure that they do not, consciously or otherwise, coerce people to forgive perpetrators of abuse. Forgiveness may, in some cases, be part of a healing process. In other cases, its promotion or advocacy could well inhibit the process of healing. For some time it has been readily accepted that feelings of anger, betrayal, rage and resentment (what have sometimes unhelpfully and uncritically been termed 'negative emotions') need to be acknowledged as part of the process of forgiving others. These entirely legitimate feelings should not be denied, condoned, buried or 'forgotten'. However, as Sanderson points out, it is the validation and processing of these emotions that leads to healing, rather than forgiveness in and of itself. Sanderson is right to question those who assert that forgiveness somehow *releases* healing; some degree of healing seems to be a precondition for forgiveness to be entertained as a possibility.

It is within this broader context of healing that alternatives to forgiveness can be considered. Helpfully, Sanderson seeks to nuance the range of responses to abuse and wrongdoing that are possible. Perhaps because empathy and compassion have been seen as necessary to the process of forgiveness (Worthington Jr. 1998; 2013), the boundaries between empathy, compassion and forgiveness have become unhelpfully blurred. However, it is entirely possible to feel compassion for an abuser *without* forgiving them. This carries significant practical weight to those involved in helping others forgive and for those seeking to forgive; not being able to forgive does not mark people out as uncompassionate and uncaring.

Sanderson is right too when she addresses a common assumption that a lack of forgiveness gives rise to resentment and the desire for revenge. Feelings of anger and resentment derive from the abuse *itself* and are compounded when abusers do not take responsibility for their actions or when they continue to abuse others. As she says, 'There is no conclusive evidence that forgiveness is necessary for healing. Some survivors find it extremely helpful, while others do not.' Her chapter is important, I think, in scaling back some of the claims made about the power of forgiveness, which may have uncritically equated forgiveness with healing.

Psychological means of promoting forgiveness

A number of chapters confirm the importance of a psychology of forgiveness to illuminate psychological processes involved in giving and receiving forgiveness and ways of promoting forgiveness where it is a desired end. For instance, Cooper notes that although Jewish teaching says it is the injured party's duty to forgive, it doesn't tell us *how* we are supposed to do that – it leaves us to our own devices. It was this very issue that gave rise to my own interest in the psychology of forgiveness almost 20 years ago, when I brought Christian forgiveness into dialogue with psychological approaches to forgiveness for my Master's thesis at Cambridge (1999). Forgiveness is so central to Christianity – and other world religions – but many are virtually silent on the practicalities of how to promote this ideal.

An exception to this is the Buddhist tradition, whose practices offer practical means of promoting forgiveness. For instance, the practice of *metta-bhavana* involves generating kindness towards oneself and other people (including people with whom we are currently experiencing difficulties). The process can be extremely helpful in promoting forgiveness – of both self and other. Vajragupta reports that for many people this meditation practice has been deeply transformative in the forgiveness process, particularly with respect to the fourth stage – which involves dealing with painful feelings towards a 'difficult' person.

From a psychological point of view, the practice of *metta-bhavana* loosens entrenched attitudes we hold towards those who have offended us, which can potentiate forgiveness. In many ways, the practice is redolent of psychological approaches to forgiveness which incorporate cognitive reframing of the offender as a means of promoting forgiveness. By thinking kindly of other people, we expand our perspective on the wrongdoer; we see beyond the offence and perceive their humanity. We might come to appreciate their behaviour in the light of what Vajragupta calls 'their conditioning and the pressures they are under in life'. This resonates closely with the approach to forgiveness advocated by Robert Enright, who calls for people seeking to forgive to reflect on the causes, both proximal and distal, for why an offender might have behaved the way they did (Enright 2001; Enright and Fitzgibbons 2000). This process of 'reframing' may take account of both the offender's upbringing and recent stressors in their lives. *Metta-bhavana* offers a practical way of unloosening the attributions of blame that hinder forgiveness. Religions like Christianity which explicitly place great emphasis on forgiveness could learn much from this practice and from psychology in terms of practical ways in which the ethical ideal of forgiveness might be realised (Gulliford 2004a; Gulliford 2004b; Gulliford 2004c; Gulliford 2016).

A frequent pastoral problem to which Hance attests is the feeling that despite the intellectual conviction they have been forgiven by God, many people simply do not feel they have been forgiven. In this connection, I have distinguished between forgiveness of the 'head' and 'heart' (Gulliford 2013). Often there is a dislocation between these elements of forgiveness, in respect of both divine forgiveness and interpersonal forgiveness. Clearly, for forgiveness to be fully and authentically realised – and transformative – the intellectual conviction of the 'head' needs to be matched by the 'heart knowledge' of truly feeling forgiven or forgiving. One way in which I suggested 'head' and 'heart knowledge' might be brought into better alignment is through rituals, both secular and religious. Hance proposes a similar solution, advocating a secular equivalent of absolution (posting a forgiveness letter) to help 'intellectual forgiveness' translate to the heart. He reports that this act is powerfully transformative.

Forgiveness and higher powers

Appropriately perhaps, the last theme to be drawn out in these chapters is the question of final judgement. Here there are some inevitable differences between the chapters representing religious traditions and those which examine forgiveness outside a religious frame of reference. The Qur'an asserts that judgement belongs to God. Similarly, Christians and Jews believe that ultimately God judges us all. Since judgement belongs to God, people with religious convictions can turn the question of forgiveness over to God. It might not be humanly possible to forgive heinous wrongs

– and so forgiveness can be 'reframed' beyond the realm of human interactions (Gulliford 1999).

What might a secular equivalent of turning things over to God look like? If you don't believe in God, into whose hands do you place forgiveness when you reach an impasse in the process yourself? Carter speaks of forgiveness being 'the discovery of a grace from beyond us to transcend even the worst evil'. What could this mean in a secular context? One possibility may be to see forgiveness - if sought – as an eventual goal and to project its ultimate realisation into an anticipated future. Another possibility would be to use the forgiveness stories of others as the inspiration and ground of our own hopes to forgive. The Forgiveness Project, a UK-based charity founded by Marina Canacuzino, employs true stories of victims and perpetrators of crime and violence to explore forgiveness and alternatives to revenge. The book arising from this undertaking 'The Forgiveness Project: Stories for a Vengeful Age' (Cantacuzino, 2015) offers a wealth of inspirational examples in this regard. These moving and powerful narratives, both from people with religious convictions and those whose standpoint is avowedly secular, bear witness to the importance of breaking the destructive attachment to revenge and embracing instead the transformative power of forgiveness.

References

Augsberger, D. (2000) *The New Freedom of Forgiveness*. Chicago: Moody.

Cantacuzino, M. (2015) *The Forgiveness Project: Stories for a vengeful age*. London: Jessica Kingsley Publishers.

Enright, R.D. (2001) *Forgiveness is a Choice*. Washington: APA LifeTools.

Enright, R.D. & Fitzgibbons, R.P. (2000) *Helping Clients Forgive*. Washington: APA.

Gulliford, L. (1999) Theological and psychological aspects of forgiveness. Unpublished MPhil Thesis, University of Cambridge.

Gulliford, L. (2004a) 'Intrapersonal Forgiveness'. In F. Watts and L. Gulliford (eds.), *Forgiveness in Context: Theology and psychology in creative dialogue*. London: T&T Clark.

Gulliford, L. (2004b) 'The Healing of Relationships'. In F. Watts and L. Gulliford (eds.), *Forgiveness in Context: Theology and psychology in creative dialogue*. London: T&T Clark.

Gulliford, L. (2004c) 'Forgiveness and faith'. *Ministry Today*, 31, 6–15.

Gulliford, L. (2013) 'The Head and the Heart of the Matter in Hope and Forgiveness'. In F.N. Watts and G. Dumbreck (eds.), *Head and Heart: Perspectives from religion and psychology*. West Conshohocken, PA: Templeton Press.

Gulliford, L. (2016) 'Psychology's Contribution to Ethics: Two case studies.' In Brand, C. (ed.) *Can Psychology Replace Ethics? On the potentials and risks of empirical research into human morality for our ethical self-image.* Springer-VS.

Jones, L.G. (1995) *Embodying Forgiveness: A theological analysis.* Grand Rapids, Michigan: William B. Eerdmans.

Watts, F. and Gulliford, L. (Eds) (2004) *Forgiveness in context: Theology and Psychology in Creative Dialogue.* London & New York: T&T Clark International.

Worthington Jr., E.L. (1998) 'The Pyramid Model of Forgiveness: Some interdisciplinary speculations about unforgiveness and the promotion of forgiveness'. In Worthington Jr., E.L. (ed.). *Dimensions of Forgiveness: Psychological research and theological perspectives.* Radnor, PA.: Templeton Foundation Press.

Worthington, Jr., E.L. (2013) Helping people REACH forgiveness of others. *Bibliotheca Sacra*, 170, 273-285.

About the Contributors

Gwen Adshead is a forensic psychiatrist and psychotherapist. She trained at St George's Hospital, the Institute of Psychiatry and the Institute of Group Analysis. She is trained as a group therapist and a mindfulness-based cognitive therapist and has also trained in mentalisation-based therapy. She worked for nearly 20 years as a consultant forensic psychotherapist at Broadmoor Hospital, running psychotherapeutic groups for offenders, and working with staff around relational security and organisational dynamics. She now works in a medium secure unit in Hampshire. Gwen also has a Master's degree in Medical Law and Ethics and has a research interest in moral reasoning and how this links with 'bad' behaviour. She has published a number of books and over 100 papers, book chapters and commissioned articles on forensic psychotherapy, ethics in psychiatry, and attachment theory as applied to medicine and forensic psychiatry. She was honoured with the President's Medal for services to psychiatry in July 2013, and was the Gresham Professor of Psychiatry 2014–17.

John Alderdice is a psychiatrist, who became Alliance Leader, one of the negotiators of the Good Friday Agreement, and Speaker of the Northern Ireland Assembly. Appointed to the Independent Monitoring Commission he was tasked with security normalisation in Northern Ireland. He has been President of Liberal International and Chairman of the Liberal Democrats in the House of Lords, and is now Director of the Centre for the Resolution of Intractable Conflict at Oxford University, Chairman of the Centre for Democracy and Peace Building in Belfast and a professor at the University of Maryland.

Anthony Bash is an honorary professor in the Department of Theology and Religion at Durham University. He is also Vice-Master and Senior Tutor at Hatfield College, Durham University. Anthony studied law at Bristol University and later practised law in Bristol. He has a theology degree from Glasgow University and a doctorate from Cambridge University. His research interests include theological reflections on forgiveness, reconciliation and remorse.

Amanda Boorman qualified as a social worker with a specialism in working with marginalised communities. She has experience of working in many care settings and is an expert in designing and creating therapeutic environments. After working in the voluntary sector, Amanda went on to adopt and long-term foster two siblings with developmental trauma and complex needs. That journey led to Amanda founding a peer support charity which campaigns for the rights of adopted and fostered people and their original families. The charity uses creative ways of raising awareness including writing, documentary, animation and art. It also provides therapeutic spaces for traumatised children and young people. www.theopennest.co.uk

Deborah Bowman is Professor of Bioethics and Clinical Ethics at St George's, University of London. Her academic interests concern emotion in ethical decision making, moral distress, therapeutic relationships, the health humanities and public engagement. She has published extensively and participated in many international projects. Deborah is a broadcaster and regular commentator in the media. She is the Chair of the Deafinitely Theatre Company. In 2016, she was awarded an MBE for services to medical ethics.

Jesse Butler-Meadows is a doctor training in psychiatry in Hampshire. A graduate from the University of Liverpool, he has experience in a variety of general hospital and mental health settings. He has a keen interest in the psychodynamics of violence and offending and is set to pursue a career in forensic psychiatry.

Marina Cantacuzino is an award-winning journalist who in 2004 founded The Forgiveness Project, a charity that works with real stories to explore how concepts of compassion, empathy and forgiveness can be used to break cycles of violence, transform relationships and restore hope. She is the author of *The Forgiveness Project: Stories for a Vengeful Age* (Jessica Kingsley Publishers 2015).

Richard Carter is a priest, teacher and writer. For the last 12 years he has worked at St Martin-in-the-Fields in Trafalgar Square as Associate Vicar for Mission, involved with the homeless, refugees and people from all walks of life. He also coordinates the education, lecture and pastoral care programmes. Before working in London, he was the Chaplain and Tutor for the Melanesian Brotherhood in the South Pacific for 15 years, becoming a Brother himself and living their community life of simplicity, prayer and service. Before studying theology, Richard was an English literature and drama teacher and continues to have a love for art, music, the theatre and learning from the traditions and wisdom of the different cultures in which he has lived in Europe, South East Asia and the South Pacific.

Stephen Cherry is the Dean of King's College Cambridge and an active writer and speaker on Christian spirituality and practical theology. He was previously a Residentiary Canon of Durham Cathedral and Director of Ministerial Development and Parish Support for the diocese of Durham. His previous books include *Healing Agony: Re-imagining Forgiveness* (Continuum 2012), *The Dark Side of the Soul: An Insider's Guide to the Web of Sin* (Bloomsbury 2016) and *God-Curious: Exploring Eternal Questions* (Jessica Kingsley Publishers 2017).

Christopher C.H. Cook is Professor of Spirituality, Theology and Health in the Department of Theology and Religion at Durham University, an Honorary Minor Canon of Durham Cathedral, and an Honorary Consultant Psychiatrist with Tees, Esk and Wear Valleys NHS Foundation Trust. He is author and editor of various books and papers on spirituality and mental health, including most recently Cook, Powell and Sims (eds) (2016) *Spirituality and Narrative in Psychiatric Practice*. RCPsych Publications.

Howard Cooper, a graduate of Sussex University (BA Hons; MA with Distinction) and the Leo Baeck College in London, is a psychoanalytic psychotherapist in private practice and the Director of Spiritual Development at Finchley Reform Synagogue. He is a workshop leader, lecturer and writer exploring religious, Judaic, spiritual and psychological themes and is the author of a number of books including *The Alphabet of Paradise: An A–Z of Spirituality for Everyday Life*. He blogs at howardcoopersblog.blogspot.com

Wendy Dossett is Senior Lecturer in Religious Studies at the University of Chester and Principal Investigator of the Higher Power Project, funded by the Sir Halley Stewart Trust, which explores the role of spirituality in recovery from addictions. Findings have been published in *International Social Work* (2013), and in chapter contributions to Bacon, Dossett and Knowles (eds) (2015) *Alternative Salvations: Engaging the Sacred and the Secular.* London: Bloomsbury; and Beckford, Harvey and Steidinger (eds) (2017) *New Religious Movements and Counselling: Academic, Professional and Personal Perspectives.* New York: Routledge.

Liz Gulliford has a long-standing interest in human strengths and is currently Senior Lecturer in Positive Psychology at the University of Northampton. She undertook her doctorate, a critical, interdisciplinary evaluation of positive psychological approaches to strengths and virtues, at Queens' College, Cambridge. Liz's interdisciplinary work has been published in psychological, philosophical, theological and educational domains.

Stephen Hance is the Dean of Derby. He was formerly Canon Missioner at Southwark Cathedral and Director of Mission for the Diocese of Southwark. Prior to that he was a parish priest for nearly 20 years. He has degrees in theology, mission and leadership, and sociology. He has written books on confirmation and (with Jacqui Hance) on parenting, and contributed to a number of others, most recently on mission action planning, and on sacramental Fresh Expressions of Church.

Dr Marian Liebmann OBE has worked in education, art therapy, victim support and probation, and has been involved in community, victim–offender and schools mediation. For eight years she worked for Mediation UK, the umbrella organisation for mediation, as director and projects adviser. She has written/edited 12 books in the fields of art therapy, mediation and conflict resolution, including

Restorative Justice: How It Works (Jessica Kingsley Publishers 2007) and *Mediation in Context* (Jessica Kingsley Publishers 2000) and contributed chapters to many others. She currently divides her time between mediation, art therapy, supervision and writing.

Steve Nolan is chaplain at Princess Alice Hospice, Esher, and Visiting Research Fellow at The University of Winchester. His peer reviewed publications on the theory and practice of spiritual care are rooted in his clinical work, and his research interests include: chaplains' case studies; practice-based research; and non-religious spiritual care. His books include *Spiritual Care at the End of Life* and (co-edited with George Fitchett) *Spiritual Care in Practice: Case Studies in Healthcare Chaplaincy* (both Jessica Kingsley Publishers).

Honor Rhodes OBE studied history then trained and practised as a social worker, before working at Tavistock Relationships, thinking about human relationships, troubled and healthy. Honor's interest is in finding effective interventions for difficult problems. She writes for practitioners, including *Knowing what you do works: measuring your own effectiveness with families, parents and children* (Family and Parenting Institute 2009) and *A short guide to working with co-parents: why we don't, why we should and how we could* (Tavistock Relationships 2012). Honor is a board member of her local NHS Clinical Commissioning Group and a founding trustee of the Early Intervention Foundation.

Christiane Sanderson is a senior lecturer in psychology at the University of Roehampton. With 26 years' experience working in child sexual abuse, sexual violence, complex trauma and domestic abuse, she has run consultancy and training for parents, teachers, social workers, nurses, therapists, counsellors, solicitors, the NSPCC, the Catholic Safeguarding Advisory Committee, the Methodist Church, the Metropolitan Police Service and the Refugee Council. She is the author of many books, including *Counselling Skills for Working with Trauma* and *Counselling Adult Survivors of Child Sexual Abuse*, both published by Jessica Kingsley Publishers.

Dr Reza Shah-Kazemi is a Senior Research Associate at the Institute of Ismaili Studies, London. He specialises in Comparative

Religion and Islamic Studies. His publications include *The Spirit of Tolerance in Islam*, *Common Ground between Islam and Buddhism*, *The Other in the Light of the One: The Universality of the Qur'an and Interfaith Dialogue*. *Paths to Transcendence: According to Shankara, Ibn Arabi* and *Meister Eckhart*.

Robin Shohet has worked in the field of psychotherapy and supervision for over 40 years. His book *Supervision in the Helping Professions,* which he co-wrote with Peter Hawkins, has been translated into eight languages. He has also edited *Passionate Supervision, Supervision as Transformation* and *Clinical Supervision in the Medical Profession*. In the field of forgiveness, he has organised two international conferences in 1999 and 2013 at the Findhorn Foundation, a spiritual community in the north of Scotland.

Graham Spencer is Reader in Social and Political Conflict at the University of Portsmouth and Distinguished Senior Research Fellow at the Edward M. Kennedy Institute for Conflict Intervention, Maynooth University. He works with a range of groups and agencies in Northern Ireland on conflict transformation and two of his publications include *Forgiving and Remembering in Northern Ireland* (2011) and *The British and Peace in Northern Ireland* (2015).

Vajragupta lives 'on the road', travelling and teaching Buddhism at various places round the world. He is a member of the Triratna Buddhist Community, a Buddhist movement making the Buddha's teaching relevant to 21st-century life. He is the author of three books about Buddhism. *Wild Awake* (a book about spending time alone in nature) and *From Now to Eternity* (a Buddhist exploration of our relationship with time) are due for publication in 2018.

Subject Index

Author Index